CANADA'S CENTURY

Maclean's

CANADA'S CENTURY

An Illustrated History of the People and Events That Shaped Our Identity

SELECTED AND INTRODUCED BY CARL MOLLINS

FOREWORD BY PETER C. NEWMAN

KEY PORTER BOOKS

Canadian Cataloguing in Publication Data

Maclean's Canada's century

Articles originally published in *Maclean's* magazine.
Includes index.
ISBN 1-55013-993-2

1. Canada — History — 20th century. I. Mollins, Carl.
II. Title: Canada's century.

FC600.M33 1999   971.06   C98-933001-X
F1033.M33 1999

The publisher gratefully acknowledges the support of the Canada Council for the Arts and the Ontario Arts Council for its publishing program.

THE CANADA COUNCIL | LE CONSEIL DES ARTS
FOR THE ARTS | DU CANADA
SINCE 1957 | DEPUIS 1957

We acknowledge the financial support of the Government of Canada through the Book Publishing Industry Development Program (BPIDP) for our publishing activities.

Acknowledgments

The first whose contributions to this book must be recognized are the 107 men and women whose works, sampled in the following pages, enriched *Maclean's*, and Canada, throughout the century. The magazine's present staff assisted actively in many ways: the editing ideas and encouragements of Editor-in-Chief Bob Lewis and those of many others who provided advice on key chapters; researchers led by Michael MacLean; library staffers Mary Jane Culbert, George Serhijczuk and Robin Selz; production whizzes Sean McCluskey and Joe Power, and Joanne Spence, who helped translate texts from yellowing old magazines into computer language. Michael Benedict, Editorial Director, New Ventures, handled business matters and copyright questions.

Of matching worth was the assistance of Key Porter staff—the book was Anna Porter's idea—in generating editing ideas and assembling the pictures. Staff at the University of Toronto's Robarts Library and the Thomas Fisher Rare Book Library helped with the archived first 30 years of *Maclean's* issues and about 75 years' worth of microtexts. Then, in immeasurable degree, stand the ideas and insights of Joan, Tracey and Julie Mollins—Julie helping to dig old articles from the Robarts and helping with the painful work of winnowing down so many verbal treasures from our history.

Design: Steven Boyle, Jackie Young / INK
Printed and bound in Canada
99 00 01 02 6 5 4 3 2 1

Key Porter Books Limited
70 The Esplanade
Toronto, Ontario
Canada M5E 1R2

www.keyporter.com

Contents

PREFACE

By Robert Lewis

IT HAS BEEN A LITTLE MAGAZINE, the size of a digest; it has been an oversized monthly that competed with *The Saturday Evening Post* and *Colliers*. It has been a monthly, a bi-weekly and, since 1978, a weekly. The very first issue in 1905 was called *The Business Magazine*, and two months later it became *The Busy Man's Magazine*. Within six years it had adopted the name of one of the founders, John Bayne Maclean, and the logo it wears proudly today in a brand new design hearkens back to the type font of years past. More important than the look, *Maclean's* has been at the heart of the Canadian experience since its launch. Some of its stands were inelegant or provocative, and at times it was even down-right offensive, as when it fretted in the old days about the flood of immigration to our shores or the emerging role of women in society. At its best, *Maclean's* has reflected the heart and soul of the nation, whether it was muckraking to challenge the establishment, as it did so many times through the century or, during the celebrated reigns of editors Arthur Irwin, Ralph Allen and Peter Newman, unabashedly promoting the Canadian identity. Under Irwin, the magazine came of age, hiring the best writers, reaching out and identi-fying itself with the issues confronting Canadians in war and, later, in peace. Allen built from that solid base, opening the magazine to a host of people who became journalistic icons, including June Callwood, Trent Frayne, Peter Gzowski, Barbara Frum and Peter C. Newman. The Newman years saw the magazine transform itself from a general interest magazine that was losing millions to a money-making entity that proved there were enough Canadian stories to sustain a weekly newsmagazine. Despite the pace of events as they now unfold in the magazine, the themes are constant: a small nation living atop one of the world's giants struggles to preserve its own identity, even as internal pressures threaten to tear apart one of the most blessed nations on earth. The pages of *Maclean's* yield the detail and color and emotion of that struggle over the past century and serve as a reminder that we have built a country that was worth fighting for – and still is.

Robert Lewis,
Editor-in-chief,
June 3, 1999

VANCOUVER: The motor car and crew with first claim to getting all the way to the West Coast from Winnipeg, 1906

THE STRUGGLE FOR NATIONHOOD

By Peter C. Newman

BETWEEN 1900, WHEN A FRESH EPOCH DAWNED over an unsuspecting Dominion, then barely a country, and the summer of 1999, when that nation finds itself on the cusp of a new millennium, Canadians could believe with some justification that the twentieth century had belonged to them. During those 10 decades they had gained not only the symbols but the substance of nationhood. Like some giant stirred by feelings of power that come late to the adolescent – not yet daunted by the failures and misgivings of maturity – the country had been populated, settled, then developed in so many new ways and exciting directions that it became the seventh largest economy on earth. From being regarded as an orphan state on the very margin of civilized geography, Canada became an envied nation, repeatedly judged by the United Nations as the best place on earth to live.

During the hyperactive century covered by this book, Canadian artists, actors, film-makers, singers and writers earned reputations that kick-started a promising and internationally recognized culture. No longer hewers of wood and drawers of water, Canada's reality took a different form; we had come of age.

What changed most of all was how Canadians perceived their homeland. They would rather eat worms than boast about their country's achievements, but those accomplishments were there for the world to see, and for Canadians to nurture and occasionally even boast about. The clearest testament to this unaccustomed state of grace were the endless line-ups of hopeful newcomers at Canada's embassies abroad. They were anxious to invest their lives in a country they recognized as having been blessed by the mandate of heaven.

The sometimes painful but mostly rewarding process of formulating and refining Canada's image of itself marked the most significant legacy of the twentieth century. That struggle for nationhood, as recorded in the pages of *Maclean's*, is reflected in the text and illustrations that follow.

This is the epic of a northern people, reared in a remarkably enduring atmosphere of national and individual modesty, overcoming that deferential heritage. The country's original European settlers got together, not to establish some proud new nationality, but simply for the sake of survival – geographically, economically and politically. With only the

OTTAWA: Three-year-old Didier Garrett shows the Governor General's Foot Guard how, 1993

OTTAWA: An overcoated Queen signs off on constitutional amendments that leave Quebecers cold, 1982

uninspiring imperative of outlasting a cold climate to spur them on – and few pretensions to manifest destiny beyond hunting down the next day's supper – the early generations of Canadians seemed satisfied with just being around, huddled together under the polar moon.

Becoming a citizen called for no dramatic conversion to a new faith or oath of loyalty to some form of pan-Canadian nationality. In fact it did not even require a salute, since the country lacked a distinctive flag for the first 98 years of its existence. Founded on social compact rather than individual allegiance, Canadian nationhood proceeded so slowly that it took 38 years after Confederation in 1867 for all the other provinces to join – except Newfoundland, which waited another half-century, just to be sure. In the final analysis, except for the Native peoples, Canadians are all boat people.

The changes chronicled in *Canada's Century* flowed from the country's newfound spirit of independence. As a result, Canadians jettisoned the final vestiges of British rule, reached a pivotal trade accommodation with the United States, and survived bitter tensions within their own borders while being drawn into two world wars and other conflicts beyond.

During this maturing process, everything changed. The comforts of hearth and home were turned inside out. Canadians shifted from their traditional unquestioning homage to authority to a mood of scepticism and impatience. The economy tobogganed from boom to bust to boom and back again, evolving from a dependence on such staples as furs, unprocessed minerals, timber, wheat and such that had earned the country its early reputation as little more than the world's storehouse of unprocessed raw materials – a kind of Manchuria with polar bears.

Part of this economic shift was due to the indisputable fact that the Old Canada, run by a sequence of self-perpetuating old boys' networks, had been replaced by a society with new imperatives: only the able were rewarded with the power that counts. Just about every human Canadian endeavor – except politics – began to operate strictly on merit. With debt-burdened governments unable to continue funding the daycare economy that had protected Canadians in the past, the big land's doughty citizens dug in, realizing they were on their own. For the most part they found their new status empowering and exhilarating.

CANADA'S EARLIEST PIONEERS, the first Europeans to explore the bleak contours of a daunting geography and to exploit its resources, chronicled their achievements with graceful diligence, by pen and ink in ledger books. Tick marks entered by clerks with fingerless gloves measured their lives, recording the acreage of farms cleared and timber felled; the depth of primitive mine shafts dug; the harvests of grain and other crops; the catch of the then-bountiful oceans. In those days, accomplishment was measured in human sweat and sinew. The hardiest and most ambitious of these pioneers eventually spawned family dynasties, uneasy collections of mutual interests based on filial benefit, assuming responsibility for individual slices of the expanding Canadian pie.

Out of these humdrum beginnings emerged business leaders such as H.R. MacMillan in British Columbia, the Richardsons in Winnipeg, the Masseys in Ontario and the Montreal money barons – Donald Smith, George Stephen, William Van Horne – who financed and built the CPR. They were joined by cadres of ambition-obsessed entrepreneurs who transformed at first Montreal and later Toronto into industrial centres, the cities' belching smokestacks providing growing evidence of faith and fortune. They thought themselves valuable and loved; in fact they were necessary and tolerated. Someone had to organize the means of production, prime the pump of enterprise, tame the wilderness, build the factories. Someone had to buy the grain, process it, sell it back again. Someone had to keep the wheels in motion.

These early tycoons faced few worries. They were nurtured by government subsidies, having entered into marriages of convenience with Ottawa by backing those politicians pragmatic or opportunistic enough to do their bidding. They traded allegiance for handouts, while the politicians turned a blind eye to their market excesses. Within this cozy context Canadian enterprise grew, multiplied and eventually claimed more solid footing in world markets. The private compacts of Canada's original commercial giants – the early "understandings" between family and state – nurtured their determination to perpetuate conservative beliefs and a self-serving agenda. Calmly in possession of power, they put down solid roots in their communities, regions and provinces, and in the country at large.

This economic evolution was an essential step in forging a vibrant economy for the new country, but it was not typical. Historically, Canadians have almost always placed collective interests ahead of individual ones – the opposite of the United States, where economic Darwinism has ruled supreme, operating strictly according to the jungle edict of survival of the fittest. In Canada that harsh ethic was tempered by government support, which provided the basic infrastructure for economic growth and a safety net for those who needed it.

WINNIPEG: A barber shop nontet, The Clarendon Hotel, 1920

DURING THE HECTIC DECADES that surrounded the birth of *Maclean's* in 1905, the Klondike gold rush reached its peak; Canadian troops were dispatched to fight the Boer War; Hull, Quebec, burned to the ground; Guglielmo Marconi received the first wireless transatlantic message at St. John's; Ontario established a 10-mph city speed limit for those newfangled motor cars; John Nash opened Vancouver's Electric Theatre, the country's first permanent movie house; Toronto's Tommy Ryan invented five-pin bowling; and Roald Amundsen crossed the Northwest Passage for the first time. It was a self-confident time of hope and consolidation. In 1903, the president of the Canadian Manufacturers' Association, Cyrus Birge, declared: "We are manufacturers not merely of articles of wood and stone. We manufacture enthusiasms, a feeling of pride in our country, a spirit of independence."

At the same time, more than half of Canadians still lived on farms, butchered their own meat, churned their own butter, and dealt with their boredom mainly by going into town on Saturday nights to play euchre. Most houses were lit by kerosene lamps, and women did their laundry on washboards. Child labor was common for girls as young as nine in the Montreal textile-trade sweatshops. Except for being maids or working in menial jobs in stores and factories, women had few opportunities. At the turn of the century there were a mere 113 women in the federal public service, cloistered in private work

MARKET SLIPP LOW WATER

SAINT JOHN, New Brunswick: Waterfront at low tide, c. 1900

rooms for fear they might be corrupted by contact with male bureaucrats. The West was being rapidly populated, its more rambunctious newcomers held in check by the Royal North-West Mounted Police, still wearing pith helmets. In 1905, two new provinces, Saskatchewan and Alberta, were created, and local government took hold.

That year, Sir Wilfrid Laurier was more than halfway through his impressive 15-year reign (1896-1911). One of the most critical issues he faced was the free-trade deal offered by U.S. president William Taft. Taft sent a negotiating team to Ottawa in 1910, suggesting a reciprocity arrangement that would give American industry free access to Canadian raw materials in exchange for near-free access to the lucrative U.S. market. A draft treaty was signed, but it was bitterly opposed by the Conservatives, who interpreted it as a first step towards political union. Branded an annexationist, Laurier lost the 1911 election, and the free-trade issue lay dormant for three-quarters of a century.

The nineteenth-century notion that the human condition was immutable, that men and women could do little to improve their lot, began to be questioned, and nowhere more so than among the newly arrived European immigrants who flooded into the western plains. There, successful farmers were organizing themselves into grain growers' cooperatives to demand higher prices for their crops. That initiative eventually gave birth to a series of agrarian protest movements, culminating in the formation of the CCF. Industrially, this turn-of-the-century, newly defiant mood was expressed in the increasing number of strikes. Labor unrest grew so disruptive that the federal government was asked to intervene. That brought into prominence William Lyon Mackenzie King, the freshly appointed deputy minister of the newly formed Department of Labor.

King eventually went into politics and in a split decision was elected in 1919 to succeed Laurier as leader of the Liberal party. A fusty bachelor who communed with the spirit of his dead mother and worshipped his pet dog, King was the great nutbar among Canadian prime ministers, a reputation not easily gained. Paradoxically, that did not disqualify him from becoming the longest-serving prime minister in Canadian history; indeed, he was probably the most successful occupant of that office. His influence spread over four decades, and even if he offered not the glimmer of a grand vision and remained allergic to any hint of statesmanship, King kept the country united during some of its most difficult years.

When King was preparing to take over the Liberal electoral machine, the focus of Canadians' concern had shifted to the muddy battlefields of France. The First World War was rooted in ancient European feuds, but one of its many unintended consequences was to turn the sparsely occupied Canadian archipelago into a nation. Hugging the French-Belgian border, near the village of Arras overlooking the plains of Douai, was a height of land known as Vimy Ridge. The Allies had been trying to capture that strategic position for more than two years. It wasn't until April 9, the morning after Easter Sunday, 1917, that the previously impregnable German positions were finally overwhelmed. The successful attackers were 100,000 Canadian volunteers, massed under Canadian command - paying a horrendous price (more than 3500 dead and 7000 wounded) for their brave assault. It was a small incident in history's bloodiest war, but it proved to the world at large that Canada was a colony no longer, and ought never again to be taken for granted.

OTTAWA: The Queen cuts the cake for Canada's 100th birthday, 1967

The postwar euphoria of the giddy 1920s, which saw the first significant urbanization and sophistication of mainstream Canada, was followed by the agony of the Great Depression. The aftershock of the stock market crash of October, 1929, spread across the economy, closing factories and bankrupting businesses. By 1933 more than one out of every three wage earners were unemployed; according to the ethic of the times, anyone out of work was a "bum." That blow to people's self-esteem was the Depression's harshest legacy.

Everything changed on September 3, 1939, when Adolf Hitler's invasion of Poland triggered the start of the Second World War. Some 42,000 Canadian men and women were eventually killed in action, an inordinate sacrifice for a peace-loving nation fighting a war on strange soil for foreign causes. The individual heroism of Canadians, fighting not to defend their turf but to preserve freedom, was remarkable. In the process, frantic efforts on the home front, as it was called, turned a hesitant and under financed economy into an industrial powerhouse. From a standing start, 5800 war planes, 487 warships and 410 merchant ships were hastily built and rushed into service. Every second vehicle used

OFF LUNENBURG, Nova Scotia: Bluenose *in full cry, 1921*

in the desert war against German General Rommel's Afrika Korps was Canadian-built. With Canada's mobilization to fight the Second World War in the early and mid-1940s, the country was finally organized along modern lines.

The war record of Canada's navy, army and air force was magnificent, quite out of proportion to the numbers of its sailors, soldiers and air crew, who time and time again played pivotal roles in the battles that produced the Allied victory. It was that impressive war effort and the creative economic reconstruction that followed which helped Canada become a world player in the postwar years. The former colony became a founding force in the United Nations and NATO, and eventually was accorded full-scale membership in the Group of Seven major industrial nations.

What brought about this dramatic leap was the psychological shift in how the country was regarded by its own citizens. Before the Second World War, Canadians had been taught, and had learned their lesson well, that the history which matters was made across the sea or over the border, and that the best Canadians could manage was bound to be an imitation. Happily, that colonial attitude was a victim of the war, which recognized individual courage and dedication on the battlefields and gave spark to the innovative talents that flourished on the home front.

Maclean's played a not insignificant part in this process. Its pages, featuring Canadian heroes, became the mirror in which Canadians glimpsed each other and came to recognize themselves. Gradually and with ever increasing reach and authority, the

VANCOUVER: Capital of The Coast

magazine became the newly confident country's house organ, providing a loose but authentic definition of Canada's blossoming identity.

The 1950s were the time of Canada's greatest flowering. Tranquil and prosperous though the country was, it was undergoing drastic social changes. Television arrived on the scene, as did superhighways, shopping plazas, the Stratford Shakespearean Festival – and John Diefenbaker. The Man from Prince Albert, as he was often called to emphasize his rural Saskatchewan roots, was the last of the great political orators. Brimming with intimations of his destiny, he became a street singer in Ottawa's corridors of power. His six hectic years in office were judged a failure, not because of any lack of passion or enlightened intent but simply because, as a man whose previous authority had never extended beyond a two-man walk-up law office, he could not handle the complicated matters of government. Yet it was entirely possible to admire his instincts without saluting his performance. When he died in 1979, a month shy of age 84, it was the stride and stance of the man that was best remembered – his guts, the brew of his laughter, the dint of his compassion.

If Diefenbaker was a three-ring circus, his successor, Lester Pearson, was a cool cat on a hot tin roof. He did as much as any man to bring peace, order and good government to the world (when he was a diplomat) and to his country (when he was its prime minister). If he did not succeed in either quest, his basic sense of decency, his wry, self-deprecating wit and his ability to soften collisions and soothe tempers were the attributes that saw him through. He was a good man in a wicked time, missed more for his personal qualities than for his political achievements.

Then came Pierre Trudeau. Elusive and exasperating, he performed the task that Norman Mailer once described as "the indispensable psychic act of a leader who takes national anxieties long buried and releases them to the surface where they belong." He breech-birthed into existence a patriated constitution wrapped around a Charter of Rights and Freedoms that fundamentally altered Canadian society. In a TV age, when most celebrities are lucky to last more than a season, Trudeau's hold on the Canadian imagination would not let go, even after he resigned in the winter of 1984. In a curious way his influence seemed magnified by his withdrawal from power. A philosopher king without a kingdom, he continues to magic us.

That was never Brian Mulroney's problem. Neither a rebel nor a reactionary, he came as close as anyone to personifying his party's oxymoronic label: Progressive Conservative. His operational code had more to do with promoting his career than with advancing any set of coherent ideas. Nevertheless, he left an impressive legacy that included the free-trade agreement with the United States and two unprecedented back-to-back Tory majorities. He was a masterful deal maker who had cobbled together a coalition (of Quebec nationalists and western isolationists) based on an impossible premise of political cooperation. An Irish charmer, he was a high-stakes player who rolled the dice and lost.

The succession of Jean Chrétien in 1993 brought almost no policy changes, but Chrétien somehow managed to capture public acceptance for his low-profile style. Given no viable, national alternative, the voters lapsed into the realization that the solutions to their problems had moved beyond Ottawa's status quo–bound politicos.

EVERY COUNTRY IS A MYSTERY COMPOSED of the lives of strangers, men and women whose official fragile link is a piece of paper proclaiming their vague allegiance to shared citizenship. In Canada by the end of the twentieth century, the nature of that compact had been dramatically altered. The country no longer operated according to its traditional mixture of creative fumbling and success by inadvertence. In uneven spurts between 1900 and 1999, Canadians had become increasingly comfortable with the notion of acting independently, of placing want ahead of need, responsibility ahead of obligation, pleasure ahead of duty.

With the weight of carrying the Precambrian Shield on their shoulders lifted, Canadians faced the new millennium with a refreshing new spirit: ready to enjoy the future instead of reliving the past. The pages that follow tell the story of how this New Canada was born.

Progress and Perils

From Growth and Grand Hopes to Pursed Lips and Parsimony

S OMETHING about Canada's entry into the 1900s generated an explosion of energy and extravagant dreams. Something about preparing to leave the century engendered official parsimony and coast-to-coast anxiety. The early surge of constructive effort is reflected in the first issues of the *Maclean's* predecessor (*The Busy Man's Magazine*, 1905–1911). In the magazine of the 1990s, uncertainties about the land, its people and its future often induced a more anxious tone. The difference in mood, manner and outlook between the first and last decades of the 1900s is just one of the staggering changes that altered virtually every aspect of life in Canada during a century that involved its people in spasms of global violence and peacekeeping missions, hard times and boom years, natural catastrophes and outpourings of benevolence, man-made disasters and creative invention.

In counterpoint to time's transformations, the century's record also reflects the maturing of enduring elements in Canadian life–the made-in-Canada approaches to constructing a society that evolved, many Canadians came to believe, into bedrock components of the national character. A dominant Canadian trait from early times, as identified in the country's literature and art, involved a determination simply to survive in an isolated setting under siege from hostile

ALTHOUGH THE MOTOR vehicle began supplanting real horse power during the early years of the century, the horse and wagon—even the occasional surviving Red River cart on the Prairies, as here, in Edmonton—persisted on country roads and city streets until the middle of the century.

IMMIGRANT RECRUITING CAMPAIGNS in the United States and Europe, run through such agencies as this storefront office in London, England, helped to produce a land rush on the Prairies and an overall record rate of population growth in Canada during the first decade of the 20th century.

elements of nature. A central story of Canada's latest 100 years is about a society coping with the perennial frictions that roil relations among its people–between the aboriginal nations and later Canadians, anglophones and francophones, the nation and its regions, Quebec and the rest. It is about surviving such divisive and potentially destructive challenges by invoking Canada's passion for civility, compromise, co-operation and communalism.

Those values are essentials of national politics, where success requires the coalescing of diverse interests. They have reinforced the construction of another of the country's distinguishing features–its racial, ethnic and cultural mosaic. They underpin Canada's health care and social welfare programs, the political creations which, by wide consensus during the century's later decades, became touchstones of national identity. And it was the erosion of standards in health care and other national services in the 1990s that helped to provoke the peevish end-of-century anxieties. During the same decade, Canada repeatedly ranked first in the world on a United Nations quality-of-life index based on standards including income, education and life expectancy. But in the 1998 UN rankings, with Canada in top place for the fifth year in a row, an accompanying new survey measuring progress against poverty placed Canada only 10th among the 17 richest nations. (Sweden was first, the United States last.) The UN report cited Canada's "significant problems of poverty" and "poorly distributed" advances in human development.

Despite periodical spells of self-doubt, and the interruptions of two world wars and economic depression, progress was the Canadian watchword for much of the

THE DEVELOPMENT OF CANADA'S multiracial, inter-ethnic society is exemplified in this 1906 photograph of African-heritage Winnipeggers about to participate in a pastime of the Great White North. However, in 1911, border officials began turning away black Americans under a federal cabinet dictum stating that "the Negro race is deemed unsuitable to the climate and requirements of Canada."

1900s. The century produced a six-fold expansion in population, three additional provinces and an ever-growing inventory of new machines and living styles. The changes made life in the predominantly urban and materialistic Canada of the 1990s utterly unlike the primarily rural and religious society of the first decade. Things long considered necessities by the century's end were barely in people's imaginings at its beginning–from cars and jumbo jets to radios and TV, from automatic washers to quick cuisine by microwave, from movies to computers. Behavior regarded as aberrant in the early 1900s became acceptable, or at least tolerated: government-run gambling; women in the work force in huge numbers; gay men and women out of the closet; openly available birth control devices, including the

THE WINNIPEG GRAIN EXCHANGE grew into a financial engine influencing global dealings in the primary product of the Prairies.

pill that helped instigate the so-called sexual revolution, and double-adjective families—two-income, no-kids, same-sex and single-parent.

At the outset of the century, Prime Minister Wilfrid Laurier encouraged expectations of a boundless future for Canada. Applauding the country's multicultural richness while addressing Nova Scotia Acadians in 1900, Laurier envisaged a nation that would be foremost among the great powers of the world. And his forecast in 1904 that "the 20th century shall be the century of Canada" (since rendered more famously as "the 20th century belongs to Canada") reflected excitement over the emergence of Alberta and Saskatchewan as new provinces in 1905, the sense of a country growing up and outgrowing its colonial status. Commentator Goldwin Smith, offering readers of John Bayne Maclean's young magazine a forecast of Canadian destiny in May 1907, asserted: "When Canadians speak of their country as being a nation, which they habitually do, they anticipate her coming emancipation."

Maclean himself belied the reputed Canadian inferiority complex in his announcement, in November 1905, that his journal would run profiles of Canadian business leaders: "There are as interesting romances in their careers as are to be found in those of the great American or British captains of industry." Earl Grey, the governor general, joined in the general excitement, and tipped his top hat to the

men who forged Confederation 40 years earlier, with a
prophecy published by Maclean in September 1907:

"I never walk in the streets of Ottawa without
remembering, and with a feeling of exaltation, that I am
treading on soil which, before the close of the present century will carry the capital city of a nation of eighty millions. I never look at the buildings on Parliament Hill
without a feeling of admiration for and gratitude to the
old boys of 1867, who planned so bravely and so well, and
I hope the example of their faith in the future of their
country will animate every successive generation from
the Atlantic to the Pacific."

Given the optimistic temper of the times, Laurier
might be forgiven for awarding what emphatically proved to
be America's century to Canada, which even then was
strongly under the influence of U.S. commerce and culture.
(Laurier's proposal to regularize that relationship in a free-
trade treaty–an aborted precursor of Brian Mulroney's 1989
trade pact–contributed to the electoral defeat of the Laurier

ON MARCH 31, 1949, the British colony of
Newfoundland became the tenth province
of Canada. As this photo suggests, there was
a lingering nostalgia for the old days.

Liberals in 1911, just as Mulroney's too-cozy relations with U.S. leaders played a part in
the demolition of his Progressive Conservative Party in the election of 1993.)

The emancipation from Britain envisaged by Goldwin Smith evolved by gradual increments: Canada gaining control of its foreign policy (1926), establishing
Canadian citizenship (1947), abolishing judicial appeals to Britain (1949), inaugu-
rating the Maple Leaf flag (1965) and patriating from Britain the power to amend
the constitution (1982).

As for Earl Grey's exaggerated estimate of population by century's end,
Canada would indeed have counted 80 million residents by the middle 1990s had
the growth rate of Grey's time persisted. Between 1901 and the 1911 census, a land
rush to the Prairies by Americans and Europeans helped expand the population
by one third (from 5.4 million to 7.2 million). Immigration paced similar surges in
production, trade–and optimism. But the population growth rate during the
century's first 10 years was unmatched in any other decade. Canada reached only
the 30-million mark shortly before the century's end.

During the later years of the century, the country experienced a creative
explosion in the arts and entertainment of all kinds and in both official languages.

IN THE EARLY 1900s, the Toronto Industrial Exhibition was already moving well beyond its original emphasis on agriculture and machinery. In 1912 its name would change to the Canadian National Exhibition, and the Ex would remain a fixture of Toronto life for the rest of the century.

THE DISTRIBUTION of Crown land to settlers in the early part of the century sometimes took the form of a race for the prize concessions. Here, landseekers are at the start of a run from Scott, Saskatchewan.

But economic prosperity was not as flourishing. In contrast to the opening emphasis on expansion, the dominating developments of the 1990s were more about retrenchment–staff "downsizing" in business and stringent bookkeeping in government as deficit financing became a political bogey. At the same time, the removal of capitalism's longtime challenger with the collapse of the Soviet Union's communist empire encouraged the triumphant western system to engage in ever greater speculative ventures at home and abroad.

In the century's closing months, anxiety over an economic downturn abroad, a depressed dollar, shrunken average incomes, persistent unemployment and fears for national unity left many Canadians fretting over the future of the country. National governance waned with the devolution of federal responsibilities to the provinces. The downsizing crusade diminished democracy itself. Ontario, for one, devalued voting power by merging boards of education and taking direct control of them, struck further at grassroots people power with similar action against municipal governments, and then eroded the value of votes provincewide by shrinking the legislature.

Optimism was in greatly shorter supply on the eve of the 21st century than during the boom beginnings of the 20th. But as the country's writers and artists had been advising for the better part of of the passing century, an educated instinct for survival is a thing Canadians share–something that east and west, Quebec and the rest, know how to do. It means coping with the periodic cruelties of a tough climate and guarding the land from spoilage. It means trying to keep the country from falling apart and withstanding the absorptive allure of the big neighbor. Such experience served as a promise that Canada, practised in surviving the passing century's fearsome wars and economic tribulations, its social upheavals and political perils, stood poised to survive a troubled transition into the new millennium.

1906 Cobalt's Undreamt-of Wealth

MAY 1906 **C**obalt is a name to conjure with today, just as Klondike was some years ago. The rich silver mines of New Ontario are yielding undreamt-of stores of wealth. This little bit of wilderness of Northern Ontario, situated by rail exactly 330 miles north of Toronto, lays claim to the possession of mines that produce the richest silver-bearing ore the world has ever known and the richest cobalt mines in the world.

Railway authorities have estimated that anywhere up to 250,000 people may find their way to the Cobalt country this season. It is said that the revenue from the mines in the Gillies timber limit alone will be sufficient to defray all the expenses of governing the province. It is safe to say that Cobalt is not a flash in the pan.

SPECULATORS AND WOULD-BE MINERS flocked in the early 1900s to the Northern Ontario settlement of Cobalt, named for the mineral that accompanied new-found veins of silver. The Cobalt craze was a follow-up to the Klondike gold rush in the Yukon Territory a decade earlier.

1906 Land Rush in the North West

OCTOBER 1906 **N**ot so very long ago our maps showed that immense tract, lying between the Great Lakes and the Rockies, as simply Prince Rupert's Land, and the popular idea saw little in it but a fur trading ground for the Hudson Bay Co. The awakening came, and from a territory that was scarcely considered in the affairs of state has emerged 600,000 square miles of fertile country. It is a great natural heritage, and wealth and energy have been freely invested, with assurance of large returns.

The greatest influx into our west has been from the United States. The thrifty Yankee from Minnesota, the Dakotas, and, eventually, many other states, found that he could sell out his property, go across the line into "Canadee," buy ten acres for every one that he had at home, and better land, besides securing 160 acres free for each of his sons and himself. He moved quick and is getting rich fast. He has become a good Canadian.

THE FERTILITY OF the Canadian Prairies and the bargain prices for property, publicized by Ottawa throughout North America and overseas, attracted thousands of migrants from eastern Canada, the United States and Europe.

To go through the west is to get the land fever. It seems to be in the air. Real estate agents are a multitude. There is money in it for the speculator and money in it for the farmer. Both should be happy. In the meantime, the Great West is prospering. Most of the settlers own their land, have money in the bank, and look forward to another big crop. The land of No. 1 hard wheat, where the climate makes it almost a crime to die of anything but old age, is filling up fast, but still has lots of room.

1996 A Seventh Lean Year in the Land

Carl Mollins – DECEMBER 30, 1996   **A** stubbornly slack economy, made meaner by toughened governmental austerity and corporate cutbacks, enlarged the toll of the unemployed to more than 1.5 million people during 1996. More than 500,000 others are dropouts from the job hunt or never managed to join the shrinking labor force. Bankruptcies ballooned. The year-end *Maclean's*/CBC News poll found most respondents resigned to the prospect of a future without enough jobs to go around or sufficient support for the jobless, the sick, the poor and the old.

Such expectations also aroused public anger and resistance. In the seventh lean year since the start of the slump in 1990, people took to the streets in protest. Efforts to gain job security provoked major strikes: 55,000 Ontario government employees early in the year and 26,000 autoworkers in the fall. Rallies against reductions in health care ranged from British Columbia to New Brunswick. On a cross-Canada crusade against cuts in social services, thousands of women marched to join a mid-June demonstration in Ottawa. Opponents of provincial policies staged mass protests in Ontario and Quebec. For many, the actions recalled a march on Ottawa and other protests during the Great Depression of the 1930s, which gave rise to social benefits—welfare, unemployment insurance, pensions and, ultimately, medicare—now decimated or endangered by budget-cutting federal and provincial governments.

In direct counterpoint to job losses, investors and the financial industry enjoyed a bonanza. Business on the Toronto Stock Exchange set records. Bank profits, and multimillion-dollar salaries to business leaders, professional athletes and entertainment celebrities, did likewise. Corporations changed hands for billions of dollars. Canadian Airlines escaped bankruptcy with bailouts from Ottawa, Alberta, British Columbia—and from its employees via another pay cut. And Ottawa reported progress in its crusade against the annual budget deficit—notably, from a huge surplus in the national unemployment insurance fund after reducing benefits.

Some market seers forecast better times ahead—but only, they advised, if consumers get over their insecurities, take advantage of tumbled interest rates and start borrowing and spending to buck up the economy.

1998 Storm Warnings

Mary Janigan – OCTOBER 12, 1998   The sheer scope of the financial calamity has become almost too large to grasp. In Russia, the Red Cross has launched an emergency appeal, warning that the nation faces mass starvation. In Brazil, the International Monetary Fund is cobbling together an emergency multibillion-dollar package of loans to shore up the nation's reserves–and to protect other imperiled South American markets. In the United States, private financial institutions are bailing out a rogue hedge fund, Long-Term Capital Management LP, which has lost billions of dollars in high-risk deals. And in Canada, investors are reeling at the news that the economy shrank for the fourth consecutive month in July, raising fears that Canada and the world are drifting into the worst financial crisis since 1929. "We are not immune from the global storm," Finance Minister Paul Martin insisted in an interview last week. "But the underlying strength of the Canadian economy has improved dramatically. The economy of the United States continues to be strong. We don't have to panic."

Even so, panic seemed to sweep across the globe. Stock markets plunged and the economic storm clouds spread so fast that world leaders scrambled to co-ordinate their

IN ONE OF A SERIES of public protests during the 1990s against reductions in social spending in federal budgets and by several provincial governments, thousands of people joined the National Women's March Against Poverty en route to Ottawa, in the spring of 1996.

rescue operations. The fear of global crisis—and the desperate need for a solution—are now palpable and powerful. The stakes for Canada mount with each passing day. There is widespread fear that the contagion will erode markets for U.S. exports—and thus damage Canada's major customer. The fall of the Canadian dollar, which closed last week at 64.73 U.S. cents, reflected fears that the economy is still contracting.

1998 Globalism Wears Thin

Deirdre McMurdy – OCTOBER 16, 1998 **N**o trend has been more red-hot in recent years than the concept of globalization, which has dominated the agendas of government and business alike. Dazzled by jargon and "strategic vision," investors have rewarded companies that have leverage by letting them into international markets. Companies have also been pushed to expand their horizons by free trade policy and government-sponsored trade missions.

But suddenly, the glamor of global commerce has worn thin. And there is a growing risk, amid calls for controls on the movement of capital and government intervention in financial markets, that a renewed fondness for protectionism will further exacerbate the economic pressures already squeezing world economies.

The biggest danger is the return of protectionism. The United States is especially vulnerable because of a trade deficit. Moreover, with other currencies devalued relative to the U.S. dollar, American producers of steel, petrochemicals, microchips, lumber and wheat have already begun to lobby Washington for protection against dumping.

Companies that have successfully capitalized on the recent fashion for global leverage are scrambling as investors turn against them. Many must now reconsider the costly mergers and acquisitions they have undertaken as part of a broader strategy to compete for business on an international scale.

A decline in globally driven corporate deals will further chill investor confidence. What is equally unsettling for

WHILE THE ECONOMIC RECESSION of the early 1990s put a crimp in major capital investment, the smallest province pushed ahead with the 12.9-km-long Confederation Bridge, Canada's longest, linking Prince Edward Island and New Brunswick. The bridge was opened in 1997.

companies that have relied on global jargon for so long is that they must now find a new management strategy. That is because in the foreseeable future, the principal global event on the horizon is a recession.

Tweedletory, Tweedlegrit

Successful National Politicians Hogged the Middle of the Road

ON the scorecard of Canadian federal politics, the 20th century belonged to the Liberals. They overwhelmed the Conservatives by a margin of two to one: Liberals occupied the Prime Minister's Office two-thirds of the time while winning almost two out of every three general elections. But in the long run of history, and on matters of ideology, policy or legislative programs, it really made little difference which of the two traditional parties held sway in Ottawa. Endurance in office generally depended on which party better managed to hold the comfortable political middle ground–and to compromise when upstart regional or reformist parties tried to cut in on the two-party minuet.

At times, a third party did exert influence, especially when a minority government required its parliamentary support to survive. The agrarian Progressive Party, favoring free trade with the United States, gained a voice in the splintered Parliaments of the 1920s (and in a 1942 merger turned the Conservative Party into the Progressive Conservative Party). The western-based Social Credit Party, the offshoot Ralliement des Créditistes of Quebec and the leftist New Democratic Party each at times exercised influence in the fractionated House of Commons of the 1960s, the NDP later able to exert balance-of-power pressure on the minority Liberal government of

SEATED BENEATH A PORTRAIT of Sir Wilfrid Laurier, the Liberal prime minister who led Canada into the 20th century, Louis St. Laurent (left) chats with William Lyon Mackenzie King, the man St. Laurent succeeded in 1948 as Liberal leader and prime minister.

THROUGHOUT HIS POLITICAL career, Wilfrid Laurier crusaded, in his own words, to promote unity and harmony and amity between the diverse elements of this country. He is pictured here at Ste. Anne de Beaupré, Quebec, on September 20, 1911, on the eve of an election that terminated his tenure as prime minister after 15 years.

1972-1974. Otherwise, apart from such mavericks as John Diefenbaker and Pierre Trudeau, the mainly middle-class leaders of the big middling parties delivered largely orderly but interchangeable governance—that is, until the 1990s.

The century's closing years brought signs of erosion in the Tory-Grit consensus. The Conservatives languished in critically reduced circumstances (as they had in the 1920s and the 1940s). They were eclipsed in opposition during the 1990s, first by the regional Bloc Québécois and then by the Reform Party, successor to the Progressives and Social Credit out of the West. At the same time, Prime Minister Jean Chrétien conveyed a sense of conformity and continuity. His Liberals seemed as solidly and blandly entrenched as were Wilfrid Laurier's during the century's opening decade, and his unexciting administration fit the dominant governing style of the 1900s. Chrétien, born in 1934, even shared the January 11 birthday of founding prime minister John A. Macdonald (born in 1815).

The 1990s also gave rise elsewhere to a political style that eschewed principles smacking of ideology and sought to balance between the electorate's apparent disillusionment with government generally and, paradoxically, the majority's evident desire for political activism on behalf of the public welfare. Commentators called it "third way" politics and cited as its pioneer practioners Bill Clinton, the chameleon-like U.S. president, and nominal social democratic leaders in Europe such as Britain's Tony Blair and Germany's Gerhard Schroeder. In Canada, the citation went to Saskatchewan Premier Roy Romanow as an exemplar of a New Democrat (a label Clinton used) practising middle-way politics. But in national Canadian politics there is nothing new about the third way. In a country of fractious regions and disparate interests, the third way has almost always been the only way to succeed electorally in federal politics.

CONSERVATIVE CHIEF R.B. Bennett (left) linking arms with his prime political nemesis, Liberal leader Mackenzie King, during a Toronto encounter midway through Bennett's early-1930s term as prime minister.

OPPOSITE:
*PIERRE TRUDEAU,
the most charismatic
prime minister since the
elegant and eloquent
Wilfrid Laurier, rode a
wave of Trudeaumania
into power in 1968 but
later alienated some
early supporters with
such behavior as flaunt-
ing an Edwardian
dandy's costume for
the 1970 Grey Cup
football game.*

TOP: *THE FIRST NATIVE of western Canada to be prime
minister, and the youngest to hold that office, Joe Clark,
born in High River, Alberta, here celebrates his election
victory on May 22, 1979. An election nine months later
cut short his time in office, but in 1998 the Conservatives
again picked Clark as party leader.*

ABOVE LEFT: *BRIAN MULRONEY KIBITZES with campaign supporters and press in the election campaign of
1984 that saw his party sweep to power with the largest
caucus of MPs in Canadian history. Despite his success in
that election and the subsequent one—the first back-to-back
majority governments for the Conservatives since the days
of Sir John A. Macdonald—Mulroney's legacy of free trade
with the United States, the GST and two failed attempts
at constitutional reform would be hotly debated till the
end of the century.*

ABOVE RIGHT: *KIM CAMPBELL, here being welcomed
home to Vancouver as the new prime minister on June 26,
1993, carried a heavy inheritance of public animosity
towards the Mulroney Conservatives into an election four
months later that reduced Tory strength from 152 MPs to
a lonely pair, not including the defeated prime minister.*

*PRIME MINISTER Robert Borden (at front right) and
leaders of other Dominions of the British Empire prepared
in London at the end of 1918 for postwar peace treaty talks
in Versailles, France. Borden, reflecting Canadian nationalism, won Canada a seat at Versailles in its own right,
and a signature on the treaty separate from the Empire's.*

1993 Prime Ministerial Minutiae

JUNE 21, 1993

First Minister Firsts

Kim Campbell, who became Canada's first woman prime minister on June 25, 1993, following her election as leader of the Progressive Conservatives, was also the first British Columbian to hold the office. As well, she was the first prime minister born after the outbreak of the Second World War (her birthday: March 10, 1947).

In the Upper Brackets

Average age of all 20 prime ministers on assuming office: 59, which was Jean Chrétien's age when he replaced Kim Campbell on November 4, 1993. The seven Liberals and seven Conservatives who served during the 20th century were younger—an average 54—upon entering office. The oldest overall was Charles Tupper, 74 when he took office on May 1, 1896, and 75 when he left it 68 days later—

IN A CENTENNIAL-YEAR cabinet shuffle on April 4, 1967, Prime Minister Pearson appointed three rising Liberal stars who were destined to follow him as head of government: Pierre Trudeau, then 47, as justice minister; John Turner, 38, registrar-general; and Jean Chrétien, 33, as a junior minister in the finance department.

JEAN CHRÉTIEN IN SHAWINIGAN, Quebec, with his wife, Aline, on October 25, 1993, when the voters awarded his Liberals power in Parliament and Chrétien the prime ministership. After a renewed mandate in 1997, the self-described petit gar de Shawinigan *seemed set to lead the country into the new century.*

the shortest term. The youngest: Joe Clark, sworn in on June 4, 1979, one day before his 40th birthday.

A Record in ex-PMs

When Kim Campbell took office, Canada had four living former prime ministers, the first time there had been more than three. She herself made it five living ex-PMs only 19 weeks later, when she joined predecessors Joe Clark, Pierre Trudeau, John Turner and Brian Mulroney.

Fertility Rates

Mary Macdonald, born on February 8, 1869, to Agnes and John A. Macdonald, was the first child born to a prime minister in office. The second came more than 100 years

*DESPITE THE SMILES AMONG
John Diefenbaker, U.S. president John
Kennedy and British prime minister
Harold Macmillan at this 1962 Bahamas
encounter, the Canadian and American
leaders disliked each other, Diefenbaker
having balked at what he regarded as
American pushiness on several fronts.*

*LESTER PEARSON, here at a salmon fish-
ing derby near Vancouver in 1965, won
the Nobel Peace Prize while external affairs
minister for his role in settling the Suez
conflict of 1956, but the Canadian electorate
never awarded him more than minority
support in Parliament as prime minister
during the 1960s.*

later: Justin Trudeau on Christmas Day, 1971. The third and fourth are also Trudeaus–
Alexandre (Sacha), also born on Christmas, in 1973, and Michel, born on October 2,
1975. The fifth and latest is Nicolas Mulroney, born on September 4, 1985, the first
anniversary of the election that propelled his father into the Prime Minister's Office.

Ottawa Knights

Seven of the first eight prime ministers received British knighthoods (Alexander
Mackenzie spurned the title). In 1919, Parliament put an end to such honors–after
the current prime minister had become Sir Robert Borden, the last to be knighted.
R.B. Bennett resurrected the practice in the early 1930s, but Mackenzie King's
government put a stop to it again in 1935 and Bennett retired to England as a plain
mister.

A Prevalence of Lawyers

Lawyers have dominated the Prime Minister's Office–in all, 14 of 20 pursued that
career, 11 of the 14 who served in the 20th century. Three former journalists who
held the office: Alexander Mackenzie, editor of the *Shield*, a newspaper in Lambton,
Ontario; Mackenzie Bowell, owner-editor of *The Intelligencer* of Belleville, Ontario;
and Joe Clark, who worked for the *High River Times* and The Canadian Press in
Alberta. The three others: Charles Tupper was a medical doctor, the first president
of the Canadian Medical Association (1867-1870); Mackenzie King and diplomat
Lester Pearson had been career civil servants.

Quebec Prevails in Ottawa

Quebecers dominated the federal leadership during the 20th Century, five men from that often reluctant province of Canada heading the national government half the time in all. The four Quebec Liberal prime ministers–Wilfrid Laurier, Louis St. Laurent, Pierre Trudeau and Jean Chrétien–together served more than 40 years, Conservative Brian Mulroney accounting for the rest of Quebec's occupancy of the country's primary post.

1997 Ranking the Prime Ministers

APRIL 21, 1997 **M**ackenzie King takes top place in a rating of Canadian prime ministers produced by a survey of 25 historians conducted by Norman Hillmer of Carleton University, Ottawa, and J.L. Granatstein, a resident fellow at the Canadian Institute of International Affairs, Toronto. The reason for King's first place? In the view of the University of Calgary's Patrick Brennan: "He was–after all the spiritualist and other jokes about his private life–our greatest prime minister. He tried to understand the country, he was capable of intellectual flexibility and change, and he attracted and held able colleagues. He was an intellectual who was sympathetic to ideas–our first."

Pierre Trudeau, second only to King in terms of time in office by a 20th-century prime minister (15 years to King's 21), ranked only fifth because, as Hillmer and Granatstein wrote, "Many academics believed that Trudeau had exacerbated difficulties with Quebec with his imposition of the War Measures Act in 1970 and the divisive struggle he waged leading to the patriation of the Constitution in 1982."

Brian Mulroney, the surveyors noted, "was seen as a Gucci-shod glad-hander in bed with the Yankees, the man who failed so dismally in his constitutional gambits and left office so hated by the Canadian public that it promptly destroyed his party in an act of calculated revenge." The historians rated Jean Chrétien, then in office about 3-1/2 years and shortly to win another term, behind Mulroney. The ranking:

GREAT:
1. **William Lyon Mackenzie King** (Liberal, 1921-1930*; 1935-1948)
2. **Sir John A. Macdonald** (Conservative, 1867-1873; 1878-1891)
3. **Sir Wilfrid Laurier** (Liberal, 1896-1911)

NEAR-GREAT:
4. **Louis St.-Laurent** (Liberal, 1948-1957)

HIGH-AVERAGE:
5. **Pierre Elliott Trudeau** (Liberal, 1968-1979 and 1980-1984)
6. **Lester Pearson** (Liberal, 1963-1968)
7. **Sir Robert Borden** (Conservative, 1911-1920)

AVERAGE:
8. **Brian Mulroney** (Conservative, 1984-1993)
9. **Jean Chrétien** (Liberal 1993-)

10. **Sir John Thompson** (Conservative, 1892-1894)
11. **Alexander Mackenzie** (Liberal, 1873-1878)
12. **R.B. Bennett** (Conservative, 1930-1935)
13. **John Diefenbaker** (Conservative, 1957-1963)

LOW-AVERAGE:
14. **Arthur Meighen** (Conservative, 1920-1921; 1926*)
   * Meighen held office for three months in 1926

15. **Joe Clark** (Conservative, 1979-1980)

FAILURE:
16. **Sir Charles Tupper** (Conservative, 68 days in 1896)
17. **Sir John Abbott** (Conservative, 1891-1892)
18. **John Turner** (Liberal, 79 days in 1984)
19. **Sir Mackenzie Bowell** (Conservative, 1894-1896)
20. **Kim Campbell** (Conservative, 132 days in 1993)

The Longest Revolution

Women Won Political Battles, Fighting Many Forms of Bias

W AY stations in the long and continuing progress toward equal rights for women in Canada may be tracked across the century in the pages of *Maclean's*. With increasing frequency over the years, the magazine published important articles about and by women, reflecting their painfully slow improvements of status in Canadian society. A report on a pro-suffrage demonstration in front of the Ontario legislature in 1909 captured the frustrations of the long struggle to convince politicians that women should be able to vote and to seek political office–rights gained federally in steps by 1920 and provincially from 1916 on the Prairies to 1940 in Quebec. Protracted litigation to include women in the law's definition of "persons"–status constitutionally necessary to qualify, for one thing, for appointment to the Senate–finally succeeded in 1929. As for achieving equality with men in other aspects of living and working, key parts of that crusade outlasted the 1900s.

From Victorian times, when women were barred from medical schools and law schools, the freedom to pursue careers in traditional male preserves expanded, if grudgingly, over the years. Despite steady gains in employment, women's earnings still lagged behind male incomes as the century drew to a

CANADIAN WOMEN BEGAN invading male preserves in the job market during the First World War, but thousands, including Vancouver shipyard welder Mary Lin, shown here in 1944, streamed into the labor force during the Second World War, increasing the female presence from fewer than one out of four paid workers in 1939 to one in three by the war's end.

close, and "the glass ceiling" imposed limits on the number of women in top management. Progress might have been even slower but for the impetus provided by the two world wars, when women proved themselves in the workforce in massive numbers and served in auxiliary military units or the home guard.

Beyond the wars, the political activism of the 1960s fuelled the feminist movement and related women's pressure groups. Their campaigning gave rise to a political turning point in 1967, when the federal government appointed the Royal Commission on the Status of Women, which issued a report three years later containing 167 recommendations urging the improvement of women's conditions related to employment, education and family law. The subsequent establishment of the National Action Committee on the Status of Women served to promote the commission's proposals and its lobbying helped persuade the government to include a minister for the status of women in the federal cabinet, to set up an Office of Equal Opportunities in the federal public service and to erase elements of the law that discriminated against women. Still, progress on other fronts was slow—notably in applying legal provisions to ensure "equal pay for work of equal value" and on repeatedly shelved political promises to establish a national day-care program for working mothers. After the 1997 federal election—76 years after Agnes Campbell Macphail became the first female MP—women constituted only 21 per cent of Parliament's membership.

CALGARY-BORN Doris McCubbin Anderson, as editor of Chatelaine *from 1957 to 1977, played a leadership role in the women's rights movement.*

On the issue of women's reproductive rights, Parliament and the courts were somewhat more responsive to pressure over a span of almost 20 years. In 1969, the government of Pierre Trudeau erased an 1892 Criminal Code provision against birth control and simultaneously legalized abortion, albeit only when a three-member committee in an approved hospital certified that the pregnancy endangered the woman's health. In 1988, the Supreme Court struck down the abortion

WOMEN WAR WORKERS, including these demonstrating steelworkers in 1945, worried about losing their jobs to returning military men. In fact, a booming postwar economy easily absorbed the women, the war veterans and a rush of refugees. From 1946 to 1959, the average unemployment rate was under 3 per cent of the labor force.

JEANNE SAUVÉ'S appointment as governor general in 1984 was a first for a woman, and followed her previous groundbreaking role as the first female Speaker of the House of Commons. With the governor general in this photo are her husband, Maurice, himself a distinguished politician, and Prime Minister Pierre Trudeau.

measure as unconstitutional, effectively handing the responsibility for reproductive decisions to the woman and her doctor.

Earlier, feminist groups successfully pressed Ottawa to include a gender-equality provision in the Charter of Rights and Freedoms, a new feature of the 1982 Constitution. Nonetheless, the fight for reform of social attitudes seemed never-ending. In May 1982, only a few weeks after the charter of rights was signed into law on Parliament Hill by the Queen, MP Margaret Mitchell stood in the House of Commons and raised the issue of violence against women, only to be greeted by laughter and raucous banter from some male MPs.

A much more sombre and troubled reaction, across the country, followed the news of the selective slaughter of 14 female engineering students in Montreal on December 6, 1989. The Montreal Massacre, as it came to be known, resonated across the country in a lasting way—with anniversary vigils and permanent memorials—as the ultimate symbol of the durable plague of violence against women.

1909 Men and Events in the Public Eye

MAY 1909 **O**ne of the important events of the past month was the suffragette demonstration at the Parliament Buildings, Toronto, on March 24, when a petition said to contain 100,000 names of Canadians favoring the granting to women of the right to vote on the same terms as men was presented to Premier Whitney by a delegation numbering nearly 1,000, mostly women. At the head of the deputation was Dr. Augusta Stowe Gullen, president of the Canadian Suffrage Association, and the first Canadian woman to take a medical degree from a Canadian University. Back about 1867, Dr. Emily Stowe, a Canadian woman, took her medical degree in a New

PIONEER SUFFRAGISTS in the Winnipeg Equality League for Enfranchisement of Women pose with pages of petition signatures in 1915: A.V. Thomas and F.J. Dixon standing, Mary Crawford seated beside 93-year-old Amelia Burrit. On January 28, 1916, Manitoba women became the first in Canada to win the right to vote in legislative elections.

York university and began practising in Toronto. Sixteen years later, in 1883, her daughter, Augusta Stowe, completed her schooling and made application for enrollment in Toronto University as a student, only to be refused by the Senate of that institution because of her sex. Trinity College, however, accepted her as a student in medicine, and for four years she suffered all the indignities and horseplay that a body of male medicals could impose upon one whom they considered as an intruder.

Memories of those years must have crowded themselves into Dr. Stowe Gullen's mind when she stepped forward to address Sir James Whitney and present the suffrage petition. "Taxation without representation," she said after a few words of introduction, "is tyranny. I never like to use the word

ON OCTOBER 18, 1929, a British court reversed Canadian rulings that "persons" in Canada's constitution meant men only. Five Albertans— Emily Ferguson Murphy, Nellie Mooney McClung, Irene Marryat Parlby, Louise Crummy McKinney and Henrietta Muir Edwards—were known as the Valiant Five for their persistence in the Persons Case.

47

THROUGHOUT THE CENTURY, technology and social pressures broadened the employment and entrepreneurial opportunities for women, from the early secretarial pool (far left) and work in the garment trade (above) to ventures such as Una Thurlow's equipment leasing operation in suburban Toronto (below) and the appointment of Maureen Kempston Darkes (left) as president of General Motors of Canada.

tyranny but I learned it from–gentlemen. The home is not only woman's sphere but man's also, and because he has been neglecting it, we women feel the need of the ballot. It has been stated that the hand that rocks the cradle rules the world but the baby does not always stay in the cradle; it goes into the office and factory. Labor needs humanizing for the women as well as for the men," said the doctor in concluding her argument. A dozen speakers supported Dr. Stowe Gullen, and Sir James Whitney in his reply stated that it was too late in the session to introduce legislation dealing with such a momentous question and he asked the ladies to "call again" another year.

1916 The Woman Soldier

APRIL 1916 **T**he enlistment of women in Canada has begun in earnest, and organizations for drill are forming in all the large cities. The Duke of Connaught [governor general] reviewed the women troops at Vancouver and gave them high praise.

It is always invidious to draw lines of sex distinction where they are not essential. Yet it is true that man most resents the destruction of property, which is his personal product, and woman that of human life.

Many persons have a confused notion that women's militarism has something to do with suffragette militancy. Nothing could be more mistaken. Many militants are pacifists. Other suffragists are ardently nationalist and militaristic.

1916 Speaking of Women

MAY 1916 *The first of numerous* Maclean's *articles by Nellie Letitia Mooney McClung (1873-1951), writer, suffragist, politician and prohibitionist, was her report on the Alberta legislature's decision in 1916 to extend political rights to women.* Maclean's *flagged the article as a counterpoint to "The Woman Question," an essay published the previous October by humorist Stephen Leacock (he caricatured the suffragist as "The Awful Woman—meddlesome, vociferous, intrusive"). In her report, McClung makes no response to Leacock, but does note : "That women are physically inferior to men is a*

THE CANADIAN SOLDIER conversing with a boy in Haiti while on United Nations peacekeeping duty in 1995 is one of thousands who served in similar situations, often in danger, in Asia, Africa and Europe, as well as the Americas, throughout the last half of the century.

strange reason for placing them under a further handicap, and we are surprised to find it advanced in all seriousness as an argument against woman suffrage. No man has the right to citizenship on his weight, height or lifting power; he exercises this right because he is a human being with hands to work, brain to think and a life to live." The Alberta bill to enfranchise women became law seven weeks after winning approval in principle on second reading.

On March 1st, at 3 o'clock in the afternoon, the Woman Suffrage Bill was given its second reading in the Legislature of Alberta, and the women of the province gathered in large numbers to hear the debate. For over an hour before the galleries were opened, women waited at the foot of the stairs; white-haired women, women with little children by the hand, women with babies in

DECADES OF CAMPAIGNING by women for the rights to vote and to seek political office preceded successes that began in 1916 in the Prairie provinces. Alberta campaign leaders Nellie McClung, Alice Jamieson and Emily Murphy join here to celebrate their franchise law.

their arms, smartly dressed women, alert, tailor-made business women; quiet, dignified and earnest; they were all there; they filled the galleries; they packed every available space. Many were unable to find a place in the gallery, and stood outside in the corridors.

"I consider it an honor to stand anywhere in the building," one bright-eyed old lady said when someone expressed regret at not having a seat for her, "and I can read the speeches tomorrow and imagine that I heard them."

When the Premier (Liberal A.L. Sifton) rose to move the second reading of the bill, the silence of the legislative chamber was tense, and the great mass of humanity in the galleries did not appear to breathe. The Premier outlined the reasons for the granting of the franchise; he did not speak of it as a favor, a boon, a gift, or a privilege, but a right, and declared that the extension of the franchise was an act of justice; he did not once refer to us as the "fair sex."

The leader of the Opposition (Conservative Edward Michener), whose advocacy of woman franchise dates back many years, seconded the reading of the bill; and short speeches were made by other members. There was only one who opposed it; one timorous brother declared it would break up the home.

A TORONTO WOMAN expresses her jubilation at the end of the war in 1945 and the availability once more of silk stockings.

1988 An Unambiguous Call from the Court

FEBRUARY 8, 1988 **T**he staff members at Toronto's Morgentaler Clinic were hoping for victory–but braced for defeat. When they learned that the Supreme Court of Canada had ruled that the federal abortion law was unconstitutional, the women leaped with joy, hugging each other and cheering. They put bottles of champagne into a tiny freezer to toast Dr. Henry Morgentaler's victory over charges of conspiracy to procure illegal abortions. They congratulated Morgentaler's companion, Arlene Leibovitch, who was visiting the clinic with their three-week-old son, Benjamin Joseph. Then, one jubilant staff member turned to a patient reclining in an easy chair outside the third-floor operating room. "Do you know," she asked, "that you have just had the first legal abortion in this clinic?"

The implications of that simple question were staggering. In a 5-to-2 ruling on January 28, the Supreme Court in Ottawa had declared that Canada's abortion law

BEFORE AND AFTER the Supreme Court legalized abortion, self-designated pro-choice (left) and pro-life (right) groups promoted their conflicting opinions in the picketing of clinics and public demonstrations. In violent attacks during the 1990s, gunfire wounded three Canadian doctors at abortion clinics.

was unconstitutional because it violated a woman's right to "life, liberty and security of the person." The decision immediately wiped the abortion law off the books– making abortion a private matter between a woman and her doctor. It put politicians in the uncomfortable position of having to find a social consensus on the divisive issue. And it indicated that the highest court in the land was prepared to use the Charter of Rights and Freedoms in bold new ways. Chief Justice Brian Dickson's sur- prisingly tough language underlined that determination: "Forcing a woman by threat of criminal sanction to carry a fetus to term unless she meets certain criteria unrelated to her own priorities and aspirations is a profound interference with a woman's body."

1989 A Nation Mourns

Barry Came – DECEMBER 18, 1989 **A**t first, they viewed it as a prank, some kind of collegiate farce in keeping with the festive spirit that marked the second-last day of classes at the University of Montreal's Ecole polytechnique. The man was about the same age as most of the roughly 60 engineering students in Room 303 of the yellow- brick building on the the north slope of the mountain in the heart of the city. He entered the classroom slowly a few minutes past 5 p.m. on a bitterly cold afternoon, a shy smile on his face as he interrupted a dissertation on the mechanics of heat transfer. In clear, unaccented French, he asked the women to move to one side of the room and ordered the men to leave. The request was greeted with titters of laughter. "Nobody moved," recalled Prof. Yvan Bouchard. "We thought it was a joke." An instant later, Bouchard and his students discovered that what they were confronting was no joke.

The young man, who would later be identified as a 25-year-old semi-recluse named Marc Lepine, lifted a light, semi-automatic rifle and fired two quick shots into the ceiling. "You're all a bunch of feminists, and I hate feminists," Lepine shouted at the suddenly terrified occupants of Room 303. He told the men to leave—they did so without protest—and, as one of the young

THE MURDER OF 14 FEMALE engineering students in Montreal on December 6, 1989, by a gunman who killed himself gave rise to annual vigils of commemoration, as here, at the University of Montreal in 1990, to draw attention to the physical abuse of women.

women attempted to reason with him, the man opened fire in earnest. Six of the women were shot dead. Over the next 20 minutes, he methodically stalked the cafeteria, the classrooms and corridors of the school, leaving a trail of death and injury. He gunned down a total of 27 people, leaving 14 of them dead, then turned his weapon against himself, blowing off the top of his skull. Most of the injured and all of the dead—except for the gunman—were women.

It was the worst single-day massacre in Canadian history. And the very senselessness of the act prompted an outpouring of grief and rage. The City of Montreal and the Province of Quebec declared three days of mourning. Vigils were mounted in cities and towns from coast to coast.

The Peaceable Kingdom at War

Waging War Won Canada Credits Abroad, but Took a Tragic Toll in Young Lives

F OR a country that nurtures a reputation as a peaceable kingdom–its own land unsullied by battle since the Métis rebellion in 1885, its soldiers famed as peacekeepers since 1948–Canada nevertheless acquired a record during the century that indicates a ready capacity for combat abroad. From the Boer War to the Kosovo war in the Balkans, Canada committed soldiers, sailors and fliers to a total of almost 16 years of fighting overseas, the equivalent of eight weeks a year.

That total counts only the conflicts where the soldier's pay came from Ottawa–the two world wars (1914-1918 and 1939-1945), an abortive intervention against the Bolshevik revolution in Russia (1918-1919), the Korean War (1950-1953) as well as the British war against the Boers in South Africa (1899-1902), the American war against Iraq on the Persian Gulf (January-February 1991) and with NATO in the Balkans (1999). In two other overseas conflicts, Canadians enlisted as volunteers. Despite a 1937 Canadian law forbidding their participation, about 1,600 Canadians fought as the Mackenzie-Papineau Battalion in the first armed struggle against European fascism, the Spanish Civil War (1936-1939). Years

CANADIANS IN THE FIRST WORLD WAR advance under bursts of German artillery fire on Vimy Ridge, in northeastern France, a heroic but costly battle in which the Canadians finally prevailed.

54

THE DISPATCH of Canadians to help Britain in the Boer War (as here, in a field hospital), provoked protests at home by nationalists in Quebec. Prime Minister Wilfrid Laurier, noting in 1900 that French and English Canadians had fought and died together and shared a South African grave, expressed a hope that "in that grave shall be buried the last vestiges of our former antagonism."

later, several thousand Canadians (estimates vary widely) joined U.S. forces in a fruitless fight against communism in Vietnam (1959-1973).

For many people on the home front, military missions may themselves provide purpose enough to justify joining the cause–turning back fascism in the Second World War or quelling hostilities in foreign war zones. And Canadian military accomplishments get credit at home not only for furthering great causes and good works abroad but also for promoting Canada's own progress to nationhood and economic maturity. At mid-century, military historian C.P. Stacey wrote that "The First World War was in many respects the most important event in Canadian history. It may also be said to have turned Canada from a colony into a nation." Of the Second World War, historians Desmond Morton and Jack Granatstein conclude in their 1995 work, *Victory 1945*: "It was, on the whole, a good war for Canada. The country emerged richer, more powerful, more outward looking than anyone could have imagined in 1939." But they also observe: "A wiser people would have found better ways to spend $13 billion than on tanks and bombers and artillery shells, and on putting a million people into uniform and sending them to die."

Canada did pay heavily. Over the course of the century, Canadian fatalities in war exceeded 104,000 people. Many tens of thousands more were left wounded in body or mind or both. Against the claims of political progress during the First World War, many Canadians weigh the 60,661 deaths and the physical and mental disabling of a generation's bravest and brightest as a deep and lasting loss to a country of barely 7.5 million people then. In like fashion, the political and economic progress gained from the Second World War is set against the loss of 42,042 young Canadian lives.

Warmaking inflicted other deep wounds on the home front. From the start, on the issue of the Boer War, French-speaking Quebecers objected to the anglophile decision to help Britain expand its imperial writ in South Africa. Both world wars rekindled the French-English dispute when Parliament—after a national referendum in the second war—imposed conscription, the enforced military service used to replenish ranks depleted by frontline casualties. Western farmers and Ontario labor unions joined Quebec francophones in their objections. But the social and regional rifts fomented in wartime between Quebec and the rest of Canada persist as a perennial Canadian affliction.

Aside from the claims of war's political and commercial byproducts, the

PRIMARILY BECAUSE COMMUNISTS allied with Spain's government against the fascists in the Spanish Civil War, Ottawa offered no aid to Canadians of the Mackenzie–Papineau Battalion, such as these wounded men in Toronto on their return from Spain in 1939.

EARLY IN THE Second World War, many young Quebecers took the public advice of Montreal's mayor, Camillien Houde, and defied the law requiring registration for potential military service. Four years of internment silenced Houde, but Canada remained deeply divided.

ON THE SIXTH OF JUNE, 1944, the Canadians pictured here aboard a landing craft were some of the more than 14,000 troops from Canada who assaulted the Normandy coast of German-occupied France in a massive amphibious invasion from England. The Canadians advanced farther than any other Allied army on that first bloody day of Operation Overlord.

exploits of compatriots who fought in foreign wars arouse admiration as well as pain. The awfulness of it all becomes clear in the company of combat veterans on the European battlefields they knew, like Vimy Ridge (10,602 Canadian casualties in five April days of 1917). At Beaumont Hamel in northwestern France, the contours of the trenches remain visible, as does the slope of the attack route into a shallow valley commanded by German machineguns that day, July 1, 1916. The Royal Newfoundland Regiment, 801 strong, obeyed orders to charge the German line. None got halfway there. The casualties: 346 dead or missing, all but 69 of the rest wounded.

Barely 100 kilometres west of Beaumont Hamel, the beaches of Dieppe and its flanking villages need only be seen to understand why, on August 19, 1942, Canadians suffered so tragically in a one-day raid on the German-occupied French seaport. With enemy firepower commanding the beaches from adjacent heights, only 1,596 of the 4,963 Canadian raiders returned to England unscathed. Among the rest, 907 died. The wounded numbered 1,154, including some of the 1,874 who spent the rest of the war as prisoners.

THE FIRST WORLD WAR was a crucible in which Canadian national independence was forged. However, the price was a terrible one: over 60,000 soldiers killed and many more than that injured, such as these men on their way from the front to a hospital in England. Understandably, Canadians were ecstatic when the Armistice was reached on November 11, 1918, and flocked into the streets for spontaneous celebrations, as on King Street in Toronto (right).

1915 The Grim News Straight from the Trenches of France

The three reports below are excerpts from stories filed to Maclean's *during the First World War by George Eustace Pearson, who had worked for a sister publication,* Hardware and Metal, *before joining the Princess Patricia's Canadian Light Infantry and going overseas.*

April 1915: As night fell, quiet-voiced orders were given and, amidst perfect silence, the regiment formed up for its march to its maiden adventure. And here we were treated to our first sight of the German star shells which shot up from the vicinity of their trenches, breaking directly over the suspected area of our territory, illuminating the whole of it within 100 yards brightly, and semi-brightly over a much larger area.

The "relief" of the trenches is not the least dangerous part of the game and each party had its own adventures on the route to the comparative shelter of their frontage. The all-too-generous supply of mud and water about was bad enough in itself, but the presence of the star shells made it doubly so. Distant shells went unheeded but those falling close by made imperative demand for "bobbin," so "bob" the Patricias did, flattening out in the muddy mess. Number 1 company in particular was so unfortunate as to fall heir to a star at a very inconvenient time, to wit, as they stood knee deep in a flooded field. But there was nothing for it, so with many a muttered interjection, down they went as if for a swim in the ice-cold lake.

In the trenches, many were the freak wounds and narrow escapes. Here, a sergeant's stripe torn off by a splinter of shrapnel; there, a pack torn bodily from a

GERMAN PRISONERS OF WAR were housed in internment camps throughout Canada during both world wars, but the locations were kept secret by the defence department. In this photo, POWs are assembled at one of these camps for Christmas festivities in 1916.

THE AGONIES OF SHELLING, bombing, gassing and miserable conditions through years of trench warfare in northern France and Belgium during the First World War were exceeded only by the human destruction when one side or the other went "over the top" in attack.

man's shoulder, tearing the coat to tatters but leaving the wearer unscathed. One bullet skinned the lip of one man, another passed through the nose of one and instantly killed a soldier at his side. And yet with due respect for Der Kaiser and his wonderful machine, let it be said here that his gunners are rotten. The noise of the bursting shells, the impact of them as they fell, the presence of flying splinters and gobs of mud was really most terrifying; but their ultimate results–nil, and out of all proportion to the energy expended.

And so the Patricias in quiet faith, born of experience and resting upon the solid foundation of mutual self-confidence, go forward to whatever the future has in store for them, ready to do their "bit" in no spirit of bravado, but of willing sacrifice.

June 1915: Is there a soldier who has fought in this gigantic struggle who does not long for the day when, his duty well done, he can desist from efforts to kill his mud-splattered brothers in the other trench–and return home?

This opens a wide field for discussion of the attitude of the soldier in the trenches. How does he stand the strain, how does he compare with the soldiers of other nations, how does he live–and how does he die? Let me speak on these points from the fullness of four months' experience in the trenches, not from the viewpoint of the correspondent who sometimes gets within a few miles of the firing line–but no closer. Let me tell this story as the soldier himself sees it.

A change of face is noticeable in most, if not all, of the men who have borne the strain of this trench fighting month after month, refusing the soft ease of hospital and conva-

CANADIANS IN THE ROYAL FLYING CORPS during the First World War included aces Billy Bishop (above), Raymond Collishaw, Donald MacLaren and William Barker, who together claimed a toll of 247 enemy planes shot down. An ace in those fledgling days of warplanes was an aviator who had downed at least three enemy craft.

lescent camps. The sick and wounded returning from those places notice and speak of the change in their friends. Young men have become old men, aged in weeks. Talkative men have become quiet. Some faces have become hard, some soft. Their owners have developed into thinkers as well as doers. The camp visitors would scarcely recognize in these quiet men the roisterers of other days. No more is *Tipperary* heard–never in this land.

May 1916: Those who have seen the most talked the least of war [in a military hospital in England]. The war had become so commonplace in its horrors that they could not adequately describe it. To do that, one must have witnessed only the fringe of action. To plunge into the vortex of it was to have lost all perspective and all vividness of impression.

They were not at all anxious to get back to the lines; a condition of mind imposed, probably, by the sick and wearied condition of the body. There was Scotty, a Highlander of bombast. He regaled us with impossible tales of gory venture that would not bear a too close inspection. He proudly admitted his keen desire to return "up the line" to the "byes." It was, however, noticed that he nursed his slight ailments as no mother ever nursed an ailing infant–but to vastly different end. Swan felt differently about going back up the line and had not even the grace to blush for that admission. The feeling of dread was very general in the hospital.

SOME OF THE NEARLY 1,900 CANADIANS captured at Dieppe. A number shown here were among prisoners of war manacled in German camps for periods in 1942 and 1943 in retaliation for similar British treatment of captured German soldiers.

1943 Assignment in Sicily

SEPTEMBER 1, 1943 *In their first major campaign of the Second World War, Canadian forces joined with British and American armies in a massive invasion of Sicily on July 10, 1943. The long-distance seaborne assault from Britain delivered more fighting men to battle than the D-Day Normandy landings in France 11 months later—almost half a million, against some 300,000 Italian and German defenders. The Allied conquest of the mountainous Mediterranean island after 38 days of fighting was the first breach in the Nazi-Fascist grip on Europe. It led to the surrender of Italy on September 3, the day that Canadian and British troops crossed Messina Strait and seized the toe of the Italian mainland. And it provided lessons for the Normandy invasion on June 6, 1944, the prelude to the end of the war in Europe on May 8, 1945.*

More than 27,000 Canadian men and women—nurses who helped set up a 600-bed hospital—took part in the Sicilian campaign. In all, 562 Canadians died in that campaign and 1,664, including 12 nursing sisters, suffered wounds.

In the first report to Maclean's *from the Sicily front, CBC correspondent Peter Stursberg recounted how he and others had worried that "it was going to be like Dieppe," the disastrous raid on the German-occupied seaport in northwest France on August 19, 1942. Stursberg's dispatch, in excerpt here, noted that, unlike Dieppe, the landing in Sicily was unopposed.*

THIS GERMAN PHOTOGRAPH OF THE CARNAGE of Canadian soldiers and tanks on the pebble beach of Dieppe on August 19, 1942, shows but a small segment of the devastation dealt out by the Germans during the ill-considered raid, a test run for the massive Allied invasion of France on June 6, 1944.

The landing craft sheared away from the big troopship which brought us from Great Britain and moved slowly through water dark blue in the early light of morning toward the grey outline of the Sicilian shore. All around us was a host of great ships—troopships and freighters and warships—and in front of us were other landing craft. There was the chatter of machine-gun fire and the louder noise of shell fire as a destroyer opened up in support of our infantry.

Then there was a sudden silence. I could see vineyards and little white houses on shore and a town on the hills behind. The sun was shining now. A few minutes later I jumped down on dry sand. I had landed in Sicily. It all seemed screwy. During the landing exercises on the British beaches we had waded ashore in water up to our

HALIFAX PLAYED a major role as a naval base for the Allied North Atlantic forces in the two world wars, both as home port for the Royal Canadian Navy and as marshalling station for convoys, as shown here in the Second World War, carrying troops, munitions and other supplies to Britain.

A TROOP TRAIN PULLS into Halifax in the summer of 1940 with soldiers of the 2nd Canadian Division set to head for Britain by sea.

chests and here I was in the real thing and not even my boots were wet.

A column of Italian prisoners passed. One of them threw his helmet into the sea. It was a gesture of finality. I lugged my pack and typewriter through vineyards, sweat pouring off me from the burning noonday heat. The second day ashore, I got a ride in a truck to Pachino. There were a few decent buildings around the main square but the rest of it was a cluster of hovels. Most towns the Canadians took during the advance were as squalid. I found civil affairs in the charge of an American lieutenant representing the Allied Military Government, although the town had been taken by Canadian and British troops. The American was aptly fitted for the job as his parents were Sicilians and he could speak the language fluently. The lieutenant told me his chief problem was food. He said, "People here are starving. Really starving."

I got a lift in a jeep. We were driving along when we almost ran down a civilian car containing two Italian officers and two Canadian officers. We trailed the car down a side road into an olive grove and then we saw the surrender of the commander of the 206th Italian Coastal Division, General Achilles d'Havet, to General Simonds [Lt.-Gen. Guy Simonds, commander of the Canadian 1st Division]. It was a strange scene, like pictures you have seen of defeated officers handing over a sword, only General d'Havet was asked to hand over his revolver. Through an interpreter, the Italian Naval commander, whom we had also captured, asked for the honor of retaining his revolver. General Simonds agreed to this and just took the ammunition. General d'Havet looked more like a restaurant keeper than a soldier. He was stout and his face was stuffy. He made a point of telling the Canadian commander that he was awarded the Military Cross by the Duke of Connaught in the last war.

We drove through towns Canadians had captured. We saw signs of skirmishes along the road, broken pillboxes, burning trucks and dead horses.

MORE THAN THREE YEARS INTO THE SECOND WORLD WAR, while Canada's naval and air forces were heavily engaged, blundering in high places had left the army only with defeats: in Hong Kong, where an entire Canadian force of almost 2,000 suffered death or capture in December 1941; and at the French seaport of Dieppe in August 1942, where a raiding force of 5,000 met a similar fate. To counter despair at home, Ottawa persuaded Britain to include Canadians in the more promising invasion of Sicily–where Canadian soldiers are shown here unloading supplies from a landing craft in July 1943.

We saw the battle of Enna which was the first real battle the Canadians fought. It began in the heat of the afternoon sun with an artillery barrage on a ridge which the Germans held before Enna. Shells screamed and made noises like an express train over our heads. When the ridge was black and smoking, infantry began the attack.

Through field glasses I watched little dots of men climbing over the dusty shoulder road close to a red house. The little dots disappeared into what looked like a vineyard. The noise of machine-gun fire became more insistent. Then a blue sputtering light burst in a wide arc across the sky. It was the success signal–the Canadians had taken the ridge.

1945 The Bombers Blazed a Short Cut to Victory

JUNE 1, 1945 Maclean's *correspondent Lionel Shapiro, whose postwar novel based on the Normandy invasion,* The Sixth of June, *won him a Governor General's Award, filed the following dispatch, condensed here, as the Second World War ended.*

The complete collapse of a great nation is a desolate thing to behold. Even though it has been your hated enemy for five years, even though its leaders and the great majority of its people have been objects of your loathing for 12 years, even though your nerves have been chilled

THE PROPAGANDA WAR was fought on many fronts, one of the most popular being the poster and billboard. This poster appeared in the Montreal area during the Second World War, encouraging both blackouts and war savings bond purchases in one fell swoop.

GOOFY EFFIGIES of enemy leaders Hirohito of Japan and Adolf Hitler of Germany played frequent parts in home-front propaganda during the Second World War, in this case forming part of the perennial Victory Bond drives whereby Canadians loaned money to the war effort.

VE DAY IN HALIFAX turned into an ugly, two-day riot of window smashing, looting and burning after authorities infuriated celebrating servicemen by shutting down beer and liquor outlets.

by the barbarities of its concentration camps, and you have retched when you looked upon the evidence of fiendish tortures and pornographic humiliation visited upon its victims, the collapse of a nation of 80 millions, once considered civilized, is still a desolate experience.

I am writing this by the window of a rural school building on the Hamburg road. For five hours, Germany, broken and panicky, has been passing in review before my eyes. Generals, admirals and rank-and-file soldiers and sailors are shuffling along the road and asking each passing British vehicle where they can surrender.

Thousands of old men, women and children are wandering in search of rest, food and shelter. Their eyes have a glazed look of utter hopelessness. Their lives have been shattered and their fortunes are dark as the clouds out of which a cold pelting rain is adding nature's ironic garland to their idiotic adventure. Behind them is the fantastic ruins of what was once the most orderly country in Europe; ahead of them lie tears and toil, humiliation and just punishment. They lent themselves to the most skilful abracadabra in all of history; now their magician is dead and his tricks have died with him, leaving only emptiness.

There is no pity in my heart for these people. I have seen too many of our graves that line the long weary road from Africa to the Elbe; I have felt too much of the colossal tragedy for which they, individually and collectively, are responsible. When I see a 70-year-old woman and two 10-year-old children dragging a cart through the rain, I remind myself of the broken bodies of the 52 British schoolchildren we dragged from the rubble of a German bombardment a year ago. When I see a grey-haired German naval captain sitting in the ditch and crying like a baby, I am not sorry; I think of the thousands tossed into the death furnaces of Maidenek and Lublin. When I look upon these thousands of German civilians wandering in the hollow halls of their great disillusion, I picture

ON MAY 8, 1945, VE Day, people almost everywhere except defeated Germany left their workplaces, homes and schools to celebrate the Allied victory in Europe, as here on Bay Street in Toronto. The parties often lasted far into the night.

these same people in the summer of 1940, laughing at the plight of the world and "hoching" and "heiling" with intense jubilation.

And my heart will not open itself to their sorrow. Yet one feels a great desolation within himself–not because Germany is ruined but because this whole pitiful episode constitutes such a blot upon our alleged civilization. Humanity in our time must have been sadly lacking in fundamental qualities that a nation of 80 millions in the heart of Europe must be virtually destroyed in order to cleanse the Western World.

This epilogue to the war is too ugly for our troops to be exhilarated. There is no tossing of caps in the air. The feeling of grim tragedy which pervades this climax is not confined to the Germans. We don't hold a gay party at an execution, no matter how just or necessary it was.

Generation Lucky

Good Fortune Rewarded Youthful Survivors of Hard Times and Battle

Generation Lucky

Robert Collins – APRIL 3, 1995   **E**ven after 50 years, my generation still measures time by what we did before, during or after "the war." The Second World War and the 1930s Depression were the pivotal events in our lives. They made us over-60s what we are today.

We were not warlike people and yet, over six years, 1,086,343 Canadian men and women joined up. For most of us, it seemed right and necessary. Millions more at home worked for the war effort, and worried and waited for people they loved to come back safely. Forty-two thousand died. The rest of us grew up in a hurry even if we had not been tested under fire. "We all had to make decisions," says Arnold Steppler, 70, of New Westminster, B.C., "and the lives of others depended on those decisions."

Steppler and I, RCAF airframe mechanics, went overseas together late in the war. He served on the Continent in the last days of fighting. I went to Bomber Group in Yorkshire and then to Germany for the first bleak winter of occupation. Like everyone else in uniform, we went home irrevocably changed and glad to be alive. We had taken a shortcut to adulthood.

At university on veterans' gratuities, we were unusual students, no smarter than others, but infinitely more motivated and mature. We challenged and argued with our

IN THE POSTWAR PERIOD, roughly 1946 to 1959, while the square-hair brush cut was popular among young males, they loved the curvilinear look in cars, and lots of chrome.

THE 1950s WAS A DECADE of unprecedented growth for the Canadian economy. The increases in output that were an integral part of the war years continued through the Fifties, a time of urbanization and industrialization. The economy of western Canada, in particular, was transformed by the oil and gas sector and by pipeline building.

professors (delighting some and alarming others). We drank the mandatory gallons of beer but, with our British pub training, kept it down and got to class the next morning. We were eager to learn, get out and make up for lost time.

Canada, too, was transformed. It entered the war as a producer of grain and ore and came out a manufacturer and trader. A nation of only 11.5 million people had become the world's fourth-largest supplier of wartime munitions and machines. Its troops had fought valiantly in every theatre of war. A million women had gone into the labor force and proved they were as good as men. "In 1945, no country in the world was more confident than Canada, or had better cause to be," wrote Ralph Allen, a postwar editor of *Maclean's*, in his book *Ordeal by Fire*.

We all shared in that pride and optimism. We expected to live in peace, get a job, get married, raise kids and have a house with a picture window and a basement recreation room. Call us Generation L, the Lucky Ones, but after a war and a depression we felt we'd earned some luck.

The Cold War was a constant frightening fact of life, but we learned to live with it. Korea was barely a blip on our consciousness, except for those 20,000 Canadians who fought in what is aptly called the "forgotten" war. We rushed straight out of uniforms and coveralls into bed, creating the baby boom: some six million children born between 1945 and 1960. Over time, most of us got houses with affordable National Housing Act mortgages. Being Depression babies with modest aspirations, we didn't

ON THE 25TH ANNIVERSARY of the opening of the St. Lawrence Seaway in 1959, Lionel Chévrier, the Seaway's first president, and William O'Neil, the president in 1984, walk away from a commemorative plaque they have just unveiled. The construction and operation of the Seaway was a major cooperative undertaking by the Canadian and U.S. governments.

expect a house immediately at marriage. The average wage in 1950 was $45.08 a week (almost exactly what I earned that year as a beginning reporter on *The London Free Press*). We waited, saved and toughed it out in basement apartments.

In 1958, six years and two children after marriage, I bought a $17,500 dollhouse in suburban Toronto with, yes, a picture window and, yes, a basement rec room built over a winter of profanity and smashed thumbs. We knew we could pay our mortgages because jobs were plentiful. From 1946 to 1959, the average unemployment rate was 2.9 per cent.

Everywhere, the country was building, discovering, bursting out: St. Lawrence Seaway, Trans-Canada Highway; Toronto subway; a river of oil in Alberta; aluminum at Kitimat, B.C.; uranium in northern Saskatchewan; nickel at Thompson, Man.; iron ore in the Ungava. We applauded it all but didn't much invest in it. The Americans did. As the Royal Commission on Canada's Economic Prospects warned in 1957, control of Canada was slipping out of Canadian hands. Between 1955 and 1965, the total foreign investment in our country almost doubled to $34 billion. Nearly three-quarters of it was American. The United States owned 90 per cent of our auto manufacturing, 70 per cent of our oil and gas, 50 per cent of mining and smelting. Our generation let it happen by default.

We socked our money away in savings bonds and banks. Debt was and still is anathema to us. Credit cards were emerging, but most of us paid the balances in full every month. We bought 3.5 million cars during the decade, but many people, like me, worked up through a succession of second-hand oil-burning clunkers until we could pay cash for a new model.

IN THE EARLY 1950s, the television set began to replace the hearth, the piano and the radio as the focus of attention and entertainment in middle-class living rooms.

In our attitude towards debt as in scores of other ways, those times seem sweetly innocent now. Political correctness meant voting Tory or Liberal. Environmentalism was not in our lexicon. When in 1957 the eerie beep of Russia's Sputnik came over my car radio as I travelled the West for *Maclean's*, I was awed, like Early Man discovering fire.

Child or spousal abuse was not talked about. We had discovered free love during the war, but, the pill being a decade away, extramarital sex was not yet rampant. We were still wrestling with prewar prurience. Divorce was rising–6,000 to 7,000 a year, triple the rate of the 1930s–but we blamed that on the American influence.

Even our crime was relatively benign. A good old-fashioned bank robbery was big news. "Swarming" was for bees and "home invasions" were for termites. We went to the office sedate in suits and skirts. Even our musical idols were sartorially correct: On Fifties album covers of The Diamonds or The Four Lads are clean-cut young guys with short haircuts, dark suits, white shirts, skinny neckties.

We entertained at home, partly because it was cheap, partly because, except in enlightened Quebec, there was scarcely a decent dining or drinking establishment from sea unto sea. A high old time in Anglo Canada meant a night at the beer parlor, where men hunched over ale-slopped formica tables and got suddenly drunk. Women, excluded from these sordid dives, had their own depressing "Women and Escorts" premises. A few restaurants let patrons bring booze in a bag and dispense it under the table.

This wasn't good enough for our 1.5 million immigrants or for veterans of overseas who had discovered convivial pubs and wine that wouldn't strike you blind. By 1959, cocktail bars and licensed restaurants had brought Canada kicking and screaming into the 20th century. The newcomers spiced our lives with their exotic foods, new accents and their fervent appreciation of the freedom we took for granted.

But we were still hard-pressed to find a drink on Sunday, except, of course, in Montreal. To many of us Anglos, Montreal with its lively bars, exquisite food and naughty night life was French Canada. Most of us had Quebec friends in the services, but were ignorant of the province's aspirations. We knew Maurice Richard and Les Habitants, but didn't know that a Quiet Revolution was quietly brewing.

We were preoccupied with jobs, families and a hypnotic new toy–television.

Our generation couldn't get the hang of government handouts. There had been "relief" in the

THE FOUR LADS, the Toronto vocal quartet who introduced do-wop to barber-shop harmonizing, hit the transborder big time in 1952 as backups for American Johnny Ray on his superhit record "Cry." Later Lads-only hits included "Moments to Remember" and "Standing on the Corner."

Depression, but most of us abhorred it. Old Age Security was passed in 1951, for Canadians 70 and older. Six years later, a federal-provincial hospital plan paid 50 per cent of specified services. But the Canada Pension Plan, universal medicare and the vast welfare state were still ahead. We were (and are) distrustful of government promises or aid.

Nor were we obsessed with Self. Throughout the Fifties, I never knew anyone in therapy (although my daughters now tell me, nudge-nudge wink-wink, "You all should have been, Dad!") But we were not harsh or unfeeling parents. Most of us clutched dog-eared copies of Dr. Benjamin Spock's *Baby and Child Care*, seeking its solace and wisdom on toilet training and tiny tots' emotional needs. We lavished everything on our kids, wanting them to have it even better than we did, and expecting them to be grateful.

So we were baffled and hurt when the first wave of boomers turned into Sixties Flower Children. Why were they rejecting all those good square Generation L values? Why didn't they want to inherit our world with its bomb, incipient pollution and passion for consumer goods?

It turned out they hadn't a whole lot more to offer. They finally shed their beads and sandals and took straight jobs. But they and we are still light-years apart. Many of them–better educated; trim from rigorous exercise, surgical tucks and low-cal high-fibre diets; postponing marriage deep into their 30s or beyond; earning more and casually spending more on things we considered luxuries–don't want to ever look or be like us.

AS WOMEN WAR WORKERS hung on in the labor force and others joined them, the food industry began providing prepared or pre-mixed food products such as the ready-mix cake, quickie macaroni and cheese, and the frozen TV dinner to make kitchen life easier for working wife-mothers and husband-fathers.

They are equally alienated from Generation X–designated by Vancouver author Douglas Coupland as a sub-species born in the late Fifties or Sixties. Some say they are really disgruntled late boomers. (The baby boom ended about 1965.) They came of age during the early Eighties depression to discover that all the good jobs and houses were gone. Their guts churn with what Coupland calls "boomer envy." Others say that, even though most Xers are over 30, they belong with the succeeding Twentysomethings crowd. One thing's sure: they all regard the main wave of boomers as fat-cat cop-outs.

While the children squabble, Generation L keeps on doing what it does best: saving money. We're prudent to the point of paranoia. We can't shake that old devil Depression. We don't know how to spend on the boomer scale. (Land Rovers at $42,000-plus to negotiate the rocky trails and towering sand dunes of Toronto? Seems like wretched excess to us, but we've got a tinge of boomer envy.)

The Xers and Twentysomethings, faced with under- or no employment, dwindling social services and a Canada Pension Plan going broke, haven't much use for my generation either. Short of setting us afloat on ice floes off the Labrador coast, they want governments to confiscate more of our alleged wealth. Yet they and the boomers stand to inherit from us the biggest windfall in Canadian history: as much as $1 trillion, if wastrel governments don't winkle it away first.

Generation L paid for the hospitals where younger generations were born, the family allowances for their childhood, the schools and universities where they stud-

AS RETURNING WAR VETERANS and immigrants formed urban and suburban homes and families, while communities provided longer hockey seasons with artificial outdoor as well as indoor rinks, after-four and Saturday hockey leagues became a way of life for kids and parents alike.

ied. Our main offence is in having lived through high employment, healthy real estate markets and a vibrant stock market—and in watching our dollars. If governments, boomers and the rest managed their affairs as well as we did, the country wouldn't be flirting with bankruptcy.

But maybe there's hope yet for the young. American business consultant and self-styled "contrarian" Harry S. Dent Jr. predicts for the rest of the Nineties a boom "astonishing in its intensity, its length and in the heights it reaches." If it happens, I suspect that the Twentysomethings would respond with a greater work ethic and sense of mission than the baby boomers ever did at that age. They might even learn to manage money. In short, they might be a lot like us.

And there's a thought that will probably ruin their day.

'The Old Game was Tougher'

The Perennial Sport of Argument: Was Yesterday Better than Today?

O NE of the few constants in the mercurial business of spectator sports is a form of nostalgia that afflicts the fan with increasing intensity as the years pass. The symptoms involve an impulse to compare the past and the present–usually unfavorably to the present. It is a phenomenon that Sprague Cleghorn, one of the pioneer professionals in Canadian hockey, tackled head on in *Maclean's* of November 15, 1934. A Montrealer then in retirement from a pro career that began in 1909 and closed in 1928, Cleghorn confronted the question at the outset of a four-part serial about his own heydays as a heavy-fisted defenceman and rushing goal-getter with seven Canadian and American teams, mostly with his home town clubs, the Wanderers and the Canadiens. The future member of the Hockey Hall of Fame spoke through writer Frederick Edwards in a series entitled *It's a Tough Game*:

> *There's a question that's always being tossed around, not only in connection with hockey but with every other major sport. Is the present game better than the game they used to play years ago? In any gathering of fans, you can start a swell argument with this innocent enquiry. An argument? Boy, you can start a riot.*

IN THE SLIPSTREAM OF Gaëtan Boucher, the native of Charlesbourg, Quebec, who dominated world and Olympic long-track speed skating in the middle 1980s, the following decade generated a squad of world beaters on the Prairies, led by Catriona Le May Doan, here winning the 1998 world 500-metre title in Calgary.

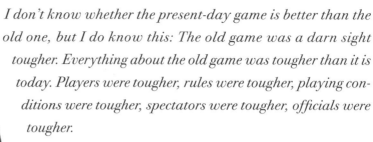

I don't know whether the present-day game is better than the old one, but I do know this: The old game was a darn sight tougher. Everything about the old game was tougher than it is today. Players were tougher, rules were tougher, playing conditions were tougher, spectators were tougher, officials were tougher.

Don't get me wrong. I'm not suggesting that the brand of hockey the boys will be playing this winter isn't tough, because it is. When you put half a dozen husky young athletes on razor-edged skates, hand them each a bladed hickory stick, and tell them to go out and mix things with half a dozen others equally husky and similarly equipped, you're starting something that is no pastime for sissies.

To my mind that's what makes hockey the game it is, and that is why hockey is today the one competitive sport growing amazingly in public favor every year in every country in the world where it has so far been introduced.

The Cleghorn brand of hockey may have been tougher—as in using his stick to open a 12-stitch gash across Newsy Lalonde's forehead in a 1912 Toronto exhibition game. But maybe not: in 1955, during a Montreal-Boston NHL game, superstar Rocket Richard took his stick to a Boston player and a lineman, provoking his suspension for the impending playoffs and a window-smashing, car-tipping riot in Montreal. In any case, the game in Cleghorn's day was probably no better than in later years. The century produced measurable improvements in terms of athletic skills, with a big assist from technology. Better hockey sticks, skates and ice in the last half of the century reinforced the natural talents of a Richard, a Bobby Orr, a Wayne Gretzky, a Mario Lemieux and others in the Hockey Hall of Fame. Players in the game's early days rarely lifted the puck, let alone fired an explosive slapshot like Bobby Hull.

Parallel changes in other sports enhanced personal talent. In competitive running, the customized footwear that became routine late in the

SPRAGUE CLEGHORN,
pictured when he played for Renfrew, Ontario, claimed years later that hockey was tougher in his day. About 70 years after Cleghorn retired, veteran sportswriter Trent Frayne concluded in a 1997 Maclean's *article that the main modern difference was in the aftermath of the bloodletting: "The wounded don't stand at the boards for a trainer with a pail of water any more. Now . . . it actually is a gleaming infirmary and a plastic surgeon wearing surgical gloves to insert stitches."*

century rendered earlier "scampers" and "sneakers" antique. The *Maclean's* report on the 1928 Olympic Games in Amsterdam (Canada's most successful Olympics in track and field, with four gold medals) notes of one Canadian marathoner: "Silas McLellan had his running shoes newly re-soled for the great event and, when he finished [26th place], the soles were completely worn off and he was practically running bare-footed."

Technology–plastics and glass fibre– provided such Canadian rowing champions of the 1990s as Silken Laumann, 1991 world champion sculler, and multiple gold medallists Marnie McBean and Kathleen Heddle with craft much lighter and quicker than any boat available to an earlier generation of world-beating Canadian scullers, including Lou Scholes (1904), Joe Wright (1928) and Jack Guest (1930). Similarly, the rediscovery of an old Dutch speed-skate design, the clap skate, tumbled records in the late 1990s, helping Canada's Catriona Le May Doan become the first woman to race 500 metres in less than 38 seconds and to win gold at the 1998 Olympics in Nagano, Japan.

Athletes and their coaches also turned increasing attention to matters of body, mind and behavior in pursuit of performances ever faster, higher, stronger, as the Olympic motto urges.

TORONTO SCULLERS Jack Guest of the Don River Rowing Club and Joe Wright Jr. of the rival Argonauts, winners of the Royal Henley Diamond Sculls title respectively in 1930 and 1928, were part of a long line of world-beating Canadian rowers.

BY 1921, WHEN THIS PHOTO of a University of Toronto group was taken, women had been involved in organized curling for almost three decades. The Scottish Roaring Game had first engaged Canadian men as long ago as the 1700s.

They enlisted professional nutritionists, psychologists and politicians to help pump up–in every sense–the competitor. Controversy chased the quest for new ways to reinforce natural ability. An athlete who considered it both logical and expedient to ingest the hormonal growth promoters of a natural diet in

concentrated and synthesized form might be punished as a cheat–or might not be. On September 21, 1998:

- An Ontario appeal court refused a plea from Canadian sprinter Ben Johnson to overturn his lifetime exclusion from competition imposed by the international track and field authority because he had used performance-enhancing steroids.
- American sprinter Florence Griffith Joyner, winner of three gold medals at the 1988 Olympics and widely suspected of using steroids, died at age 38 of what her family said was heart failure.
- American baseball giant Mark McGwire, an admitted user of a hormone booster banned in some sports but not in baseball, gloried in the public adulation aroused by his obliteration of a 37-year-old record of 61 home runs in a single season, his tally having reached 65 the previous day on the way to achieving 70 by the end of the season six days later.

Performance improvements had long since begun being measured by ever narrower gauges. After 1968, for example, sprints were timed in hundredths of a second instead of tenths. The 100-metre world record of 9.84 seconds run by Donovan Bailey on a rubberized track at the 1996 Atlanta Olympics was only about a half-second quicker than the 10.3 world mark set 66 years earlier on cinders in Hamilton by compatriot Percy Williams, double gold medallist at the 1928 Olympics. (American sprinter Maurice Greene beat Bailey's mark on June 16, 1999, with 9.79 seconds–Ben Johnson's disallowed time at the 1988 Olympics.)

By the 1980s, hundredths of a second began to be used for the mile run and its metric counterpart, the 1,500 metres. When England's Roger Bannister ran the mile on May 6, 1954, in less than four minutes–a physical and psychological barrier for decades–he inspired a spate of breakthroughs by other runners, including Australia's John Landy only 46 days later. That set up a showdown, quickly promoted as "the mile of the century," at the Empire Games in Vancouver. There, on

FORMATION OF THE National Lacrosse Association two months after Confederation gave rise to the myth that lacrosse is Canada's national game. Immensely popular in the century's early years, the game later faded from public favor.

DONOVAN BAILEY, here beating Frankie Fredericks of Namibia at the 1996 Atlanta Olympics in world record time of 9.84 seconds, extended a Canadian pattern of world-beating sprinters. Percy Williams was a record-breaker in 1930, Harry Jerome in the 1960s, Ben Johnson in the '80s and Bruny Surin, with Bailey, in the '90s.

CANADIANS WERE MORE INCLINED towards skating that scored goals than to what used to be called fancy skating until the arrival of Barbara Ann Scott, the sweetheart of her home town Ottawa and of all Canada. She won the world title at her first overseas competition, in 1947, and the Canadian, U.S., European, world and Olympic championships in 1948.

BRIAN ORSER knocked on the door for a long time before getting in: he was 2nd at the 1984 Olympics, 2nd at the world championships that year, then 2nd again in 1985 and 1986 before finally winning the crown in 1987. Here, the reigning world champion carries the flag into the Calgary Saddledome at the head of Canada's Winter Olympics brigade in 1988. He would finish 2nd again.

August 7, 1954, the runners proved the aptness of the advance billing. On the final turn into the home stretch, Bannister overtook Landy and beat him by five yards, clocking 3 minutes 58.8 seconds to Landy's 3:59.6.

Not everything in sport got faster and steadily better in the 20th century—not even, in every case, the professional's paycheque. The first pro hockey league, launched in Michigan in 1904, paid its Canadian stars as much as $500 a game— $125 more than the average Canadian industrial worker took home in a year. In end-of-the-century dollars, that works out to almost $62,000—more than the average per-game rate regularly paid to the 23 National Hockey League stars who played for Team Canada at the 1998 Winter Olympics. (The Team Canada players received on average $4.7 million for an 82-game NHL season.)

As tastes and fancies shifted through the century, a highly popular sport in one stretch of years might be another decade's dud, hockey remaining the enduring

AT THE 1998 WINTER OLYMPICS in Nagano, Japan, Ross Rebagliati of Whistler, B.C., won the snowboarding event at the sport's inaugural Olympic appearance, lost the gold medal for evidence of marijuana use and then regained it on a plea that the dope in his system was from other people's smoke.

exception. The Canadian Football League and its Grey Cup championship flourished with new vigor after fans of the Calgary Stampeders turned the week before the 1948 cup game in Toronto into a festival. Three decades later, the CFL seemed destined to share the fate that befell lacrosse, a game seldom seen or played after the middle of the century despite its status in federal law as Canada's national sport. Curling reached its apogee as both a spectator and participation sport in the 1960s and early 1970s, then faded until it became a medal game at the 1998 winter Olympics. Golf, by contrast, grew in popularity as the century advanced.

Individual athletes cashed in on transitory crazes that their world-class performances often helped generate–among them, Tom Longboat in long-distance running before the First World War, Torchy Peden in a bicycle-racing rage of the 1930s, Marilyn Bell as a long-distance swimmer during the 1950s, Jacques Villeneuve in racecars in the late 1990s.

A quartet of Canadian Alpine skiers picked off Olympic gold medals–Anne Heggtveit (1960), Nancy Greene (1968), Kathy Kreiner (1976) and Kerrin Lee-

Gartner (1992). Three Canadians dominated the men's world figure skating championships over a span of more than 10 years, beginning with Brian Orser in 1987, followed by Kurt Browning and Elvis Stojko.

Increasingly for athletes, especially after the mid-century advent of television, product endorsements augmented prize money and paycheques–or made up for their absence in defiance of prevailing rules of amateurism. The amateur purity rules came under attack in *Maclean's* just before the 1948 Winter Olympics. In the issue that February 1, which featured defending world champion figure skater Barbara Ann Scott on the cover, sportswriter W.G. Hardy reflected widespread Canadian indignation when he grumped that the superstar, "in order to retain her status as an amateur for Olympic competition, was compelled to give up an automobile which her fellow citizens in Ottawa had given her in good faith." Worse, Hardy went on to lament, the rules effectively barred Canada from sending its best hockey players to take on the world.

KERRIN LEE-GARTNER of Calgary, shown here after winning the downhill skiing gold medal at the 1992 Winter Olympics, was among a parade of Canadians who turned in world's-best performances over the years.

That issue arose with greater impact after 1954, the year the Soviet Union sent a national team to the annual world hockey tournament for the first time, and won the championship. In 1955, the Penticton Vs wrested back the title for Canada, but in roughhouse style and amid Cold War rhetoric. By the 1960s, with Soviet teams routinely retaining their world title year after year, the Canadian cry was to send in the pros. That they finally managed to see in the storied Canada-USSR tournament of 1972. Team Canada's return-from-the-dead victory proved to many citizens to be such a perfect affirmation of hockey supremacy that it was cheered anew on silver dollars and postage stamps 25 years later.

By then, a century of debate over amateurism and professionalism in sport had been resolved. Due largely to the irresistibly lucrative influence of the entertainment industry and its television viewers, the Olympic Games and other international sports endeavors were not only opened to highly paid superstars but effectively required them if their sport hoped to survive as a serious contender for an audience in the international marketplace. One result was the reduction of the CFL into a de facto subsidiary of the U.S. National Football League. Another was to endanger the financial stability in Canada of Major League teams, especially when a devalued Canadian dollar made it highly costly to compete for players against U.S.-based clubs.

As sport evolved into big-league business, the two major money centres of eastern Canada, each with lengthy histories hosting second-level baseball teams, qualified to join top-rank American associations–first Montreal, with the National League Expos in 1969 and then, in 1977, Toronto and the American League Blue Jays. The Expos came close to glory several times, winning their division in 1981 and seeming set to make the playoffs in 1994 when a players' strike cut short the season. The Blue Jays had just conquered all in winning the World Series championships in both 1992 and 1993. Bred-in-Canada big-league stars, however, remained a relative rarity, although Ferguson (Fergie) Jenkins of Chatham, Ontario, gained eminence as a Chicago Cubs pitcher, winning the Cy Young award in 1971 as top performer in the National League. And out of Maple Ridge, British Columbia, Larry Walker, who honed his batting and fielding credentials with the Expos, went on as a member of the Colorado Rockies to be voted the National League's most valuable player in 1997 and, the following year, became the first Canadian to win a Major League batting championship (average: .363).

AFTER A RATHER DISAPPOINTING National Hockey League career–only one game as a player, and several seasons as coach of the Boston Bruins, who could never get past the Montreal Canadiens in the playoffs–Don Cherry turned to commentating on Hockey Night in Canada, *building a huge fan base and becoming one of the most popular and recognizable figures in Canada.*

As for winter sports, Canada's professional game had been all but totally taken over by others. In a World Cup hockey tournament of pro national teams in September, 1996, the United States beat Canada's best for top honors. The Canadians achieved a measure of vengeance at the Nagano Olympics–the first where NHL players were able to represent their countries–by beating the United States in round-robin play. But the Europeans, playing the kind of canny but low-scoring game that was fast losing favor on American television, shut both North American teams out of the medals. Otherwise at Nagano, Canadians reaped a national record tally of 15 medals–6 gold, 5 silver, 4 bronze–some of them in sports new to the Olympics as medal events: curling, snow-boarding and women's hockey.

The NHL, meanwhile–its headquarters long since moved to New York from Montreal, its proportion of Canada-born players sliding in three decades to barely 60 per cent from 97 per cent in 1967–authorized expansion to a 30-club league by century's end, at least 24 of those based in U.S. cities. Major multinational entertainment corporations with American TV and professional sports interests purchased ownership stakes in NHL teams and competed for rights to televise games.

As the league expanded into unfamiliar territory in middle America and the Deep South, the new fans seemed to favor hard-knocks hockey to accompany the razzmatazz of cheerleaders, mascots, raucous music and rock-concert lighting. NHL governors adopted rule changes designed to encourage more action and higher scores. The sport thus seemed poised to turn full circle as the century was closing. It would entail a retreat from the swift, skills-based style taught by the Russians in 1972 and employed by the Europeans at Nagano. It would mean a return to a Sprague Cleghorn's cruder brand of Canada's durable game.

1928 Canada at the Olympics

AT THE 1928 SUMMER OLYMPICS, Canadians won four gold medals in track and field, the country's best performance in the marquee events of the Games. The stars were sprinter Percy Williams, a double winner, and the women athletes, competing in the Olympics for the first time. Maclean's *published reports in October, 1928, by Alexandrine Gibb, the women's team manager, about the women's contests and by Bobby Kerr, winner of the 200-metre race at the 1908 Olympics, on the men's events.*

This year at Amsterdam, Holland, for the first time in athletic history, women athletes were given an official and definite place on an Olympic program. That they made good beyond all shadow of doubt is admitted wherever there are broadminded sportsmen. Canada's women athletes were tried as they never had been tried before. And they won the world's track and field championship. It is no exaggeration at all to say that it was an amazing achievement.

Six girls from Canada—Jane Bell, Ethel Catherwood, Myrtle Cook, Bobbie Rosenfeld, Ethel Smith and Jean Thompson—were pitted against the cream of the women athletes of 21 countries, against a total of 121 competitors. The United States team totalled 20, the German 19, the Belgian 14, the French 13. And when the last race was run, the unofficial score stood: Canada 26, United States 20, Germany 18, with the rest trailing nowhere near the leaders.

THIS YOUNG SEXTET posing in front of coaches and manager at the 1928 Amsterdam Olympics, the first where women competed, comprise the entire Canadian women's track and field team. They were dubbed The Matchless Six back home after winning two gold medals, a silver and a bronze.

In the 100 metres final, in the opinion of a number of people at the finish, Bobbie Rosenfeld either won it or it was a dead heat with Betty Robinson of the United States. [A majority of the finish-line judges awarded the American first place.] Ethel Smith was undoubtedly third. In the 400-metre relay, the Canadian team [Rosenfeld, Smith, Bell and Cook], all from Toronto, won with a comfortable margin–there could be no argument about that win at any rate! And we won in a record time of 48 and two-fifths seconds.

And when Ethel Catherwood of Saskatoon won another first in the high jump, our joy knew no bounds. Miss Catherwood, tall, with beautiful eyes, pretty hair and what the French call a photo-filmic face, had been unofficially crowned Beauty Queen of the Olympiad. When she defeated the hometown favorite, Miss Gisolf, the Hollanders, disappointed as they were, came across with real applause for our pretty Canadian. In the five events [including the 800-metre run and the discus], we secured two firsts, one second, a third, a fourth and a fifth.

TRIUMPHANT VANCOUVER SPRINTER Percy Williams is hoisted aloft at the 1928 Olympics, where he won gold medals in both sprints for men before going back home, where he set a world record for the 100 metres two years later in Hamilton.

At the 1928 Olympic Games, it was a big thrill to see the red maple leaf go to the top of the mast twice in token of the fact that, for the first time in history, a Canadian, Percy Williams of Vancouver, had won a double world's championship with victories in the two major sprint events of an Olympiad.

With all his triumphs, Williams remains a modest, unaffected lad. After he had been carried off the field on the shoulders of his comrades following the winning of his second championship, he grinned as he watched Canada's flag flutter and said: "And four years ago a doctor man told me I had a leaky heart. Look at me today. It is to laugh."

He was the outstanding hero of the games. A slender, frail-looking lad, Williams competed eight times in four days, running one of his heats in the 100 metres in world's record time of 10 and two-fifths seconds.

Williams has beautiful style. He has smoothness and grace in his running, is a fairly fast starter, and a wonderfully strong finisher. In fact, in some of the heats at the Olympics, he seemed to be beaten 50 yards from home, when he would gather himself and literally fly at the tape.

Percy Williams will be placed with the greatest sprinters of all time.

1955 The Vs Won a Hockey Game, Not the Holy Grail

Ralph Allen – APRIL 16, 1955 **N**ow that the Penticton Vs are home resting on their laurels as world hockey champions, we congratulate them on their victory and urge them to spare themselves the trouble of doing it again. We address a like message to their sponsors, the Canadian Amateur Hockey Association, and to the millions of grim Canadian patriots who joined in rooting the Vs home.

We have always thought it a dangerous thing to mix politics and religion. The recent hockey tournament managed to mix politics and religion and sport. The result was, to put it as mildly as possible, awful. Everyone knew from the start that the tournament was really a two-team contest between Canada and Russia. It was no surprise when the Communist press made more than the most of the fact that Canadians play hockey much rougher than Europeans do. Since Russia had won the championship with ease last year and expected to win it with ease again this year, it was also to be expected that the Communists would encourage their followers to believe a good Marxist team can lick a good capitalist team any day.

West Germany, where the tournament was played, got behind the Vs–vocally and in the press–and with a vengeance. The Penticton players suddenly found themselves cast in the role of a guest-star Siegfried. In this illusion they were sustained by exhortations from home–exhortations to defend the honor of Canada, to defend the cause of freedom, to strike a blow against tyranny and evil.

In the final game, they walloped the Russians, 5 to 0. One official of the team, his voice choked with emotion, came on a trans-Atlantic radio network shortly afterward and attributed a good deal of the credit to God. Later, another official of the team said thoughtfully: "This is a great thing for democracy."

If the future of democracy, or any part of it, depends on the skating ability of a dozen or so young stalwarts from B.C., then democracy is in a bad way indeed. If God spends any of His time fixing hockey games, then we had better start looking to some more responsible source for our salvation. But of course the recent contest between the Vs and the Russians had precisely nothing to do with God or democracy or the soundness or unsoundness of any set of political or spiritual values. But since it has led millions of normally sane human beings to hold the opposite belief, however momen-

THE RICHARD RIOTS in Montreal on March 17, 1955, began in the Montreal Forum hockey arena as a violent protest against the suspension of hockey hero Maurice (Rocket) Richard for whacking Boston Bruin Hal Laycoe with his stick and attacking a linesman who intervened during a game in Boston four days earlier.

tarily; since in so doing it sorely increased international tensions, we believe Canada ought to pull out of the world hockey tournament and stay out until the world—ourselves included—has learned a good deal more about the difficult art of being sensible.

1972 Team Canada in War and Peace

Jack Ludwig – DECEMBER 1972   **C**anadians, men and women, held to the credo that hockey was *our game*. When the Soviet Union and Czechoslovakia started winning in international competition and in the Olympics, no Canadian had any doubt that we could absolutely demolish the opposition if we would only put our best hockey players together on one team and not the tenth-raters classed as "amateurs" who had been wearing Canada's colors in recent sad international hockey years.

We wanted a series between the USSR and a team of NHL stars not to prove anything to ourselves. Our convictions required no proofs. We wanted that contest only as a means of teaching the usurpers what hockey was really all about.

Most of us thought the match would never come off, that fools in the international federations and fools in the NHL would never find a way to make this match happen. Suddenly, however, the NHL and the NHL Players' Association and Hockey Canada put together this Team Canada; just as suddenly the confrontation devoutly to be wished was here. We couldn't wait to see the USSR wiped out on the ice.

That was the script we turned out to see on September 2, 1972, in Montreal. We saw another script unfold. We saw Canada lose 7-3. We watched an entire nation plunge into the depths of terrible doubt: if we weren't the country who could do it all in hockey, who were we? If our illusions about ourselves on the ice were so palpably false, what was there that we could cling to as true?

By game four, in Vancouver, which Team Canada lost 5-3, the Canadian myth hung by a hair: by game five, the first played in Moscow, in which Team Canada blew a three-goal lead and ended up losing 5-4, Canada's situation seemed hopeless. A once-mighty hockey nation acted as if it had been castrated. But then, out of a seemingly hopeless situation, down in the series three games to one, with one game tied, Team Canada regenerated itself, and regenerated this nation. Three games in a row we won—each one with Toronto's Paul Henderson scoring the winning goal.

Oh how the unmighty had risen!

Canadians in Moscow shot champagne corks into the night air. Our nation was restored. The myth still hung by that thin hair. Our manhood, our macho, our national selves were, even if pounded a bit, still intact. Drunk or sober, show a Canadian in Moscow even a lapel flag and he was just as likely as not to break right into *O Canada*. Canadians at home went even wilder. People jigged a dance not seen since World War II ended. The Team Canada players who had been bums and bushers and lushes and louts now were only heroes, and Canadians were the baskers in victory's heroic lights.

But all the questions raised by the series yet remained. Was hockey still our thing the way we thought it was before this series began? Were our players getting all the help they required in order to make the most of their talents?

I suggest a partial answer. I suggest that hidden behind the show biz shoot-it-in-and-chase-it hockey played by the NHL was the natural hockey talent Team Canada players didn't always have to use in the NHL. I suggest that in the days that followed that 7-3 loss in Montreal, each and every one of the players painfully dredged up his memories of hockey past.

That someone like Phil Esposito, who in the past years had become a crease-parker, turned himself back into a brilliant all-round hockey player who, in spite of the fantastic speed of the USSR men, forechecked with them and back-checked with them and did his own digging in the corners. That Paul Henderson pitched his performance at the high level set by Valeri Kharlamov and Aleksander Yakushev, driving himself relentlessly from shift to shift in ways nobody had seen him perform, either as a Detroit or a Toronto NHLer. That, in short, the Team Canada players went to school to the USSR team, that they learned and adapted and did this by giving up the bad habits picked up in the lazy years of NHL show biz.

And thus the Canadian identity crisis passed with only a long "Whew!" On the brink of a national wipe-out, the team gave up its carousing, heavy-drinking, John Wayne image and, like the Soviet team, played hockey.

A MOMENT IN MOSCOW on a date—September 28, 1972—that lives in fame throughout Canada: Paul Henderson after scoring the winning goal in the clinching game of Canada's come-from-behind triumph in the first hockey series between Canadian professionals and the stars of the Soviet Union.

1992 Baseball Heaven

Bob Levin – NOVEMBER 2, 1992 Eight days, six baseball games–that is all it was. But it was so much more. Never mind that the first World Series on Canadian soil was played on shiny Astroturf, under a steel roof. Never mind that the paid gladiators who packed SkyDome with flag-waving Canadians were all Americans, Puerto Ricans or Dominicans. For one stunning week, a game played with a stitched ball and a wood bat managed to unite Canadians from coast to coast even as the constitutional referendum was dividing them [referendum voting and the World Series celebration parade were both on October 26]. More than 11 million of them tuned into some contests, and non-Torontonians did not even seem to mind that the centre of their televised attention, puffed up with pride, was hated Hogtown. And in the nation's largest city, the Blue Jays' 4-2 Series triumph over the Atlanta Braves, wrapped up in gut-twisting style down in Dixie, sent a half million people pouring into the streets in a world-class frenzy. "When the final out registered, the city roared," marvelled Toronto police Insp. Gary Grant, watching over the dancing, singing throngs. "I must have high-fived 2,500 people by now–my arm will be on the disabled list tomorrow."

For the Jays themselves, the road to victory was paved with fine pitching, timely hitting and steely nerves. Ed Sprague's ninth-inning homer in Game 2 in Atlanta, Devon White's wall-banging catch in Game 3, Jimmy Key's precision pitching in Game 4, Pat Borders's Most Valuable Player performance throughout the Series. And Dave Winfield's 11th-inning double in the cardiac-arresting Game 6 that let the celebrations begin. And no one had more to celebrate than Cito Gaston, the much-criticized Jays skipper who, amid the clubhouse champagne showers, stood a vindicated man. "I'm churning inside with joy and happiness for all of us," he said. "I don't hold any grudges."

To some Torontonians, the wonderful World Series avenged an earlier Atlanta victory: the right to host the 1996 Summer Olympics, a prize Toronto had also sought. For all their recent rivalry, though, the two cities have much in common. Both are painfully insecure, wary of their portrayals in the U.S. national media. As sick as Canadians are of Americans' image of them as dog-sledding moose-hunters, so Atlantans are tired of their stereotype as tobacco-spittin', hell-raisin' rednecks. Just as Toronto wants to be a "world-class city," Atlanta strives to be an "international city."

The team, the city, the country–all will feel the effects. No one will ever again accuse the Jays of choking. No one will say Canadian fans are too sedate. "No one," said Tom Noble, 35-year-old security supervisor for the Jays, blowing his trumpet in the post-Series street celebrations, "can ever take this away from us."

AT 11:39 p.m. on October 23, 1993, in Toronto, Blue Jays star Joe Carter hit a three-run homer in the bottom of the ninth inning of Game Six of the baseball World Series to produce a dramatic 8–5 victory over the Philadelphia Phillies, thereby winning Toronto's second straight championship.

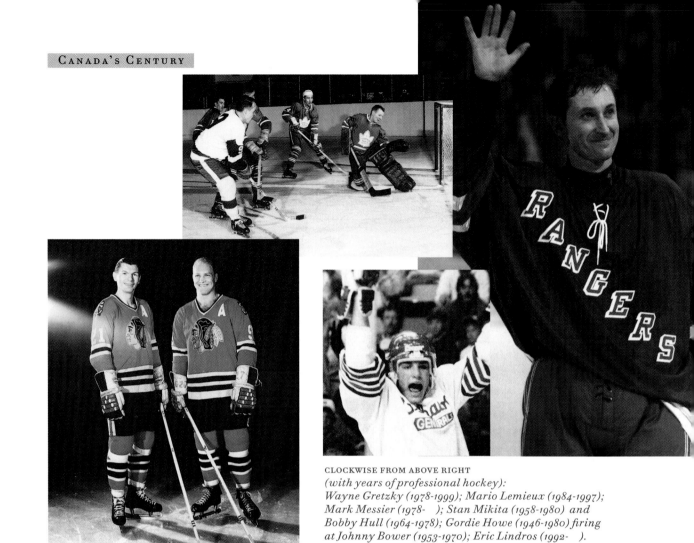

CLOCKWISE FROM ABOVE RIGHT
(with years of professional hockey):
Wayne Gretzky (1978-1999); Mario Lemieux (1984-1997);
Mark Messier (1978-   ); Stan Mikita (1958-1980) and
Bobby Hull (1964-1978); Gordie Howe (1946-1980) firing
at Johnny Bower (1953-1970); Eric Lindros (1992-   ).

CLOCKWISE FROM LEFT:
Jacques Lemaire (1967-1979) and Yvan Cournoyer (1963-1979);
Bobby Orr (1966-1979); Ken Dryden (1970-1979);
Maurice (Rocket) Richard (1942-1960); Manon Rhéaume,
Canadian women's star goalie in the 1990s.

A Question of Survival

In a Land of Wide Horizons the Gurus Stress Communication

I N 1907, Confederation's 40th anniversary year, entrepreneurs and governments were busy building new lines of communication across the country and overseas. Two new east-west railway links, the Canadian Northern and the Grand Trunk Pacific, advanced across the Prairies, augmenting the 22-year-old Canadian Pacific. The cranky new autombile began to be used for inter-city contacts. The Marconi company launched the first commercial overseas radio-telegraph service from a station built with $80,000 in federal aid near Glace Bay, Nova Scotia. At nearby Baddeck, Alexander Graham Bell pushed aviation experiments that produced vital flight controls and landing-gear designs. At the same time, the market heated up for the telephone, Bell's invention of three decades earlier, in the wake of a 1906 federal price-control law.

But in the midst of all that effort to knit the young country together, reinforcing its sense of nationhood, an eminent Canadian thinker of the day expressed serious doubts about the strength of the country's communications network and, because of that, the prospects of Canada's long-term survival. Goldwin Smith, once a leading Canada First nationalist, concludes in a lengthy assessment of the confederation in *The Busy Man's Magazine* of May, 1907, that "natural forces" of

PERHAPS NOT SURPRISINGLY for a man whose homes ranged from Edinburgh, Scotland, to Brantford, Ontario, and from Boston, Massachusetts, to Baddeck, Nova Scotia, Alexander Graham Bell, here with his wife near Baddeck in 1914, devoted his talents to defeating distance with his telephone and his contributions to flight.

RADIO NETWORKS BEGAN operating some 20 years after inventor Guglielmo Marconi's reception of the first transatlantic wireless message in Cabot Tower on Signal Hill in St. John's, Newfoundland, as pictured here, on December 12, 1901.

communication point toward Canada's eventual union with the United States. Noting powerful north-south traffic in people, commerce and information, Smith observes: "In fact, nothing separates the two portions of the English-speaking people on this continent but the political and fiscal lines."

Throughout the century, the concerns of Smith became common themes, at times preoccupations, among pundits and scholars. The powerful social impact of communication and the perennial internal and external challenges to Canada's very survival are recurring features in the works of such internationally influential Canadian thinkers as economic historian Harold Innis (1894-1952), critic Northrop Frye (1912-1991) and Innis disciple Marshall McLuhan (1911-1980).

FROM ITS BEGINNINGS, the Information Highway went through bursts of growth, as in the first years of the century, when this Bell Telephone Company work team was photographed, to what Bell Canada termed in the closing years of the century the data-centric economy.

Survival, a potent subtext in Frye's writings on the role of primal ideas and myths in molding human cultures, is the focal point of other Canadian gurus, including philosopher George Grant (1918-1988). He writes of "the impossibility of Canada," concluding in his 1965 work, *Lament for a Nation: The Defeat of Canadian Nationalism*, that the country is a branch-plant society which surrendered its independence in defence and foreign affairs to the United States.

The notion of the Canadian as loser is seen as one of several manifestations of the survival theme in writer Margaret Atwood's 1972 study, *Survival: A Thematic Guide to Canadian Literature*. The century has produced a generally pessimistic or ironic literature, she notes, "but surely the Canadian gloom is more unrelieved than most and the death and failure toll out of proportion."

Survival of the French fact in predominantly Anglo-Saxon North America formed the primary theme of Quebec nationalist Lionel-Adolphe Groulx (1878-1967). While Grant articulated the worst fears of Canadian nationalists, historian Groulx and the journals he edited inspired both Quebec's Quiet Revolution of the 1960s, a creative flourishing of francophone culture, and the political sovereigntists who gained power from that movement.

INFLUENTIAL SCHOLAR-WRITER Goldwin Smith—here at the entrance of his Toronto home, The Grange, in 1907—espoused Canada's autonomy from Britain but also its eventual absorption by the United States. Both notions evolved from a belief in Anglo-Saxon superiority further besmirched by an anti-Jewish subtext.

Forces that menace the survival of urban societies is a central element of Jane Jacobs's *The Death and Life of Great American Cities*. Her 80th birthday in 1996 inspired a month-long conference in Toronto, her longtime residence, an "international gathering to create and share knowledge" on a wide range of social issues. But as Jacobs says in *Maclean's* on October 20, 1997, "It is not ideas alone that can stop injustice, oppression and idiocies like urban renewal or slum clearance. It is people who have to do that."

Jacobs's advocacy of active people power matches the approach to social and political problems espoused by George Woodcock (1912-1995). In comments reported by *Maclean's* on December 28, 1992, the Winnipeg-born writer, who

PHILOSOPHER GEORGE GRANT'S conclusion in his slim but potent 1965 treatise Lament for a Nation *that Canada was destined to be swallowed by an American global society gave rise to such organized nationalism as the Committee for an Independent Canada in 1970 and its successor in 1985, the Council of Canadians.*

JANE JACOBS ARGUED that the way to find out how to help human communities work well is to observe "very small-scale things—neighborhoods and streets, the immediate things—and what you learn from them."

spent his later years in Vancouver, applauds civil disobedience as a communication technique that "has changed the attitudes and destinies of nations." With the anarchist's mistrust of governments, Woodcock argues that "You have to get power in the right hands—and the right hands are those of the people."

People power, in some opinions, is a victim of western society's idolization of technological progress. Grant denounces "the dictatorship of technology," arguing that it suppresses human values and "does away with human purpose." McLuhan, in a *Maclean's* essay (January 7, 1980), predicts that, with electronic communication hastening change, "there will be a general awareness that the technology game is out of control." He adds:

"Excessive speed of change isolates already-fragmented individuals and the accelerated process of adaptation takes too much vitality out of communities. By sheer attrition the social group is reduced to the condition of an anemic individual without the energy to adapt to the demands of survival."

Perhaps fittingly, there is something of all his predecessors in the messages of writer-philosopher John Ralston Saul (*Reflections of a Siamese Twin: Canada at the End of the Twentieth Century*, 1997). Observations from the century's first years find echoes in Saul's words during its closing decade. Saul disputes the suggestion of Goldwin Smith, and many who followed that writer, that the natural lines of communication run north-south. But Saul, as Smith had done in 1907, cited the dominance of the American information industry in Canada. In a presentation before a Senate committee in 1994, Saul pointed out that, in Canada, only 4 per cent of films shown and 17 per cent of books and publications sold were Canadian.

Saul's emphasis on the importance of communication, and the communicators, in placing social values ahead of commercial and political competition is recorded by *Maclean's* on November 25, 1996. In an extract from his

DAVID SUZUKI, the Vancouver geneticist who crusaded through the last third of the century on a series of radio and TV programs for better science policies and cultural enrichment, often lamented public laxity on both counts. "The problem is not a lack of material wealth," he said; "we simply lack faith in ourselves."

IN A MACLEAN'S *essay on January 7, 1980, Marshall McLuhan, pictured here on a tandem bicycle with his wife, Corrine, discussed the impact of an environment of instant information, predicting that North America "will become a society of non-achievers, intent on being, rather than on becoming."*

acceptance speech earlier that month at the Governor General's Literary Awards—his *The Unconscious Civilization* was honored as the year's best nonfiction book—Saul argues that the corporate mentality in the bureaucracies of business, government and other special interests undermines society as a whole:

Corporatism reduces civilization to the sum of its interest groups. We are all reduced—culture, public education, child care, medicare—to warring with each other for crumbs from the public purse and for charity from the private purse. If we accept that formula, we are back to the public good as nothing more than a beggar at the tables of the kings and the rich. If the writers—the people of language—can't draw back from this false struggle of interests, then who can? The real battle for the public good today is one of language and ideas. If we accept the language of these great dominating false truths, then we accept the naive and destructive ideologies that follow. I believe that what society wants from us is that we embrace that central idea of the writer as a communicator between all types of communities. I feel that the obligation which lies upon us is to ensure that the corporatist language of fear mongering and economic superstition does not stand.

A NATIONAL DEFINITION PRESENTED in 1997 by John Ralston Saul held that "Canada is above all an idea of what a country could be, a place of imagination. In spite of a recurring desire to find outside inspiration, it is very much its own invention."

AMID EFFORTS BY OTTAWA to promote national unity, George Woodcock observed in Maclean's *in December 1977: "Canada is historically and geographically incapable of being molded into a centralized nation-state of the kind that is now proving unviable even in Europe, its place of origin."*

1991 Glimpses of a Boundless Mind

FEBRUARY 4, 1991 *Just eight weeks before his death, Northrop Frye discussed a wide range of subjects, including the debate over the future of Canada, in a conversation at his home in Toronto with Carl Mollins of* Maclean's.

If a sculptor were to make a statue of a patriotic Canadian, he would depict somebody holding his breath and crossing his fingers. There has never been a time when Canada has not thought in terms of disintegration. I think that Confederation was a terribly remarkable achievement, but its great disadvantage was that it was culturally impoverished. What happened after the Second World War was the growing awareness of the fact that Canada needed a kind of reconfederation on a better cultural basis.

If I were living in Quebec, I would be a strong federalist because I think of Quebec as a political unit and therefore a province like other provinces. On the other hand, I think that French-speaking Canada is a tremendous cultural force in its own right. And I think that a reunited Canada is the inevitable context for Quebec because of the tendency of the economy to unite.

Whenever there is a minority, the feeling of cultural identity grows. Oppress the blacks in 19th-century United States and they revolutionize music. You ignore

A Scholar's Thoughts
Northrop Frye April 5, 1982

On Nationalism: Canada has passed from a pre-national to a post-national phase without ever having become a nation.

On the Canadian Identity: We are being swallowed up by the popular culture of the United States, but then the Americans are being swallowed up by it too. It's just as much a threat to American culture as it is to ours.

The Canadian identity is bound up with the feeling that the end of the rainbow never falls on Canada.

On Language: There is only one way to degrade mankind permanently and that is to destroy language.

On Writing: The most technologically efficient machine that man has ever invented is the book.

On Separatism: Separatism is a very healthy movement within culture. It's a disastrous movement within politics and economics.

On Tradition: The rear-view mirror is our only crystal ball–there is no guide to the future except the analogy of the past.

the Eskimos and they turn out to be a nation of tremendous creative genius in sculpture and painting. And you treat the French-Canadians as a minority and they produce a literature of great power. Then, finally, the last thing anyone would believe happens: English Canada comes to life and produces a specific culture that is respected and studied all over the world. They [English-Canadians] are a minority in their own context, which is a North American one. And because they feel that, it throws them back on the sense of cultural identity.

I am convinced that if I had gone to Harvard or Princeton or Oxford [to live and work], what I have produced would have been quite different in tone and context. I became a Canadian scholar in the same way that Margaret Atwood or Robertson Davies or Alice Munro have become Canadian writers–through not trying to be Canadians. They simply write about what they know.

Creative culture is infinitely porous–it absorbs influences from all over the world. That is what differentiates a genuine culture from nationalism. Nationalism is the parody of the reality of cultural identity.

The Mosaic and the Glue

Newcomers Played a Prime Role in Creating Canada's Character

FOR many of the 12.5 million immigrants who arrived in Canada from the beginning of the century until 1996, the country was merely a way station en route to their ultimate destination, the United States. In all, for every 100 new arrivals, about 51 people moved away, mostly to live south of the U.S. border. The coming and going resulted in more than a net Canadian gain in population. The migrations–despite recurring entry restrictions arising from official and personal racism–also strengthened the country's ethnic and racial diversity. The immigrants thereby helped create the cultural mosaic which, before the century was out, became Canada's boast and pride.

An immigration boom during the century's first decade set the pace in population growth. Canadian leaders agreed that attracting more immigrants, and the economic dividends they produced, remained a priority need in the sparsely populated land. Clifford Sifton, Minister of the Interior, waged a recruitment campaign in Europe, subsidizing shipping companies to transport settlers to free land in the Canadian West. The Prairies quickly developed into a composite of many ethnic groups. People from north, central and eastern Europe, including adherents of persecuted religious sects, joined homesteaders from the British Isles and the United States.

DURING THE FIRST 10 years of the century, when this shipload of Prairie-bound Europeans crossed the Atlantic, Ottawa spent heavily on immigrant recruiting offices. That helped reverse the pattern of the previous four decades, when more people moved out of Canada than moved in.

AN OFFICIAL EXPRESSION of long-standing Canadian animosity towards non-white people took place in 1914 in Vancouver harbor when Canada's brand-new navy, amid cheers from Vancouverites ashore, forced the ship Komagata Maru *and its almost 400 would-be immigrants from India to leave Canadian waters.*

But not all immigrants were welcome, an official bias noted in a 1928 *Maclean's* article by teacher-novelist Frederick Philip Grove in his comment that Canadian governmental agencies invite "members of all white nations" to move to Canada. Discrimination against visible minorities ranged from a federal commission's conclusion in 1902 rating Chinese and Japanese residents of British Columbia "obnoxious" and "dangerous," through the imposition of crushing, race-based head taxes to deter unwanted Asian migrants and the denial of voting rights to Chinese and Asiatic Indian people. Statutory racism persisted for most of the century: residents of Asiatic origin and descent gained federal voting rights in 1947, but it was another 20 years before Ottawa removed the last of the discriminatory immigration restrictions.

Other immigrant groups and their descendants experienced prejudicial treatment. Black Canadians whose ancestors came to Canada as United Empire Loyalists in the late 1700s and as fugitives from American slavery in the 1850s often suffered treatment similar to the racism of the American South. After somewhat more than 1,000 black Americans took up Canadian offers of land on the Prairies in 1905, the federal cabinet yielded to pressure groups in Alberta and passed an order in 1911 that barred "any immigrants belonging to the Negro race, which race is deemed unsuitable to the climate and requirements of Canada." From the earliest days of the century, influential intellectuals—notably, commentator Goldwin Smith in English Canada and Abbé Lionel Groulx

IN 1907, British Columbian hostility towards Asians exploded into outbursts of harassment and property damage, as in the window smashing depicted here. The same year, Ottawa pressured Japan into imposing a limit on male migration to Canada.

THE CANADIAN NAVAL OFFICER questioning Japanese Canadian fishermen in Esquimalt, British Columbia—two days after Japan attacked U.S. naval ships in Pearl Harbor—is the beginning of the roundup and detention of almost 21,000 British Columbians of Japanese ancestry, the confiscation of their property and their dispersal in the name of national security.

in Quebec—openly fostered anti-semitism. Appeals to Ottawa on behalf of Jews seeking to escape persecution in Europe during the 1930s and 1940s went unheeded until after the Second World War, when Canada began admitting Jewish survivors of the Nazi Holocaust among other refugees collectively known as DPs, the displaced persons from a devastated Europe.

Public prejudices flared in later years. Amid campaigning for the federal election in October 1972, debate arose over a flood of "visitors" from the Indian subcontinent and Latin America using a legal loophole to seek immigrant status. The outcry prompted the Liberal government to plug the loophole. Immigration Minister Bryce Mackasey resigned by way of atonement. In the 1980s, politicians received complaints when federal authorities granted entry to high-paying Asiatic passengers dropped off Canada's Atlantic shores by unscrupulous foreign shippers—155 Tamils from Sri Lanka into open boats off Newfoundland in August 1986, and 174 Asians, mostly Sikhs, at night in shallow water off southern Nova Scotia in July 1987. Women of the nearby village of Charlesville, as *Maclean's* reported at the time, made tea and muffins for the Sikhs.

By the mid-1990s, with Asians and Africans regularly making up more than two-thirds of total immigration running to about 200,000 annual admissions, British Columbians resurrected the racist sentiments that blemished Canada's

THE STRICTLY MALE ROOMING-HOUSE gathering in Vancouver's Chinatown in about 1906 is typical of its time and for decades afterward. A heavy head tax on immigrants from China made the entry of wives a rarity, and a city bylaw confined the Chinese to Chinatown.

record early the century–albeit much more discreetly than had participants in the 1907 anti-Asiatic riots in Vancouver. A *Maclean's* cover report of February 7, 1994, records complaints about the monster-homes and other offending habits of Chinese immigrants, many of them rich enough to take advantage of a program whereby an investment of $100,000 or more bought a front place in the immigrant line. Then, in 1995, the federal government provoked accusations of racism and discrimination against poor would-be immigrants and refugees from Third World countries by imposing a counterpart of the old head tax–a $975 right-of-landing fee on top of a $500 application levy for each adult applicant seeking entry to Canada. As Immigration Minister Sergio Marchi explained in announcing a subsequent overhaul of immigrant selection rules: "We want the immigrant to be a success in a shorter period of time and get integrated . . . a heck of a lot quicker."

A notion more appropriate to the official espousal of Canada as a cultural mosaic may belong with the words in the *Maclean's* of October 13, 1986, by Ken MacQueen, an Ottawa correspondent. That year, the government launched an immigration drive to counteract a lagging birthrate and stimulate economic growth. The result over the following decade, compared to the previous 10 years, was a near doubling in the number of newcomers. That, at a time of high unemployment, prompted public grumbling. But as MacQueen observed in his cover story: "Canada is a nation of immigrants. Its trees were felled, its prairies cleared and its cities built by successive generations of misfits and refugees. In the suspicious view of the ruling majority, they often spoke the wrong language, wore the wrong clothing or worshipped the wrong God. But while they were exploited and isolated, they were also allowed in by the hundreds of thousands, the necessary raw material for the nation."

Perhaps, then, the true future of Canadian immigration lies in the example

MORE THAN 40 YEARS after Canada turned away a shipload of Asiatic Indians in Vancouver, authorities and hospitable local greeters welcomed 174 Indians—some pictured here—who were dropped at night into shallow water off southern Nova Scotia in July 1987 by a people-smuggling shipper.

of the Nova Scotian women who made refreshments in the night for the weary Sikhs who waded through the surf to Canadian soil—and received a welcoming kindness of muffins and tea.

1908 Some Settlers Canada Can Do Without

J. T. Ardley – JULY 1908 **C**ertain misfits and failures of other lands are proving rather too heavy a burden upon the exchequer of the Dominion. The foreign population of Canada—those who come from other countries—constitutes about 20 per cent of the number of inhabitants in this peaceful and prosperous land. But in 1907 in Ontario, 38 per cent of those committed to jail and 30 per cent of admissions to insane asylums are foreigners.

In connection with the Toronto Asylum, Dr. C. K. Clarke, Medical Superintendent, furnishes some rather startling figures of the strong tendency to degeneracy on the part of those of foreign birth, who have evidently come from squalid and submerged communities in the Old Country.

One cause of so much insanity and crime among the foreign born who come to Canada is that a large majority are brought out by steamship companies or immigration societies, bonuses frequently being paid to bring the new settlers to this land.

We have enough of our own to look after without having foisted upon us the derelicts from other countries. Canada should exclude from her shores all who are not healthy, active and willing to work.

ALTHOUGH EARLY IMMIGRATION POLICY favored people from the British Isles, Ottawa contracted with a firm called the North Atlantic Trading Company in 1904 to recruit other Europeans, preferably Scandinavian, Dutch, German, Russian and Swiss. The government terminated the contract after only two years on the grounds that the company had been recruiting too strenuously in eastern and southern Europe. The immigrants pictured here are waiting to disembark in Quebec City in 1911.

1919 The Problem of Our New Canadians

Nellie McClung – SEPTEMBER 1919 The West has had for many years a "Foreign Problem," caused by the great influx of people from other countries who have come hither, attracted by the free land and the resultant opportunities for home-making. They come here unable to speak the language, unacquainted with our customs and in many ways dependent upon the kind offices of our people. In the public schools where the foreign children have attended, there have been many teachers with real vision and real kindness of heart whose good work cannot be measured. But no particular effort was made in the way of special help to the foreign schools until about four years ago in Manitoba, when Mr. Ira Stratton, of Stonewall, was appointed "Official Trustee."

Once, addressing a gathering of Polish farmers, among whom he had gone to organize a school, Mr. Stratton urged them to give their children the proper equipment for battling with the world: knowledge of the English language, and drove it home to them in this way: "I not say English language best language in world–maybe it is–maybe not; but anyway, one good tool for make living in this country." This simple parable went home, and the school was duly organized without opposition.

It is Mr. Stratton's great delight to take visitors to his schools, and especially those who are disposed to doubt the value of educating the "foreigner." For we have, unfortunately, still a few very excellent people so imbued with the belief that the Anglo-Saxon people are the pets of the Almighty, that they are apt to question the wisdom of giving the foreign child exactly the same chance as we give our own. One eminent divine who, while not actively opposing the education of the foreigner, had not shown any enthusiasm over it, was so impressed by the sight of the eager little faces in one of Mr. Stratton's schools, that he cried out in astonishment to his travelling companion: "Why they would pass for a group of Scotch Presbyterian children!"

Surely there can be no higher word of praise than that!

1928 Canadians Old and New

Frederick Philip Grove – MARCH 15, 1928 *Writer Frederick Philip Grove, born Friedrich Greve in 1879 and raised in Germany, travelled widely as a young poet and settled in 1913 in Manitoba. After 10 years as a schoolteacher, he took up a writing career following the success of his early books (*Over Prairie Trails; Turn of the Year*). He won a Governor General's Award for Literature in 1946 and died two years later at Simcoe, Ontario.*

Like the statues of the ancient Roman deity Janus, this article is going to have two faces, one turned to those who, being born in this country or having lived here long enough to be fully acclimatized, invite through their governmental agencies members of all white nations to come and to make their homes among them; the other, to those who have just arrived in pursuance of that invitation, or who, having arrived some time ago, did not find all they may have expected to find in the way of a welcome. It involves a subject which we commonly summarize under the heading of "assimilation of the immigrant."

Firstly, then, Mr. Canadian Citizen, let me tell you a few truths about yourself as well as about your guests. What, at the present moment, do you, the average citizen of this country, do in order to make the newcomer feel at home? First of all, you call him a "foreigner." It is

WITH FREE OR NEARLY FREE Crown land for the taking, most early immigrants—such as this family trudging to town in about 1900—favored farming. But in the century's later decades, the big cities were the main draw, with Toronto, Montreal and Vancouver absorbing three-quarters of Canada's immigrants by the 1990s.

SUCH WELL-AGED URBAN LANDMARKS as Kensington Market, a crisscross of midtown Toronto streets pictured here in 1926, reflect changing layers of immigration. Kensington retains reminders of its time as a European Jewish centre during the first 50 years of the century, followed by Portuguese, then West Indians and Vietnamese.

ICELAND PROVIDED a small but vibrant stream of migrants to Canada after devastating climate changes, volcanic eruptions and epidemics in the late 19th century drove hundreds of families to seek a new homeland, mainly in Manitoba. The community of Gimli, where these early 20th-century Icelandic Canadians are playing croquet, was briefly a self-governing settlement.

well-known that this title, within the British Isles, has from time immemorial had a sinister sound.

Yet, if the national status of Canada means anything at all, then it surely means this: that here, in Canada, we cultivate an attitude toward life and its various phases—economic, intellectual, spiritual—distinct from that of a mere British Crown colony. In such Crown colonies the foreigner may be tolerated; we invite him. The Britisher coming to these shores is as much a "foreigner" when he lands as any man arriving from Central Europe.

The present writer knows a good many districts in the west of this vast Dominion where there are "little islands" of English or Scotch immigrants who offer as their contribution towards the evolution of a new Canadian mentality chiefly acrid criticism of the destructive kind. So-called "foreigners" rarely make themselves obnoxious in that way.

Again, what, Mr. Citizen, do you do in order to welcome the "foreigner" whom you invite? Oh, well, you assign him 160 acres of land in the bush or a job in a factory or work on the road-bed of a transportation line, and thereafter you leave him icily alone. He meets with other "foreigners"; and if they are farmers, there is soon a "foreign settlement"; if they are factory hands, there is a "foreign quarter" in some city; if men of the pick and shovel, there is a "foreign gang." The adults are very apt to hang onto their vernacular; they have little opportunity to acquire any other, especially the women. They have no desire for isolation; but it is forced onto them.

THROUGHOUT THE FIRST THIRD of the century, Canadian policy encouraged the entry of white Americans and Western Europeans to develop farming and natural resources in western Canada. As indicated in this photo of Ukrainian women cutting logs in the Athabasca region of Alberta around 1930, the need to tame the land required a willingness for hard work by people of any ethnic group, and of either gender.

Their ways may be strange and even repulsive to you; so are your ways to them. In such a settlement I have heard a Russian farmer speak of Canadian farming methods as "slovenly English ways."

Another thing. We speak a great deal of "Canadian Ideals." But so long as we advertise our country abroad as a good place to come to, there cannot be anything that may properly be called a Canadian ideal; at best it is only a provisional one; for that ideal is still in the making; and when you invite anyone to become a new citizen of this country, you invite him also to help in the making of it.

Do you, Mr. Canadian Citizen, think that these people have no contribution to make to our intellectual and spiritual life?

Don't forget that these people who come among us have pluck and enterprise; or they would not be here. Do not forget that they have brains; for most of them were the underdogs in Europe; and it is precisely the underdog who develops his brains. Look at your rural schools in mixed districts: which children lead their classes, yours or those of these "foreigners"? No, assimilation can only be mutual. Only if you take from them, will they take from you.

1948 'We Can't Go Back'

Eva-Lis Wuorio – JUNE 1, 1948 To Canada, Displaced Persons are so many strong backs. To DPs, our Canada is a dream of freedom and plenty miraculously come true.

Georges Lukk got up at five that morning but already the other 23 men in the triple-bunked cabin of the S. S. *Marine Falcon* were stirring. "Fog," he said, "can't see anything." They took pains at washing and shaving and dressing. Not many had coats and pants that matched. Those who had two shirts had saved the clean, least frayed one for this morning. Georges went up to the deck slowly although he wanted to run. He told himself this was a great moment, but his mind was curiously blank. And then to the right a lighthouse lifted out of the fog. The last he had seen of Europe, after they'd left Wesermunde, port to Bremerhaven in Germany, had been a lighthouse.

The decks were now filling with people. Georges recognized Jan Zaramba, the Polish lawyer, with his family. He was going to St. Georges de Beauce to be a mill laborer. And the quiet, dark Tadeusz Piekutowski, ex-engraver, who had signed up as a construction worker. Around him were his friends—young Estonians like himself, whose destination was Campbell Red Lake Mines Ltd., Ont. He fingered the tag on his lapel. The printed address, a definite destination, gave him a feeling of security.

The dolorous sound of the foghorn emphasized the unreal silence. In the slowly moving throng there was hardly a sound. Four hundred and thirty-one displaced persons, the doors closed to their Northern European homelands because they knew, and hated, Communism, turned strained eyes this spring morning of 1948, toward the still hidden shore of Canada. Ten thousand DPs had come before them. Another ten thousand would follow to fill the quota Canada had decided to let in by three separate Orders-in-Council. Another million men and women and children, in the bleak camps of Europe, would wait for the nod they might never receive. On board now are DPs in five main categories:

1. Those who are vouched for by close relatives already in Canada.

2. Workers brought here by Canadian employers—garment workers, miners, lumbermen, metal workers, etc. who have been assured jobs in these various trades, with the approval of a Government Immigration-Labor Committee. (Employers are required to promise they will provide employment for a period of one year at rates of wages and under working conditions no less favorable for the DPs than those prevailing for Canadian workers in similar occupations.)

3. Domestics, sponsored by the Ministry of Labor.

4. Jewish orphans, looked after by a Jewish refugee committee.

5. Ex-soldiers of Poland brought out with a two-year contract as farm laborers.

All these people may hope for Canadian citizenship in five years.

Shortly after eight o'clock the fog began to undulate. They had stood on the decks for three hours. Now busy tugs, tooting importantly, came to tow the liner in. Above the fog a hill emerged, a flat fortification crowning it. Then a long quay wall with grey high sheds running down the length of it. Halifax. Canada. The people lined the shoreward decks.

"It's a pity there is no way to say welcome," someone on the dock said. "Even a band."

"They don't need a band," someone else said. "The fact they're allowed to come here is good enough. They should be grateful."

A.G. Christie, inspector-in-chief of immigration in Halifax, a quick-moving, slight man, took a couple of swift steps forward. He lifted his hand and the smile that breaks up his whole thin face came out. "Welcome," he shouted and waved.

The two solid lines of brightened faces, the sudden wave of motion as though the still people had been brought to life, was literally like light bursting out of a thick cloud bank. With almost hurting eagerness the people on the ship answered him in a universal smile.

Now the loudspeaker on the ship was shouting in Polish, in Estonian. Orders were given for the grouping of the miners, the garment workers, the construction workers, the domestics. Tagged, numbered, accounted for, they could be more easily cleared through the immigration, Customs, package check. It was sheeplike but efficient.

Finally they started moving off the ship, carrying their hand luggage and their smallest children. Down the ramp they went and up the stairs, to wait on the long yellow benches for a doctor's examination. To many it was the fifth or sixth medical since they got tentative permission to come to Canada in a DP camp in Germany. "Screened," was the word they used for it. "We've been screened," or, "We've been processed, often." This time it's just a slow line moving past a Canadian doctor, whose sharp eyes and long experience could tell him when to pull a man or a child out of the line for a more thorough examination.

At the doorway to the Customs corridor there is the Imperial Tobacco Co.'s stand. Every DP is handed a couple of packages of cigarettes and some tobacco, the gift of the company. The majority of the displaced persons do not own a single Canadian cent.

NEW CANADIANS WHO SHUNNED farming in favor of city life received negative ratings in a 1914 report. Among the citations: European Jews ("pre-eminently dwellers in cities") and Italians ("when times are slack the Italians flock to the cities"). Here, Italian Canadians in Toronto muster for First World War military service.

A CNR train is pulled up beside the shed. This is a DP Special, as the one which had taken the upright, wooden-shoed Dutch off the *Kota Inten*, earlier in the week, had been a Settlers Special. (Settlers pay their own fares.) The cars are allotted– members of the domestic workers' schemes up ahead, then the car for families travelling together, coaches all of these. There is a sleeper for the Canadian officials accompanying the party, two dining cars, and at the back the colonists' cars for the men going to mines and other manual jobs. From here on, the bill for transportation and food is footed by firms who have undertaken to employ the new arrivals. This, ultimately, will come out of their wages, refunded in 10 months, if the DP is still then in the company's employ.

Displaced Persons are truly people naked of the past, with no goods to bring, with memories they want to forget, seeking a chance to start again. Some bring hatreds—hatred of the Russians and Communism and the Germans—but even these are diluted in the deep well of tragic experiences they have known. You can suffer so much. Hate so much. Fear until the very fear is dead. Then, dully, you must begin to build up your dead reflexes again. That is the impression a Displaced Person gives you.

As the train leaves Halifax for the bare rocky lands and spruce forests of the Nova Scotia interior, I look for Georges Lukk again. He is 29, a six-foot-two, slender man, with blue eyes behind horn-rimmed glasses, and a sombre face, until it lightens with a frank young smile. The tag on his lapel says No. 136. He waves a hand at the magnificent, lonely landscape. "Like Estonia," he says with an unexpected smile. "Like home. Father told us it would be so."

His father, owner of a large glass factory in Estonia, had once spent some time in Calgary and come back to tell his family of a fabulous land where "there is no fear." With the idea of migrating to Canada, the Lukk family began to learn English. Today, Georges speaks the language fluently.

Here are the steps that went into the making of Georges Lukk, 29, Displaced Person, and brought him on a spring Sunday in 1948 to a westbound train from Halifax:

A happy boyhood in the ancient walled city of Tallinn, during Estonia's young years of independence. Later, as a scholarship student, he went to the Vienna Technical University, where he did research on how coal is converted into petroleum, and won his science doctorate in 1941.

He returned to Estonia but by then the ordinary way of life was broken. Russian armies had entered in 1940, Germans invaded in 1941, Russians would take over again in 1944. He had married during his last year in Vienna and managed to get back there to his young family. When the Germans ordered him to enlist he went into hiding until his former professors got him a permit to work in the university's research branch.

The Austrian town in which he was living was liberated by the Americans on May 4, 1945. All foreigners were instructed to report to UN officials for repatriation. Estonia under the Russians was not Georges' goal, so he marked down his preferred destination, "Canada." The family was sent in crowded lorries from Austria to Mannheim in Germany. Later, with two babies now, they made their way to the seaport of Hamburg where Georges ultimately found a post with the newly founded Baltic University for refugees. Because of his position, the family lived in luxury—a 250-foot square hut, all to themselves.

Canada began accepting DPs as immigrants in the spring of 1947. (The first ones got here that July.) The first scheme was for single men only. Twenty men in each DP camp in the British and American zones of Germany could go. Georges tells how the element of luck entered right there. You were fortunate to even hear the news—there weren't enough printed notices or registration blanks.

Three factors could eliminate you, even though a non-German: If on your arm you wore the blood-category scar of the Hitler SS with which good party members were branded; if you had served in the German armed forces; if you had been a collaborator. Screenings were thorough. You accounted for each move of the war years.

One day word came that five families could enter. The Lukks were selected as one. Georges' wife and two small daughters were launched into the screening process.

Medically speaking, DPs immediately eliminated were those suffering from TB and venereal diseases and crippled persons. Not more than half of those who had first indicated their desire to go to Canada got beyond the preliminaries. Of the semifinal group of 150, only 40 passed the last screening. The rest "were not strong enough." There were tragic eyes of many good friends that lucky Georges Lukk didn't like to meet. He says now: "In the camps there are many sensitive, famous men and women. They have suffered more than we who were young and less conspicuous. No one wants them now. They'll never get out. What will happen to them?"

Yesterday, I had a letter from Red Lake, which is a barren mining town in Northern Ontario, near the Manitoba border. Georges Lukk and Karl Ohmet write it and their 15 friends sign it. In part they say: "The best of it is, today, the bread we eat we earn. We have left behind the DP status. We are free men in charge of our own lives. It is good to greet each new morning as individuals, ordinary human beings."

1952 Why are We Afraid to Grow?

Ralph Allen – OCTOBER 1, 1952 **T**he true measure of our national imagination–the measure of our belief in Canada's capacity to play a better and more fruitful part in a better and more fruitful world–will be, for many years to come, the measure of our willingness to grow and to accept the risks of growth along with its rewards. In no field are we so ready for growth as in population. In none are the rewards so apparent, in none the risks so meagre. Yet we are still burdened by the dismal hope that we can somehow cash in on the rewards while avoiding almost every element of risk.

After gradually overcoming its early postwar caution, Ottawa recently put the brakes on immigration again. The new and temporary regulations virtually slammed the door on all new settlers except those from the United Kingdom, France and the United States. The new policy will reduce the immigrant intake for this year by fifty thousand.

There has been no lack of justification for the policy. It is precisely the kind of justification that might be expected from a timid and race-conscious bookkeeper: the current restrictions will arrest the disruption of our traditional ethnic structure, reduce the dangers of temporary unemployment and help to hold the line on housing. These are all excellent arguments to a bookkeeper. To a nation halfway through the century with fewer than fifteen million inhabitants, they're just plain silly.

1958 In a Racial Sore Spot

Sidney Katz – JANUARY 18, 1958 **T**hree weeks ago, with headlines bannering yet another in the fear-and-hate-filled series of racial incidents in Little Rock, Ark., I went back to the sleepy southern Ontario town where in 1949 I wrote an article called Jim Crow Lives in Dresden. I wanted to see what the intervening years had done to the Canadian town [home to descendants of Southern slaves who fled to Canada in the 1850s] where Negroes couldn't eat in local restaurants, have their hair cut in barber shops or play in pool rooms.

There have been changes, most of them the result of Ontario's Fair Accommodation Practices Act passed in 1954. Today, the restaurants are open to everyone. Morley McKay, who owns the town's largest, led the fight for segregation. In 1956 he was fined for refusing to serve a Negro. Since then, he has been serving everybody, but few colored people patronize him. "They know they're not welcome," he told me. "Would you go where you're not wanted?" Mrs. Matt Emerson, of Emerson's Restaurant, says, "Our own Negroes don't give us any trouble. It's the outsiders from Toronto and Detroit."

Outside Negroes had the Fair Accommodation Law successfully tested in court. Did she think it was a good law? "I'm not a lawmaker," she said curtly. In answer to the same question, Mayor Doug Weese replied impatiently, "I won't talk about it. I don't want to start trouble." Many citizens, like Jack Neil, Kinsmen president, say, "I think the law is fair. That's the way it should be."

Certainly the law has boosted the Negro's morale. "I'm no longer ashamed to tell people I'm from Dresden," says Bill Carter, a farmer active in the struggle for equal rights.

Although barber shops are now required to serve all, Negroes still don't use them. Mrs. William Rickman, who cuts her husband's hair, explains: "We know the barbers don't want us." Mayor Weese says, "You might pass a law forcing a barber to cut hair but you can't force on him the kind of haircut he's liable to give." I asked barber George Wellman point blank if he would defy the law by refusing to cut a Negro's hair. "There are other ways of handling it," he said. "There's no law against using dull tools, is there?" Then he denounced the law. "A bunch of guys sit at their desks in Toronto and try to tell me how to run my business," he said. "It's not democratic, I was in uniform for five years fighting against dictatorship. It's all been wasted."

Pool halls (also included in the law) appear to be open to colored people, but most proprietors don't seem happy about it. When I questioned one owner, Harvey Sutton, he shouted: "Get out of here, and never come back!"

The reception was almost as cool at the house of Rev. Lawrence Newton, a Presbyterian minister who heads the Dresden Ministerial Association. For fifteen minutes I stood on the doorstep on a bitterly cold afternoon while he told me: "The more

BEFORE THE GRADUAL removal of racial discrimination from immigration policy after the Second World War, black Africans who settled in Canada were mainly fugitive or freed slaves from the United States and their descendants. A Halifax settlement named Africville, pictured here, disappeared under demolition orders in the 1960s, its people ejected with little compensation. Thirty years later, as Maclean's *reported in June 1995, "The city's 8,000-strong black community remains mired in poverty and anger."*

discussion, the worse this thing becomes. Fellows like you do a lot of harm." Rev. Newton does not favor legislation as a method of promoting minority rights: "You can't pass laws about that sort of thing. You've got to work on the human spirit."

Dresden's colored people still don't belong to local clubs–except the Canadian Legion. Jack Neil, Kinsmen president, says, "we've never received any applications. We might accept a colored applicant if he had a good character. That's a requirement for everybody." But Neil foresaw difficulties at social functions where women were present.

Behind objections to mixed race social affairs is fear of intermarriage. I was asked more than once, "How would you like your sister to marry a Negro?" Since my last visit, there have been eight or nine mixed marriages. Usually the man is colored, the woman white. Most of the couples have moved away. When they remain, they are more closely identified with the colored community than the white. "Practically all the mixed marriages have been successful," says Joe Hanson, secretary of the Colored National Unity Association.

I asked what impact the events in Little Rock, Ark., had had on Dresden. Bill Carter replied, "We colored people talked about it a lot among ourselves. But I couldn't get a white person to discuss it with me." Mayor Doug Weese said, "Little Rock gives you an idea of how well off the colored people are in Dresden."

In Dresden, where the tombstone of Harriet Stowe's model for Uncle Tom is the town's most prominent monument–"The Grave of Rev. Josiah Henson the original Uncle Tom of Uncle Tom's Cabin by Harriet Beecher Stowe," says the memorial–most Negroes and many whites agree with Mrs. William Rickman, a colored housewife, who told me, "The anti-discrimination law was a good thing. The principle was just. But it won't do everything. God will have to take the prejudice out of men's hearts."

1998 Face of a Nation

Danylo Hawaleshka – MARCH 2, 1998 **S**tatistics Canada's groundbreaking report on ethnic origin and visible minorities had barely been released, and already television executives at CFMT International were busy crunching numbers. A lot was at stake. The station broadcasts in 22 languages throughout southern Ontario, and the Statistics Canada report shone a revealing spotlight on its target audience. For instance, the station learned that fully one-quarter of Toronto's visible minority population is Chinese–about 335,000 people in total. Knowing the size of the market is important for landing lucrative commercials aimed at particular ethnic groups, says Madeline Ziniak, the station's vice-president. "This report," she adds, "will reinforce with advertisers the need to communicate with these communities."

IN 1964, SOME CANADIANS were moved by the civil rights movement in the United States to demonstrate in sympathy with U.S. blacks–and to demand recognition of minority rights and an end to discrimination north of the border too.

The federal survey unit's snapshot of Canada's ethnic makeup will be a boon to business people. But not everyone is as pleased. The report, based on the 1996 census, is the first in Canadian history to ask people so sensitive a question–to identify themselves as, for example, Chinese, Filipino or Vietnamese.

Some of the findings: more than one in 10 Canadians–11.2 per cent, or 3.2 million people–identified themselves as members of a visible minority group. Of those:

- About 30 per cent were born in Canada.
- Chinese are the most numerous–860,000, or 27 per cent of all visible minorities.
- South Asians are next (671,000, or 21 per cent).
- Blacks place third (574,000, 18 per cent).

Statistics Canada says the data are needed to enforce the Employment Equity Act, which tries to ensure visible minorities fair access to jobs under federal jurisdiction. But MP Deepak Obhrai, the Reform Party's critic for citizenship and immigration and an opponent of the act, says Canada is becoming dangerously like the United States, where everything from births to crime are tabulated along race lines. Obhrai, an East Indian born in Tanzania, also says that using Statistics Canada numbers to ensure fair hiring practices will only create resentment and prompt people to ask: "Why is this group getting special treatment?"

More political jousting resulted from rather unexpected findings in Quebec. For the question about a person's ethnic origin, Statistics Canada for the first time listed "Canadian" as a possible choice among others such as French, English,

IN THE LATTER half of the 1990s, according to Statistics Canada, immigrants constituted about one-third of Vancouver's population and more than two-fifths of Toronto's. Here, in Vancouver's Chinatown on June 30, 1997, performers of a dragon dance celebrate the return of Hong Kong to China after 156 years of British colonial rule.

Micmac and Portuguese. Across the country, almost one in five respondents, 19 per cent, said their ancestry is exclusively Canadian. Another 17 per cent said British Isles. But in predominantly French Quebec, only 29 per cent of the province's residents identified French as their roots, while a surprising 38 per cent said their background is Canadian. Some federalists quietly mused that perhaps Quebecers had developed a sudden love affair with Canada, a suggestion that Bloc Québécois Leader Gilles Duceppe quickly tried to shoot down.

"They're trying to play politics with Statistics Canada just like they're trying to play politics with the Supreme Court," said Duceppe as the high court considered Quebec's right to declare independence unilaterally. "This is very childish."

Whatever a person might call it, the report offered an intimate and unprecedented look at the nation. While the 1861 census identified "colored" persons, and the 1901 census designated a person either white, black, yellow or red, the 1996 accounting of the population was much more specific, asking people to identify themselves as one or more of 10 categories, including Chinese, South Asian (such as East Indian, Pakistani, Punjabi, Sri Lankan) and black (African, Haitian, Jamaican, Somali and so on). Canada's 1.1 million aboriginals were tabulated separately.

The report concluded that virtually all visible minorities (94 per cent) live in metropolitan areas, mostly in and around Vancouver, Toronto and Montreal. Among Vancouver's visible minority population, nine out of 10 were Asian, with Chinese the largest group. Montreal was found to be home to 92 per cent of Quebec's visible minorities, with blacks—many of them Haitian—the city's largest group.

The Forces of Disunity

Quebec's Historic Discontent Forms a Defining Feature of Canada

A S the century opened, widening policy differences festered between Prime Minister Wilfrid Laurier and his brilliant young protegé in Quebec, Henri Bourassa, who objected to Laurier's decision to send a Canadian military contingent to help the British fight the Boers in South Africa. Bourassa, who founded the Montreal newspaper *Le Devoir*, advocated a united and truly bicultural Canada, a country independent of ties to the British Empire. For that reason he opposed Ottawa's decision in 1910 to establish a navy—a force many Quebecers regarded as a Canadian branch of the British Royal Navy. Bourassa's opposition helped split Laurier's Liberal Party and contributed to its defeat in the 1911 federal election. Yet he joined forces with Laurier in 1917 to attack military conscription during the First World War.

By the 1920s, moderate Bourassa nationalists faced a challenge from a more radical brand of nationalism, a Quebec-centred movement with secessionist leanings. And in the century's final quarter, autonomy had become the ascendant political faith in francophone Quebec, despite the successes of federalist counterforces led by Pierre Trudeau from the 1960s into the 1980s.

Separatism received stimulus from both positive and negative factors. In the 1960s, following the death of Maurice Duplessis, "Le Chef" for 15 years, Quebec

HENRI BOURASSA, grandson of Louis-Joseph Papineau, leader of the 1837 rebellion in Lower Canada, was a power in Quebec and Canadian affairs for half the century—and remains so. He planted the seeds of the Parti Québécois in his isolationist Nationalist party and in his living legacy, the Montreal daily newspaper he founded in 1910, Le Devoir.

underwent profound changes. The Quiet Revolution in thought and attitudes generated a new climate of francophone self-assertion, confidence and creativity–in the arts, commerce and industry. In the 1970s, the essential failure of a federal "B and B" campaign discouraged moderate Quebecers who had harbored hopes of building the kind of bilingual-bicultural nation espoused half a century earlier by Henri Bourassa.

In the midst of those developments, the October crisis of 1970–provoked by the kidnapping of British consul James Cross in Montreal and the murder of Quebec cabinet minister Pierre Laporte–cut both ways. The terrorist tactics of the Front de Libération du Québec tarnished the separatist cause among mainstream Quebecers for a time. But the response of federal and Quebec authorities in suspending civil rights and jailing reputed separatists lent support to arguments that an assertive francophone Quebec risked oppression. A subsequent federal inquiry into RCMP activities exposed evidence that the force had engaged in clandestine operations against the sovereigntists, including the break-in theft of a Parti Québécois membership list and a barn burning meant to implicate separatists.

MAURICE DUPLESSIS, *Quebec's premier for all but five years between 1936 and 1959, dominated the province with his Union Nationale until his death in 1959. He fought labor unions and trampled civil liberties in campaigns against communists and critics of Catholicism.*

It was Quebec nationalism, plus the charisma of Parti Québécois leader René Lévesque, that produced Lévesque's election in 1976 at the head of the province's first openly separatist government. Despite the PQ's successes at election time (1981 and 1994), the sovereigntist option went down to defeat in two Quebec referendums, first in 1980 and then–by 50.6 to 49.4 percentage points–in 1995. The federal government subsequently asked the Supreme Court of Canada to say, in effect, how the country and Quebec should proceed if a future referendum went the other way. In 1998, the court essentially threw the issue back to the politicians, stating that they should decide precisely what referendum question and result

MONTREAL RIOT POLICE *watch over a fire beneath a "Oui" sign after Quebecers, by a hair-thin margin, opposed Quebec's secession in a referendum on October 30, 1995.* Maclean's *reported: "Quebec's non-francophone population voted overwhelmingly against Premier Jacques Parizeau's independence plan, raising the prospect of a society perilously split along language and ethnic lines."*

BOMBINGS IN THE SPRING OF 1963 at federal buildings and mailboxes in Montreal by radicals of the Front de Libération du Québec killed a night watchman and disabled an army explosives expert. Here, police survey bomb damage. Men later convicted in connection with the bombing death received jail sentences ranging from 6 months to 12 years.

would constitute a clear "yes" to separation and then, if Quebecers chose secession, the province and the rest of Canada should negotiate the terms.

In the interval between the two referendums came repeated attempts to accommodate Quebec in a looser Confederation under a 1982 constitution enacted over Lévesque's objections. Federal and provincial leaders twice negotiated constitutional proposals—the Meech Lake Accord of 1987 and the Charlottetown Accord of 1992—that attempted to reconcile Quebec's desire for constitutional recognition of its unique status with the insistence of some other provincial leaders that all provinces are constitutionally equal. Meech failed by a pair of provinces (Manitoba and Newfoundland) to win unanimous legislative approval by the mid-1990 ratification deadline. Just over two years later, on October 26, 1992, majorities in both Quebec and the rest of the country displayed a rare sharing of common purpose by voting down the Charlottetown Accord in a national referendum.

Almost exactly a year later, the electorate produced a democratic absurdity. In the federal election of October 25, 1993, the Bloc Québécois, the three-year-old separatist party led by former federal cabinet minister Lucien Bouchard, finished second to the victorious Liberals and thereby provided Parliament with an Official Opposition dedicated to the destruction of Confederation.

The following excerpts from *Maclean's* trace a century's testimony to the pre-eminent role in the life of Canada played by Quebec's relations with the rest of the country. The record suggests that—regardless of whether or not Quebec remains in Confederation—the dictates of geography alone ensure that the Quebec question will persist as a defining feature of Canada.

1909 A Day with Canada's Premier

C.B. Van Blaricom – JUNE 1909 **I**n an address before a Western Ontario audience during the election campaign of 1908, Sir Wilfrid Laurier made use of these words: "My days cannot be very long now. But whether they are long or short, I shall always treasure as the most holy thing in life–if I may say so–the confidence which has been placed in me by men who are not of my own kith and kin. When my life does come to an end, if my eyes close upon a Canada more united than I found it over twenty years ago, when I assumed the leadership of the Liberal Party, I shall not have lived in vain, and I will die in peace and happiness."

SIR WILFRID LAURIER achieved his record of serving the longest unbroken term as prime minister–15 years–by finding a balance between the nationalist pressures exerted from his native Quebec and the prevailing anglophilia among English-speaking voters, until 1911, when defections by former supporters in both camps helped defeat his Liberal government.

1928 What the French Canadian Wants

Louis A. Taschereau – JANUARY 1, 1928 *Louis Taschereau served as premier of Quebec from 1920 to 1936. (He spoke to Leslie M. Roberts for* Maclean's.*)*

Three words have been handed down to us by the Mother of the French-speaking race in Canada, words that a man grows to love for the depth and significance of their meaning as he utters them, or thinks of them: Liberty, Equality, Fraternity. In those three words you have alpha and omega, the be-all and end-all of what beats in the heart of the French Canadian, and the answer to the ever-asked question, "What does the French Canadian want?"

You may say, therefore, that the riddle is solved, and, speaking broadly, you will be right. The French Canadian has Liberty, the liberty that is the heritage of all of us in this land and under this flag. Equality he shares with all good citizens of this Dominion. He enjoys the Fraternity of broad-minded men and women everywhere.

But liberty, equality and fraternity will fall to the ground unless, first, you have understanding. Unless we can understand each other and draw more closely together with the years, liberty, equality and fraternity— or any other labels which tag our national aspirations—can be nothing but catchwords.

Lack of understanding has been our greatest drawback and stumbling block to harmony in Canada. Here, sectionalism has reared its ugly head; there, inter-racial jealousies have festered and grown sore for want of the wise surgeon's knife.

EVEN THOUGH LIBERAL Louis Taschereau promoted the notion of provincial autonomy as premier of Quebec from 1920 to 1936, his moderate politics provoked the hostility of both Quebec nationalists and their anglophone opponents.

The ghost of bigotry must be laid if these two races are to know each other as they should and love and admire each other as they ought and as, in the broad conception of things, they do.

Some of the expressed opinions about the Province of Quebec have been weirdly funny, but altogether too pathetic for laughter. In some schools of opinion, one might almost glean the view that Quebec is a sort of huge reservation, almost uncultivated and inhabited by a quasi-aboriginal race, which makes up for what it lacks in civilization, culture or education by the rabid quality of its views and opinions. Perhaps this will have the ring of gross exaggeration to the reader, but it is, nevertheless, an accurate summing up of the so-called viewpoint of that charming fellow, the non-thinking bigot.

It used to be proclaimed by these zealots–perhaps it is still proclaimed–that the English-speaking minority in the Province of Quebec lives in a condition bordering on persecution. They speak of French Canadian domination of this and of that, of "blocs," of what the West wants to cram down the throat of the East and of all manner of things that could never exist if we ruled out hyphens and geographical considerations. The question of "domination" or "control" may be dismissed at once. If it exists, it is the first that I have heard of it, other than in the ranks of non-thinking bigotry.

Consider another angle of the "domination theory" that has been put to me. I was asked if the growth of French Canadian settlements in the Northwest does not signify the possibility of predominance of the French-speaking race in other provinces as well as in Quebec; if it is not true that these northwesterly settlements are bases whence, in the years to come, the French Canadian horde will swoop down, quite peacefully, of course, on the southerly portions of the western provinces until

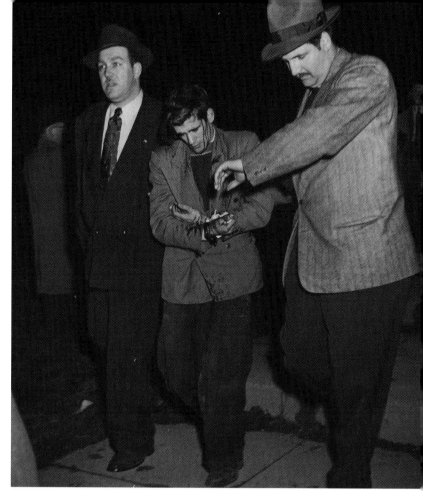

A FOUR-MONTH STRIKE EARLY IN 1949 by about 5,000 Quebec asbestos miners, and the brutality of the police reaction under the aegis of the Duplessis government, became a pivotal political event leading to a social reformation in Quebec.

THE CANADIAN ESTABLISHMENT'S paranoia over communists – especially in Quebec, with its anti-union traditions–prompted Ottawa to recruit American union thug Hal Banks in 1949 to drive out the Red-led Canadian Seamen's Union. The result was years of bloody, club-swinging violence in Canadian ports and ongoing labor unrest. Here, Banks (on the left) marches his union down Notre-Dame Street in Montreal in 1963.

BEFORE HE ENTERED politics in 1960, became founding leader of the Parti Québécois in 1968 and served as Quebec's premier (1976-1985), René Lévesque worked as a correspondent with Radio-Canada. In this photo, taken 10 days before his 29th birthday, he interviews a Canadian soldier in the Korean War, in August 1951.

they become the racial and linguistic overlords of Canada. I smiled broadly, I confess, at this new poser. The French Canadian race is one of the large elements which make up the Canadian race of today, and Canada, I take it, belongs to all Canadians. There is no reason, therefore, why they should be confined to the Province of Quebec.

The French Canadian seems to be disliked by some people because he speaks French. That is always the cry of the man who is the super-patriot of words, who will tell you that, if the French Canadian is so loyal a subject of Canada and of the Crown, he should forfeit the language of his forefathers and speak only English. To such gentlemen I would point out that the use of the French language in Canada is the French-speaking citizen's right and gift, under that very charter of British liberty which the super-patriot pretends to hold so dear. The French tongue is one of the two languages that are "official" in this Dominion.

If we are all Canadians in truth and in fact, opportunity awaits the English-speaking citizen in "French Quebec" just as surely as it awaits the French Canadian in British Columbia. If our Canadianism is of other texture than this, we had better entrench ourselves in our ditch-ringed islands of provinces and admit, forever, our insularity, bigotry and narrow-mindedness.

There is no room in this country for biases of section, race or creed. From east and from west, from prairie and seaboard, English and French, we are all Canadians, men who may meet anywhere on common ground as citizens of Canada. Only by drawing apart and keeping to ourselves can we fail to understand each other.

1961 The French Revolution, Quebec 1961

Peter C. Newman – APRIL 22, 1961 The revolution in Quebec is no longer racial anger; it is nothing less than an earnest challenge to this country's English-speaking citizens to compete, or be satisfied with a secondary position. With this new spirit of freedom has come a wave of popular protest against old-line Quebec politicians for failing to lead the province into the twentieth century. "It was a waste of time for our politicians to teach us to spit on the English," says Pierre Elliott Trudeau, the backer of *Cité libre*, a Montreal journal whose burgeoning following closely reflects the new mood in Quebec. "It's not the fault of the English that we're a backward province. We're responsible for our own mess. But from now on, we'll contribute more than inhibitions to the Canadian federation."

Many of [Premier Jean] Lesage's ministers– particularly René Lévesque and Georges Lapalme– can sit back and think, with a great deal of justification, that Lesage would never have gained power without them. Lévesque, who was Quebec's most popular television commentator before he took up politics, is the rallying point for most of the young idealists who voted for Lesage. He was so hated by the Union Nationale that they promised if elected to set up a provincial broadcasting network in order to combat his influence. He's been spearheading the Liberal anti-patronage drive in the job as minister of public works and now of natural resources. "The ideology of the Liberal party is historically non-existent," he snorted when I saw him in his office. "We're starting from an ambiguous base, with a wide rage of opinions in cabinet. I'm on the far left, of course. If the government does not reflect the views of the left, it won't be here long."

JEAN LESAGE, shown here shortly before his retirement from politics in January 1970, devoted himself as Quebec's premier (1960-1966) to reformist policies and programs that became known as the Quiet Revolution— changes that affected education, labor law, women's rights, social welfare and election rules, furthering the cause of making Quebecers masters of their own house ("maitres chez nous").

1964 Trouble in the Streets

A clash between police and separatist demonstrators in Quebec City during a visit by Queen Elizabeth on October 10, 1964, prompted a debate about Quebec.

PRESIDENT Charles de Gaulle of France encouraged Quebec separatists and offended his official hosts in Ottawa by crying out "Vive le Québec libre" in a speech delivered from a balcony of Montreal's city hall in 1967. Prime Minister Lester Pearson issued an official rebuke and de Gaulle went home.

***Maclean's* Ottawa Editor Blair Fraser** (December 2, 1964): Quebec wants to change the constitution, and this is new. Always in the past, Quebec has led the resistance to change, jealously guarded its power of veto, fended off encroachments by Ottawa and the English-Canadian majority. Now it's the French Canadians who want to use the new powers of amendment in Canada, and construct a new basis for nationhood. To succeed they will need maximum good will, maximum sympathy, maximum generosity from the rest of Canada.

Historian A.R.M. Lower (December 14, 1964): Instead of recoiling in horror at the possibility of an independent Quebec, I believe English Canadians should be seriously considering whether their interests would be better served with Quebec out of Confederation.

I am not advocating separatism and I am not indulging in a hymn of hate against "the French," but I am suggesting that the so-called dialogue between Canada's two peoples might be a great deal more fruitful if we considered separation at least as a possibility and tried in a hard-headed fashion to see what it involved.

Novelist Hugh MacLennan, author of *Two Solitudes* (December 14, 1964): We all know that we must share this country sensibly or lose it like fools. Those Anglo-Canadians who talk glibly about joining the United States, if life with Quebec becomes too uncomfortable, ignore the fact that the Americans have no intention of taking us in. Those Quebec politicians who talk dreamily about two associated states in a single state must know that no such arrangement could work.

We all know that Canada's two solitudes can never be welded. We should also know that, if this is to be a country valuable to mankind and pleasant to herself, there must be some love between the two cultures of which she is composed.

THE OCTOBER CRISIS OF 1970, ignited by the kidnapping of British consul James Cross and Quebec labor minister Pierre Laporte—later murdered—prompted Ottawa to place the army on police duty and suspend civil rights, permitting the arrest of more than 450 Quebecers without charge. Here, a girl makes shadow puppets under the watchful eye of a soldier.

1971 War Measures

Ron Haggart and Aubrey Golden – FEBRUARY 1971 The War Measures Act swept 453 Quebecers into jail. Editors. Singers. Intellectuals. Unionists. Even a piano tuner. It was done with the overwhelming approval of the Canadian people. But later–perhaps too late–came a profound questioning that challenged the wisdom of the action.

"These are strong powers," the Prime Minister of Canada said late on the night of the day they took singer Pauline Julien to jail, "and I find them as distasteful as I am sure you do. They are necessary, however, to permit the police to deal with persons who advocate or promote the violent overthrow of the democratic system."

After the invocation of the Act by the federal cabinet at four o'clock in the morning on Friday, October 16, 1970 (but not fully revealed in the House of Commons until

DEMONSTRATORS ON BEHALF OF "POLITICAL PRISONERS"–people arrested in connection with Quebec nationalist activities–paraded to the Montreal courthouse on March 24, 1971. Authorities later suspended proceedings against 32 persons arrested the previous October under the War Measures Act.

11 a.m.), hundreds of Quebecers were rounded up by the police. The average period of detention was about a week. All but a handful were released without any charges laid and, in most cases, only perfunctory interrogations. But the most noticeable characteristic of the detainees was their diversity, ranging from Pierre Vallières, the philosopher patron of violent revolution, to university student Les Lascau, who was doing nothing more suspicious when arrested than canvassing an apartment building with a public opinion poll for the McGill sociology department.

One of the results, intentional or otherwise, was to blur the distinction between all the varieties of dissent in French Canada. Newspapers fell into the habit of referring in their headlines to the "FLQ sympathizers" in jail, and to the roundup of "suspected terrorists." Some were. But, as Pauline Julien said, 99% of those who ended up in jail opposed terrorism.

1976 Time to Start Thinking the Unthinkable

Graham Fraser – NOVEMBER 29, 1976 **A**t the candidate's headquarters in a small shopping plaza in Longueuil, across the St. Lawrence from Montreal, campaign workers went wild when the first poll in Taillon riding was announced at 8:10 p.m.: René Lévesque, 60 votes; his Liberal opponent, 27. It was a sign that was to hold good for the rest of election night, in Taillon and across Quebec. When the victory of his Parti Québécois seemed assured–and Robert Bourassa, the Liberal premier defeated after 6 1/2 years in office, had, with surprising graciousness, conceded defeat–Lévesque appeared before ecstatic supporters at a Montreal arena. "Politically, it is the most beautiful and perhaps the most important evening in the history of Quebec," he declared. Then, after a congratulatory telegram from Quebec chansonnier Gilles Vigneault in Paris was read, Lévesque walked out into the crisp, snowy night–perfect weather for election day in the province of Vigneault's nationalist song, "Mon Pays (c'est l'hiver)."

For others, such as Pierre Marois, a newly elected PQ member, it "felt like spring–maple sugar time. This is the beginning of a new spring in Quebec." The climate across Quebec was electric. Cars honked their way across the predominantly French-speaking eastern half of Montreal and champagne flowed in the newsroom of Montreal's largest daily, *La Presse*. Quebecers who delightedly savored the moment had several reasons for doing so–some, probably a small minority, because the party dedicated to leading Quebec to independence had taken power after an eight-year struggle, others because the deeply unpopular and discredited Bourassa regime had been trounced.

Among Montreal's anglophones, there was concern. Said James Molloy, a salesman: "I'm not going to panic, yet, though I believe there is a great threat to

THE CHARISMATIC RENÉ LÉVESQUE, here addressing a Montreal victory rally after leading his Parti Québécois to power for the first time on November 15, 1976, won re-election in 1981. However, the party developed divisions over the independence issue. Lévesque resigned in 1985 and died two years later.

English-language rights." For the third time since he came to office in 1970, the colorless, calculating Bourassa had sought victory by playing on fears of independence. By contrast, Lévesque's PQ campaigned in a deliberately low-key style, and played down, without denying, its separatist stand. Whatever the future may hold, Lévesque could not help but be keenly aware that a referendum on separation has no hope of passing until he has proved that his party can provide good government.

The final result: PQ 69 seats; Liberals 28; Union Nationale 11; Creditiste 1; Parti National Populaire 1.

1992 Trudeau Speaks Out

Sᴇᴘᴛᴇᴍʙᴇʀ 28, 1992 *Former prime minister Pierre Trudeau waded into the debate over the Charlottetown Accord a month before a scheduled national referendum rejected the proposed revision of the constitution.*

Commenting on Quebec nationalist politics in the first issue of *Cité libre* 42 years ago, I wrote, "The country can't exist without us, we think to ourselves. So watch out you don't hurt our feelings. . . . We depend on our power of blackmail in order to face the future. . . . We are getting to be a sleazy bunch of master blackmailers." Things have changed a lot since then, but for the worse.

Consider that in the past 22 years the province of Quebec has been governed by two premiers. The first [Robert Bourassa] was the one who coined the phrase "profitable federalism." We'll stay in Canada if Canada gives us enough money, he argued. The other premier [René Lévesque] was the one who invented "sovereignty-association." He demanded all the powers of a sovereign country for Quebec, but was careful to arrange for the sovereign country not to be independent. Indeed, his referendum question postulated that a sovereign Quebec would be associated with the other provinces and would continue to use the Canadian dollar as legal tender. Money, money, money!

So for 22 years the Quebec electorate has suffered the ignominy of having to choose between two provincial parties for whom the pride of being a Quebecer is negotiable for cash. And if by some stroke of ill fortune the rest of Canada seems disinclined to go along with the blackmail, as happened over the Meech Lake Accord, it is accused of humiliating Quebec.

PIERRE TRUDEAU, here voicing his opposition to the Meech Lake constitutional accord before a Senate committee on March 30, 1988, argued then—as he had as prime minister—that shifting ever more power from Ottawa to the provinces would surely "erode the very essence of the Canadian state."

The Quebec nationalist elites falsify history to prove that all Quebec's political failures are someone else's fault: the Conquest, the obscurantism of Duplessis's time, slowness to enter the modern age, illiteracy, and all the rest. It is never our leaders' fault; it has to be blamed on some ominous plot against us.

Nationalist thinkers in Quebec have used terms like "distinct society," which succeeded "sovereignty-association," which followed "equality or independence," which was preceded by "special status." None of these terms stands up to serious scrutiny. It is a truism to assert that Quebec is a distinct society, since the Constitution we adopted in 1867 has permitted it to be a distinct society.

QUEBECER LUCIEN BOUCHARD, who served in the 1980s as Canada's ambassador to France and as a federal cabinet minister, emerged from the separatist closet in 1990 and formed the Bloc Québécois with fellow defectors from the Conservative parliamentary caucus. Three months after the narrow defeat of the sovereigntist cause in the Quebec referendum of October 1995, Bouchard replaced Jacques Parizeau as Parti Québécois premier and led that party to re-election in late 1998 with the promise of another referendum on independence when the time seemed ripe.

As far back as memory serves, French Canadians were essentially asking for one thing: respect for the French fact in Canada and incorporation of this fact into Canadian civil society, principally in the areas of language and education, and particularly in the federal government and provinces with French-speaking minorities. The Offical Languages Act was passed in 1969 and minority-language education rights were entrenched in the Charter of 1982. The gates had suddenly opened and institutional bilingualism was recognized in Canada.

Then, equally suddenly, the Quebec nationalists no longer wanted the French language to be made equal with English throughout Canada. They denounced bilingualism as utopic. Quebec declared itself unilingually French and abandoned the cause of French-speaking minorities in other provinces, the better to marginalize the English-speaking minority in Quebec.

It has become clear that all the demands made of Canada by the Quebec nationalists can be summed up in just one: keep giving us new powers and the money to exercise them, or we'll leave.

"French Canadians have no opinions, they only have feelings," Sir Wilfrid Laurier said. For unscrupulous politicians, there is no surer way of rousing feelings than to trumpet a call to pride of race. French Canadians will be rid of this kind of politician if the blackmail ceases, and the blackmail will cease only if Canada refuses to dance to that tune.

Passing Fads and Fleeting Fancies

In the Changing World of the Latest Craze, the Only Fixed Thing is How to Have Fun

FROM ragtime to rap, from the yoyo to the hula hoop, 20th-century fun and games constitute a kaleidoscope of fads and fancies. Excerpts from *Maclean's* offer glimpses of a few of the things that–to borrow drug-culture jargon from the 1950s and 1960s–turned people on, or, in some cases, off.

1908 The Delightful Pastime of Tobogganing

MARCH 1908 **O**f the many exhilarating sports which enable the long Canadian winter to be passed so pleasantly, and at the same time so healthily, tobogganing must certainly be considered among the foremost in rank. Truly the sensation enjoyed is most delightful, whether it be on an elaborate, artificially prepared ice track, such as the noted Park Slide in Montreal, or on a natural slope. The thrill of excitement experienced as the toboggan gathers momentum, the invigorating swish through the keen air, the breathless negotiation of the various jumps–presuming there are any–and the

THE HIP-SWIVELLING ART of hula hooping–as in this 1952 photo of Toronto hooper Beth Morris–became a sexy recreational rage throughout North America in the 1950s, the postwar wonder material plastic replacing bamboo in the adaptation of an exercise hoop used in Australian elementary school gyms.

peaceful easing up at the bottom after the torrential rush, combine to give a kaleidoscopic enjoyment that is lacking in other pastimes.

On a natural snow slide with its soft surface, a flat bottom toboggan is necessary, but on an ice track the conditions are reversed. Two kinds of runners are now used—one made of lignum vitae [tropical wood], and the other of horse bone. The bone runner is faster and more durable—and more expensive. The number of toboggans that are made indicate the hold that this fascinating sport has upon the athletic community. Long may the hold remain to add to the many other winter amusements which make Canadians an object of envy to those in other climes who are denied similar pleasures.

A speed is obtained on the toboggan of today that is nothing less than a breathless one. Official timing has shown 2,250 feet to be travelled in 45 to 50 seconds. No wonder that Mark Twain is reported to have said, after analyzing his sensations in the peace and safety of the clubhouse, that he would not have missed the trip for $100—but he would not repeat the experience for $1,000.

THE SPINNING YO-YO, as in this 1937 photo from Toronto, is said to have been around for thousands of years. The name itself is traced to a Filipino word for a returning weapon used to whack prey from a tree. The toy was a hot item for Canadian kids from the 1930s to the 1950s, and then made a comeback, appropriately, in the 1990s.

1920 Fight the Drug Menace?

Magistrate Emily F. Murphy – FEBRUARY 15, 1920 **A** person addicted to its habitual use is known as a cocainist. In a later stage they are described as cocainomaniacs. When on the verge of suicide for need of the drug they are said to have "the cocain leaps."

Cocaine is usually retailed to the victims by illicit vendors in small paper packages of about the size and shape of a postage stamp. These are called "decks," and contain a couple of snuffs. Ordinarily, these cost a dollar apiece, but if the purchaser is distempered for need of it, the vendor may extract two dollars or even more.

The general rule is that addiction is present mainly in youths from 16 to 21 years of

IN A WINTER COUNTRY, what better than to get out on the hills or the purpose-built chutes with the family toboggan (the word and the design itself borrowed from Canadian Micmac, Algonquin and Tlingit people)? In the 1990s, such early-century chutes as these, in Toronto's High Park, were still providing spills and thrills, if only on plastic sliding machines.

THE PEDAL VEHICLES shown off here by the Winnipeg Bicycle Club in about 1905 were already antiques by then. The iron-tired boneshaker in penny-farthing figuration had made way for the basic bike still in style at the end of the century. Until the Second World War, riding the two-wheeler flourished as a spectator sport as well as a means of transport and recreation.

age. Narcotics hinder development, and boys and girls are forever wrecked. Distracted parents come pleading for aid and advice. The complaint is always the same—"If we only knew the first sign of this dreadful curse we could have saved the boy."

1949 Do Whistling Wolves Bite?

Ray Gardner – FEBRUARY 1, 1949 **O**nce upon a time the wolf was merely a four-legged animal that went after Little Red Riding Hood's grandmother. But in this fifth decade of the 20th century the term is more often applied to the questing male with the low whistle and the high-speed line who isn't interested in anyone's *grand-mother*. As such, the wolf has become a symbol of social significance, a key to the study of our changing sex customs.

Those experts who make it their business to decide whether we are on the short-est road to hell—the psychologists, sociologists, boys' counsellors, social workers and teachers—say that our sex customs are constantly changing and that the modern variety of wolf is a product of this evolution. He has had may predecessors, each one usually a trifle more bold than the last.

The "masher" of the early 1900s has his place in the genealogy of the wolf, says Prof. J.D. Ketchum of the psychology department of University of Toronto.

"He was dressed to kill and gave a wicked look out of the corner of his eye," Prof. Ketchum recalls. "That wicked look has descended today to the whistle. The end in view is the same."

In the 1920s, the wolf was the Latin lover who slicked down his hair and gave a sickly impersonation of Valentino. Further back, the man who made the ladies duck behind their parasols was the man who made goo-goo eyes.

The phrase "to see a wolf"–meaning to be seduced–was a colloquialism in 19th-century England. It is only since World War II that wolf has assumed its present meaning. Hank, a 29-year-old RCAF veteran and fourth-year student at University of Toronto, has in mind the latter type of wolf when he says, "A wolf is a guy who goes out after *one thing*."

1953 My 12 Hours as a Madman

Sidney Katz – OCTOBER 1, 1953 *As a participant in a study into schizophrenia at a Saskatchewan hospital, journalist Sidney Katz voluntarily took LSD. He later wrote about his experience for* Maclean's.

On the morning of Thursday, June 18, 1953, I swallowed a drug, LSD, which, for twelve unforgettable hours, turned me into a madman. For twelve hours I inhabited a nightmare world in which I experienced the torments of hell and the ecstasies of heaven. I will never be able to describe fully what happened to me during my excursion into madness–the sensations I felt or the visions, illusions, hallucinations, colors, patterns and dimensions which my disordered mind revealed.

I saw the faces of familiar friends turn into fleshless skulls and the heads of menacing witches, pigs and weasels. The gaily patterned carpet at my feet was transformed into a fabulous heaving mass of living matter, part vegetable, part animal. The texture of my skin changed several times.

But my hours of madness were not all filled with horror and frenzy. At times I beheld visions of dazzling beauty–visions so rapturous, so unearthly, that no artist will ever paint them. I lived in a paradise where the sky was a mass of jewels set in a background of shimmering aquamarine blue; where the clouds were apricot-colored; where the air was filled with liquid golden arrows, glittering fountains of iridescent bubbles.

1965 Dig Those Crazy Skurfers

Jack Batten – JULY 24, 1965 It's hard to avoid skateboarding and skateboarders these days. I mean it's physically hard to avoid them. The sidewalk on my street slopes

YOUTH BEING THE ENEMY of sitting around, such pastimes as tossing the Frisbee and cramming the telephone box were certain to be invented, as demonstrated here by 11 members of the pharmaceutical department at Victoria General Hospital in Halifax during the hospital staff's annual party on July 14, 1988.

south to north and when I walk home at night, north to south, I walk into an avalanche of careening kids whistling past me (hopefully, past me), precariously mounted on two-foot-long by seven-inch-wide wooden slabs which are in turn mounted, more or less securely, on a set of wheels that resemble roller-skate wheels.

Skateboarding is this summer's hottest fad among young Canadians. And, as far as I'm concerned, it is popular for very good reason. I took a couple of plunges down the street on a board recently, coached by Susan Crozier, the street's Pavlova of the skateboard, and I found the experience exhilarating, scary, breathtaking, and a lot more fun than, say, shaking a hula hoop around your sacroiliac.

Skateboarding–or skurfing, as it's also called–was started four years ago in California. Perhaps the surest sign of skateboarding's success is that it has already attracted detractors. The city council in Ottawa is considering a resolution to outlaw the sale of boards. And there's a

WHEN SPRING 1997 turned up in February in Kelowna, British Columbia, skateboarder Robyn Gullachsen did what has come naturally to schoolkids coast to coast since about 1965: he caught some air in flight downtown.

spoilsport Toronto alderman who regularly issues statements of doom about: "the skateboarding menace." Menace. Well, I'm relieved he doesn't represent my and Susan Crozier's ward at city hall.

1969 Some of the Best People Smoke Pot

John Ruddy – JANUARY 1969 **W**e have all heard that marijuana, once the "noxious," "crippling" and "degrading" preserve of criminals, jazz musicians, delinquents and, latterly, hippies, has shown a tremendous upward mobility in the last few years. It's no pipe dream–it's here. The virtues and dangers of marijuana are debatable but its wide acceptance is obvious. I know a lawyer who says, "Half the law students in the country smoke pot. It is just a matter of time until our legal institutions are comprised mainly of pot-heads. Do you think it will be illegal then?"

THE LUCK OF MARGARET (formerly Trudeau) Kemper was such that in 1981, when many people were thinking it was high time that police gave pot possession a rest, the Mounties went to the bother of taking out a search warrant to find a pack of marijuana in her Ottawa home and charge her with having some.

Police, in resolutely confining their investigations to intractable youth, have not only failed to check pot's upward mobility, they have failed to grasp it. "I think we have pretty good control of the problem," says the head of a 20-man RCMP drug section in Toronto. He adds: of more than 300 Toronto marijuana arrests last year, not one involved a member of the professional classes.

The biggest enclaves of these newly typical pot smokers are in Vancouver and Toronto, although Montreal, Winnipeg and several other cities have their share. The smokers are mostly in their 20s and 30s, affluent, articulate and prepared to do anything to promote the legalization of marijuana, short of risking the seven-year jail term they could still conceivably get for possession.

1971 Eighteen People in the Nude— and why they matter to you

Pat Annesley – FEBRUARY 1971 **F**irst there was the party. Most of them got drunk fairly early on. That was Sunday night. Monday morning, I went into a screening room, tired and hung over, to watch a movie. What we saw that morning, and in the next four days, was the uncut version of a feature called *Out of Touch*. An entire weekend marathon encounter on film. Forty-five hours of it.

Encounter groups are those get-togethers where people let their hair down, peel back the layers of self-protection and try to get back to some kind of basic, honest human contact. It was inevitable that, when touch therapy became nude therapy, someone would put it into a movie. They did, with startling results. What was to have been just a job for actors became real, in scenes that say much about alienation in us all.

At least 3,000 people will attend sessions in Montreal this year, and this winter the expected attendance at various groups in the Vancouver area is close to 2,000. In Toronto, 15,000. The sessions may last anywhere from an evening to a month. Proponents of the continent-wide "growth movement" see it as a solution to the problems of alienation: today the individual, tomorrow the world.

1981 Rock without Roll

Bart Testa – AUGUST 10, 1981 **L**ights flash, smoke pots explode and a fierce industrial roar erupts from the sound system. The singer, caparisoned in hair and leather, unleashes a banshee wail. Blue Oyster Cult has opened another show, which will build layer upon layer of thick guitar chords as the 17,000-strong audience (composed mostly of teen-age boys) punches the air with its fists.

THE FAD OF STREAKING through a public event in nothing more than footwear may have achieved its zenith in Canada when a prancing young male nude joined in the closing ceremony of the 1976 Olympic Games. The interrupter of an NHL game at Maple Leaf Gardens in 1980, pictured here, bereft of skates, was quickly caught.

This is heavy-metal music, the most extreme form of lumbering hard rock and the most durable travelling music of the '70s that is now emerging as the dominant sound of the '80s. It could be termed rock without roll–the screaming guitars, brutishly pounding rhythms and overwrought sex-crazed vocals. The classic heavy metal of Rush, Van Halen and AC/DC and the more pop-oriented dilutions of REO Speedwagon, Loverboy and April Wine are reaching gold (sales of 500,000 copies in the U.S.) and even platinum (sales of one million) status almost as they hit the record racks.

From 'Curiosity' to 'Love Affair'

Canada Takes to the Road

T HE 20th is the century of the airplane and space travel, of motion pictures, radio and television, of the electronic computer, the Internet and other paraphernalia on the information highway. But it is hard to argue against labelling the 1900s the century of the automobile. The motor car's birth coincided almost exactly with the start of the century. By 1901, early prototypes had evolved into vehicles propelled by the still-familiar power systems–the internal combustion of vaporized gasoline inside a row of cylinders. A manufacturing boom in 1905 and 1906 began to establish the automobile's enduring role as an engine of the national economy and international trade, as well as a staple of households and lifestyles, a way of getting groceries, reaching friends, taking vacation trips, supporting a host of other activities.

A number of Canadian companies were quick off the mark. The very first issue of John Bayne Maclean's new magazine in October, 1905, carried an article on Torontonian T. A. (Tommy) Russell, "who has put his name on one of the most perfect cars ever made." Advertisements for the Russell in later issues offered three models of the cars, built by Canada Cycle and Motor Co. (CCM), starting at a two-cylinder runabout for $1,600. The top-of-the-line four-cylinder machine cost $3,750–four times the average annual industrial wage. Tommy Russell was only a

WITHIN A FEW YEARS of this show of new Russell automobiles in front of the then-young Toronto City Hall around 1905, with CCM general manager Tommy Russell behind the wheel of the first car, the manufacture of his and other Canadian cars had yielded to Ford and other American firms. And the steering wheel moved to the left.

TO BE BOTH MODERN AND SPORTY during the infant years of the century meant being in a motor car such as this Beattie Parkdale machine. Car and occupants are pictured in about 1906 in front of Toronto's King Edward Hotel, itself then only about three years old and, unlike the Beattie Parkdale, still operating at the close of the century.

few years out of the University of Toronto when he was appointed general manager of CCM, the magazine reported. "He might have been a lawyer, but he chose to be a twentieth century man out and out and put his name on an automobile."

He was far from being alone. Just as CCM began building the Russell, R.S. McLaughlin was starting to make cars bearing his surname in a family wagon-building plant in Oshawa, Ontario. But the Canadians did not last long. They were small fry in a prolific industry that spawned more than 200 North American automakers in the first dozen years of the century. Almost all of them had to shut down or merge with the biggest Americans after 1908. That was the year that Henry Ford, who had established a branch plant on the Ontario side of the Detroit River in 1904, transformed the industry with the assembly-line Model T at budget prices.

The McLaughlin Motor Car Co. lasted until 1918, when it merged with the Chevrolet Motor Car Co. of Canada to form General Motors of Canada Ltd. The

DURING THE GREAT DEPRESSION, some motorists, unable to afford fuel for the family car, reverted to real horsepower and, in a jab at R.B. Bennett's Tory federal government, christened the hybrid transportation the Bennett buggy. In this 1933 photo taken in Sturgeon Valley, Saskatchewan, Bennett's political opponent, Liberal Mackenzie King, is driving such a contraption.

expanding Canadian market for cars, plus the industrial skills of Canada's automakers, kept automobile branch plant factories humming, mainly in southern Ontario and later in Quebec. That arrangement was reinforced by the U.S.-Canada Auto Pact of 1965, which essentially required the American manufacturers to make at least as many vehicles in Canada as they sold in the country. European and Asian car makers generated additional manufacturing and assembly operations in Canada.

Against the benefits brought by the automobile came serious detriments as the motor car produced proliferating hazards to health and to life itself. Polluting exhaust fumes poisoned urban environments and human lungs. Efforts to counter the plague with tightened emission standards and more fuel-efficient cars barely kept up with the proliferation of traffic on streets and highways. (Even international politics interfered with anti-exhaust efforts: in 1998, trade treaty rules forced Canada to lift a ban on the import of a U.S.-made gasoline additive faulted for reducing the effectiveness of automotive anti-pollution mechanisms.) Another liability: the traffic accident, a leading cause of premature death in the country. Under the headline "Death on Wheels," a *Maclean's* report on February 15, 1946,

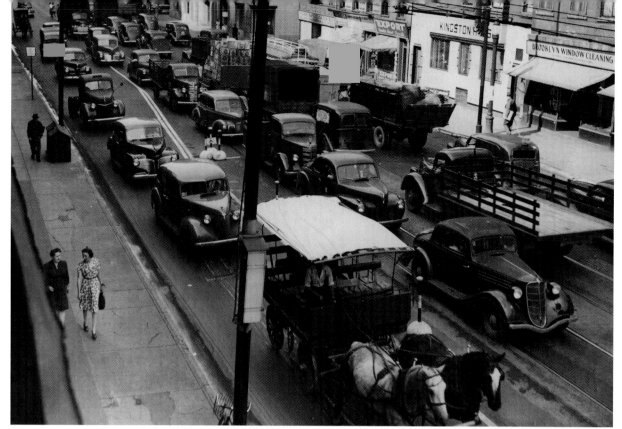

AS LATE AS 1944, the horse had not been completely driven off the streets of Montreal.

blamed "the careless driver" for the expected 1,500 deaths that year in traffic accidents. Fifty years later, the annual toll was more than double the 1946 rate, but down sharply from a peak in the 1970s. As the magazine reported in its issue of July 15, 1996, technology helped reduce slaughter on the avenue:

> *As people's love affair with the car intensified, so did the realization that a new killer had been loosed on the world. Seat-belts and air bags have helped reduce the grim statistics: last year, traffic accidents in Canada claimed 3,313 lives, compared to 6,061 in 1975. The electronic component of an automobile is expected to double to about 20 per cent of the total value—much of that devoted to new features that will enable the so-called smart cars to see, hear and communicate with one another and with the roadway itself.*

1954 How the Auto Beat the Horse

R.S. McLaughlin – OCTOBER 1, 1954 **B**y 1905, there were a couple of dozen cars in Toronto. They were still much of a curiosity, a sporting proposition for adventurous people. In the United States, the Ford Motor Co. was two years old. The Buick Motor Co., also two years old, had just been taken over by William C. Durant and, in this year, would produce 750 cars. Cadillac, three years old, was offering a one-cylinder car with the motor under the front seat. Among other cars for sale were the

Locomobile, Mobile, Winton, de Dion, Columbia and Gasmobile. But the real titan was R.E. Olds, whose curved-dash, one-cylinder Oldsmobile outnumbered all other cars on America's dirt roads and rutted gravel highways.

I started a campaign to persuade my brother George that automobiles had a place in the world, and pretty well convinced him. We never did convince the Governor [their father], though. He honestly believed that the automobile would never replace the horse-drawn carriage; certainly not in his time.

I had to move warily. When my vacation came I went to Buffalo, where Richard Pierce was making a car that was beginning to be heard about. Mr. Pierce showed me around his plant where the Pierce-Arrow was being manufactured, painstakingly by hand operation. This stately, courteous gentleman of the old school then made a startling statement in a quiet, matter-of-fact voice: "Cars like this have no future, Mr. McLaughlin. I would advise you against trying to make them."

He stated that McLaughlin's should use its experience in the mass production of carriages to enter the low-priced car field. I went over to the E.R. Thomas Co., also in Buffalo, for a look at the Thomas Flyer. Mr. Thomas couldn't talk business with me, he said, because he already had commitments with the Canada Cycle and Motor Co. in Toronto. This made me all the more interested in getting a line on some arrangement to make cars in Canada, before competitors got the jump on us in our own country.

Not long afterward, while eating breakfast in Jackson, Mich., [before visiting a local manufacturer], William Durant and his factory manager had walked into the dining-room. I had known Durant for ten years, having met him at conventions of carriage manufacturers. He and his partner, Dallas Dort, had built a $50 stake into Durant-Dort, then one of the biggest carriage and wagon companies in the United

AN EARLY-SPRING SPIN outside Sarnia, Ontario, in a McLaughlin, the car manufactured in a former wagonmaking plant in Oshawa from 1905 to 1918, when the McLaughlin Motor Car Company became General Motors of Canada.

IN 1974 AND 1975, American entrepreneur Malcolm Bricklin—financed heavily by New Brunswick taxpayers—built 2,857 Bricklin sports cars in Saint John and Minto. After difficulties with the car's distinctive gull-wing doors and other technical problems, the project collapsed when the province turned off the cash flow and private investors steered clear of Bricklin.

BY THE 1950s, Canadians' love of big cars was beginning to create near-gridlock on city streets, as here, in Montreal.

States. Just about the same time I started to get interested—and concerned—about cars, Durant had been persuaded to buy the Buick company.

Before accepting Durant's invitation to "come and see me," I bought a Model F two-cylinder Buick in Toronto for $1,650. Before I was halfway to Oshawa I knew it was the car we wanted to make in Canada. I wired Durant and went to see him. We agreed on most points—and then reached an impasse. We just couldn't agree on final details of the financial arrangements. I went home to Oshawa and George and I worked out our alternative plan—to make our own car.

We needed a first-class engineer to supervise the manufacturing. My choice was Arthur Milbrath. We equipped [a building] with automatic lathes and other machine tools, planers and shapers—dozens of machines. I put all I had into designing the most beautiful car I could dream of—the bodies, of course, would be made by the same artisans who had been making our carriages for years. The car was to be more powerful than the Buick. We had everything we needed for our first hundred cars, and had the first car all laid out and practically ready for assembly, down to the beautiful brass McLaughlin radiator on which I had spent many hours, when disaster struck. Milbrath became severely ill with pleurisy.

I wired William Durant, asking him if he could lend us an engineer. His answer came back promptly: "Will you be home tomorrow? I'm coming over." In five minutes we had a model agreement. Chiefly, it covered the terms under which we had fifteen-year rights to buy the Buick engine and some other parts. We would build and design our own bodies.

I have heard people regret that we had to put an end to the project to produce an all-Canadian car. Any regret on my part is tempered by the hard facts of the automobile industry, by the very great probability that if we had proceeded with our plan to make our own cars, we almost certainly would have taken a header.

One of the strangest facts about the automobile business in North America is that in its 50-odd years no fewer than 2,400 different makers have manufactured and offered cars for sale. And today you can count on the fingers of two hands the car manufacturers who have survived.

1959 'Car Craziness': A Menace to Our Teenagers?

Eric Hutton – JUNE 6, 1959 **M**ost parents worry to some extent when their offspring are out in cars. Understandably, they worry about damage or injury to car and contents–dented fenders, broken bones, fatal smashups. They worry, too, about what unchaperoned boys and girls may be up to. But the motoring teenager has become much more than a family problem. In the past few years as youth-at-the-wheel has become a major phenomenon of Canadian life, a lot of other people have become concerned about much wider implications they attach to the apparently simple act of a teenage boy driving a car. Police view with alarm the truly gaudy record of teenagers as traffic hazards and accident causers. Many teachers regard teenagers' preoccupation with cars as a menace to their education. Sports officials, physical-fitness authorities and doctors deplore the influence of the automobile on teenagers' agility and even their health. Psychologists paint the gloomiest picture of all. Some of them warn that the teenager's car, as the chief symbol of soft living, may debase him mentally, physically, spiritually and morally to the point where, like the enervating public baths of ancient Rome, it leads to the decline and fall of the nation.

1967 The Car as a Toy

SEPTEMBER 1967 *What's going to happen to the car in the future? Maclean's asked Marshall McLuhan, Canada's communications oracle, and he came up with a pretty pessimistic answer. "The car's future isn't rosy, it's not rosy at all," he told us. Physical movement of people and goods may be totally replaced by "information movement," he believes. "Already you can send almost anything anywhere by telegraph. Why have personal transportation when we have the videophone?" The future, McLuhan says, belongs to decentralization.*

The wheel created the road–yet the airplane puts its wheels away when it takes off. It doesn't need them. The wheel's becoming redundant even in physical transportation.

IN THE 1950s, AN ASTON MARTIN was a highly desirable vehicle to be seen in—even if it had to be pushed.

Kids today know that cars are for fun—they've got completely different sensory and spatial preferences from their predecessors. They want to get deeply involved in situations such as driving. Sports cars are involvement—kids are crazy about them because they can be involved in the power and the energy of the machine. The ultimate of this is the Honda: your legs are right on the wheel, the road—you become almost part of the road. This delights the TV generation.

The American is proud of his car because of its visual effect—the way it looks. The European tends to be prouder of the way it feels. It's like a miniskirt: exposure equals involvement. Everything's unexpected, adventure, surprises, dialogues, encounter. The British car is like a pet. The Volkswagen is the German's ideal image of space: it's a wraparound, secure little thing—its special form is a little pavilion of German culture, Expo-style.

Car designers have been aware of all these things in various ways, but I don't think they've been too ingenious in solving the problem. All this stuff about the car as mistress, as wife, as companion . . . . Sex is taking on new meanings in the electronic age. The old movie-era meaning of sex is hot. Today, everything's cool. Reading sex into cars is all a rather desperate effort.

SIX YEARS BEFORE these young people were pictured lolling around in a sporty convertible, Maclean's *writer Eric Hutton reported that some psychologists were warning that "the teenager's car, as the chief symbol of soft living, may debase him mentally, physically, spiritually and morally."*

The Edsel! It was just hopeless. Everything about it was hopeless, including the radiator which was designed to look like a toilet seat. How could all these things have happened under the watchful eye of experts?

[Some people] talk about cars having personalities–this is a little too abstract for me, too ethereal. From my point of view, I want to know: what are the senses played up by this or that type of car? That's where the answer is.

Remember all those old images of all those guys sitting at the wheel of a car with their caps turned back-to-front? This was real turned on, real hot. But the modern driver puts on his cool rather than his cap. You wouldn't expect a modern sports-car driver to have something lyrical to say about driving. He's so involved he gets fulfillment right in the act. That's why the car's great for fun, a plaything. You're an enormously increased human being, several times larger, when you get behind a wheel. You're packing a mighty big wallop. This is the fun-and-games aspect. But as serious transportation–who'd want to drive for pleasure in New York? I'd take a cab, anything but drive.

What do I drive? A Toronado. It's my wife's choice–she likes the tremendous feeling of power. She's very happy with it. Personally, I don't like driving much. I'd rather walk.

CONSUMERS TURNED AWAY from big, fuel-wasting cars towards more compact models such as the General Motors Chevrolet Vega, pictured here in 1970, during subsequent energy crises, when world oil prices quadrupled in 1973-1974 and nearly tripled in 1979.

1970 Can a High-powered Pitch Sell a Low-powered Car?

Albert Tremblay – NOVEMBER 1970 The introduction of Detroit's new "baby" car poses some intriguing questions. Most fascinating, how will they be sold? Detroit car dealers have for years been extolling the virtues of big cars—roominess, massive horsepower, constant newness. They will still have to do so to sell the standard-sized cars. And they will then have to turn around and promote the babies on the ground they're small, low-powered and of a design that won't be changed for years. The Chevrolet Vega 2300 epitomizes the problem. It is a totally new car and yet it is classically traditional, with lines reminiscent of the GM-owned German Opel cars.

1998 Big Wheels

Tom Fennell – JULY 20, 1998 As vacationing Canadians hit the highway this summer, what's up ahead is frequently a long line of big trucks—four-wheel-drive behemoths and gas-guzzling people-haulers churned out by upwards of a dozen foreign and domestic manufacturers. Across Canada, sales of new vehicles are stronger now than at any point since 1988, and nothing underscores the sector's revival more than the surging demand for light trucks, the industry's catchall term for everything from SUVs (sport-utility vehicles) to minivans, full-size vans and pickups. This year, light trucks are expected to account for a record 48 per cent of all new vehicles sold or leased in Canada, up from 31 per cent a decade ago. The result is a sea of smiling faces in the auto industry—and a raging debate over the truck boom's impact on road safety and the environment.

To Douglas Leighton, who teaches a course on the car and society at the University of Western Ontario, the enormous popularity of trucks echoes the car-mad 1950s, when neighbors competed to own the largest set of wheels on the block. Says Leighton: "People are wearing these things like badges to show that they've arrived."

The industry has also begun to sell environmentally friendly electric cars, largely because of pressure from government regulators. And there have been some successful launches of smaller niche vehicles, such as Volkswagen's New Beetle. For the most part, however, North American auto executives are emphasizing big muscular trucks in their efforts to appeal to the huge baby boomer market. Ironically, the generation that disavowed materialism in the 1960s and helped give birth to the environmental movement in the 1970s now leads the charge to the largest and most powerful vehicles on the market.

Ken Zino, director of product development for Ford Motor Co. in Dearborn, Mich., says the demand for trucks is in some ways a reflection of an earlier, more carefree age. Before the Arab oil embargo in 1973, the top-selling cars in North America were family-sized cars which boasted V8 engines and ample cargo space. Government regulations and consumer demand for smaller, more fuel-efficient vehicles gradually killed off those lumbering dinosaurs. But strong economic growth and falling oil prices this decade—adjusted for inflation, gasoline is cheaper now than at any time since the 1950s—have taken the industry full circle to the time when big wheels ruled the road.

The trend to heavier and more brawny vehicles has drawn plenty of criticism. Consumers Union, the Washington-based consumer advocacy group, has denounced light trucks as "heavy, gas-guzzling behemoths that in accidents wreak havoc on other vehicles and otherwise take a particularly heavy toll on the environment." The outcry from safety advocates grew louder last month when the U.S. National Highway Traffic Safety Administration released a study of 5,259 fatalities in crashes involving a light truck and a car. In 81 per cent of those cases, the people killed were the ones riding in the car.

Environmental concerns focus on the weaker pollution control standards on most light trucks, as well as their relatively poor gas mileage. To draw attention to the issue, the Vancouver-based David Suzuki Foundation ran a series of newspaper ads in April depicting a family wearing gas masks while picnicking beside their SUV. The vehicles are unquestionably dirtier than sedans. According to the U.S. Environmental Protection Agency, a typical light truck emits at least 75 per cent more nitrogen oxides, a major cause of global warming, than a large family car.

Suzuki Foundation executive director Jim Fulton sent Finance Minister Paul Martin a brief last September urging him to introduce a plan to reduce the emissions from larger vehicles. Without a dramatic shift to more fuel-efficient cars, Fulton says, Canada will not meet its international obligations to cut greenhouse-gas emissions. Ford's Zino, however, says that unless fuel prices spike upward in the near future—something few analysts expect—environmentalists are destined to lose their battle. "Consumers want power, and that's what vans and SUVs give them."

When Things Go Fatally Wrong

Calamities of Nature or Machinery are Cues for Generosity of Spirit

WHEN the century's industrial technology and science went wrong, it often seemed to wreak more mayhem than did nature's ways of meting out death and destruction by flood, fire and storm. Traffic accidents, plane crashes, ship collisions and even pharmaceutical blunders took thousands of lives. The tragedies wrought by the failures of human inventions aroused active compassion, as did the crash of Swissair Flight 111 on September 2, 1998, among the Nova Scotians who searched the sea in vain for survivors after the crippled plane crashed off the Atlantic shore of Peggys Cove with 229 people aboard. But in Canada, it has been more often the calamities committed randomly by the elements that wielded the power to move the charitable spirit of communities, often the entire country.

The populace rallied with material and personal assistance for survivors when comparatively few lost their lives in such destructive events as the massive landslide that killed 31 people in the Quebec town of St-Jean Viennay on May 4, 1971, but left many more bereft of shelter and food as well as kin. The devastating floods of Quebec's Saguenay River in the summer of 1996 and along Manitoba's Red River the following spring together took only about a dozen lives but generated nationwide generosity toward those whose lives, and often their livelihoods,

THE FREEZING RAIN STORM that knocked out electric power in Quebec and eastern Ontario in January 1998 forced some people to rely, as many did at the beginning of the century, on wood fires, candles and oil lamps.

A HEAVY SUMMER STORM in the Saguenay and Lac-St-Jean region of Quebec in July 1996 caused flash floods that overflowed inadequate dams—as here, in downtown Chicoutimi— taking seven lives and forcing the temporary evacuation of some 12,000 people.

were shattered. It happened again in 1998 when a destructive January icestorm toppled hydro lines and blacked out Quebec and Eastern Ontario, leaving hundreds of thousands of people without heat or light.

It was as if there was a sense that disasters delivered by weather and flood should not happen in the technological age, which surely had tamed nature. Hugely expensive dam reservoirs and defensive flood canals—those built in Manitoba after the 1950 Winnipeg flood, for instance—are not supposed to overflow. Freezing rain in a winter country that virtually invented hydro-electric power simply should not bring down towering pylons. Electronic alarms and computerized sprinklers, not to mention safety regulations, were meant to render obsolete such horrors as the deaths of 76 children, mostly by asphyxiation, from a fire in the Laurier Palace Theatre in Montreal on January 9, 1927. But big fires remained a threat to lives in the 1990s.

Likewise, modern-day mining deaths—such as those in the Westray coal-dust explosion of May 9, 1992, that killed 26 coalminers near Stellarton, Nova Scotia—ought somehow to belong to olden times. Such tragic episodes seemed a throwback to the nearby, long-shut Springhill coalmines, where 424 men in all died in a history of misfortunes, the last on October 23, 1958. Or else to times even more distant—back to June 19, 1914, the date of the worst single mining accident in Canadian history, the coal-dust explosions that took 189 lives beneath Hillcrest, Alberta.

Post mortems often faulted human error for overriding technical safeguards. As *Maclean's* reported on December 15, 1997: "Justice Peter Richard of the Nova Scotia Supreme Court, in his long-awaited public inquiry report, described the Westray tragedy as a tale of, among other things, 'incompetence, apathy, cynicism, stupidity and neglect' on the part of mine managers and their government overseers."

The science and practice of flight failed hundreds in major airliner accidents—the crash of a Trans-Canada Air Lines DC-8 after takeoff from Montreal's Dorval Airport on November 29, 1963, killing all 118 aboard, and an Air Canada DC-8 that exploded and crashed, taking 109 lives on July 5, 1970, during an attempt to abort a landing at Toronto international airport. But it was a terrorist bomb planted aboard an Air India 747 jumbojet bound for Bombay out of Toronto and Montreal that blew the plane out of the sky south of Ireland on June 25, 1985, killing all 307 passengers, mostly Canadians, and the crew of 22. The deadliest crash on Canadian soil happened on December 12, 1985, near Gander international airport in Newfoundland when a refuelled DC-8 jetliner carrying home troops of the U.S. 101st Airborne Division from Egypt crashed on takeoff, killing all 256 people aboard.

Violence wrought by weather runs in a terrible line from an avalanche in the Rogers Pass of the Rockies on March 5, 1910, that killed all but one of 62 men clearing an earlier snowfall off the CPR track, through to the eastern Canadian ice storm of

NOVA SCOTIA COAL-MINING COMMUNITIES were racked throughout the century by underground cave-ins and explosions that produced tragic death tolls, including (from top) New Waterford in 1917, Springhill in 1936 and Westray in 1992.

TORNADOS STRUCK REGINA IN 1912, Barrie, Ontario, in 1985 and Edmonton in 1987, but the century's worst inland storm in Canada was hurricane Hazel in 1954, which cut a swath of death, destruction and flooding in the Toronto area.

January 5, 1998, that was blamed directly for about two dozen deaths and more than $2 billion in damage. A Regina whirlwind on June 30, 1912, killed 28 people and left some 2,500 residents homeless. A fire triggered by a lightning storm on July 29, 1916, killed at least 228 people and razed the northern Ontario towns of Cochrane and Matheson. Hurricane Hazel caused at least 81 deaths in and around Toronto on October 15, 1954, and left a swath of destruction. A tornado that swept through Edmonton neighborhoods on July 31, 1987, took 27 lives and injured hundreds. At sea, a raging Atlantic storm toppled and sank the towering *Ocean Ranger* oil rig off Newfoundland on February 15, 1982, killing 84 men.

Some historians rated the wreck of the *Ocean Ranger* at the time as the worst Canadian marine disaster since the Second World War. That discounted the loss of lives aboard the luxurious Great Lakes cruise ship *Noronic*, albeit while docked in Toronto harbor, in the small hours of September 17, 1949. A blaze of explosive speed caught many of the 669 passengers and crew asleep. In all, 118 people died. The toll also included the ship and, effectively, the Great Lakes cruise business.

Marine disasters in Canada or close by killed thousands during the century's second decade. There were the 1,522 people lost when the British Royal Mail Ship *Titanic*, struck by an iceberg off Newfoundland on its maiden voyage from Southampton to New York, went down in the early hours of April 15, 1912. The Canadian connections to the storied accident spanned 85 years, from the burial of 121 of the victims in Halifax, the nearest seaport, to the partial filming in the same city of the 1997 Hollywood megamovie on the tragedy by Canadian director James

Cameron. There was even a peripheral link between the *Titanic* and Canada's first foreign embassy: the diplomatic mission in Washington was housed for some 70 years in a mansion acquired from the widow of a local hunt club's master of the hounds, a man lost in the *Titanic* along with a pack of dogs he had bought in England. And then there was Newfoundland-born poet E.J. Pratt's *The Titanic*, the epic 1935 poem that accords heroic status to the Arctic iceberg that sank the liner:

> *Silent, composed, ringed by its icy broods,*
> *The grey shape with the paleolithic face*
> *Was still the master of the longitudes.*

Barely more than two years after the *Titanic*'s doom, Canadian Pacific's *Empress of Ireland*, outbound from Quebec on May 29, 1914, sank in the lower St. Lawrence after a Norwegian coal freighter sliced open the liner's hull, a colli-sion that cost the lives of 1,012 of the *Empress*'s 1,477 passengers and crew. A similar fate befell CP's *Princess Sophia*, which broke up on a reef during a storm and sank on October 25, 1918, en route to Vancouver from Skagway, Alaska, losing all 343 aboard. Most devastating of all was the Halifax explosion of December 6, 1917, when a collision involving a muni-tions ship in the city's harbor spewed a wide swath of death and ruin—more than 1,600 people killed and damage exceed-ing $35 million.

STORMS IN CANADA'S *three oceans have taken a heavy toll of fishing folk and sealers over the years, but the modern phenom-enon of the offshore oil hunt took 84 lives off Newfoundland—here, searchers return one of the bodies to land—when a February storm in 1982 sank the huge* Ocean Ranger *oil rig.*

In ironic but substantial ways, the science of medicine was responsible for calamities, offsetting in part its century of life-giving pharmaceutical discoveries, from insulin to antibiotics. Thalidomide, a "wonder drug" out of Germany, licensed for sale in Canada from April, 1961, until March, 1962, was prescribed for pregnant women suffering from nausea. It helped with the morning sickness, but spawned an epidemic of birth deformities that afflicted an estimated 12,000 babies in all, more than 100 of them in Canada. (Twenty-five years after Ottawa revoked the drug's licence, membership in the Thalidomide Victims Association of Canada numbered 125.)

A more widespread blight infected Canada in the 1980s. Blood banks run by the Red Cross since the 1940s became contaminated by viruses for which no sure

IN WARTIME HALIFAX HARBOR, on December 6, 1917, the Norwegian vessel Imo *struck the French munitions carrier* Mont Blanc, *triggering its cargo of more than 2,500 tons of explosives. The blast "smashed against the town with the rigidity and force of driving steel,"*

as novelist Hugh MacLennan, a Halifax boy at the time of the explosion, would later write in Barometer Rising, "shattering every flimsy house in its path." That included all the wooden, waterfront homes of Africville, the north-end Halifax community, as depicted here.

THE RED RIVER FLOOD in Manitoba in 1950 forced 100,000 Winnipeg residents to flee their homes and invaded other communities as well, including here in St. Boniface. The damage estimate exceeded $100 million.

antidote was known–HIV (Human Immunodeficiency Virus), which causes AIDS (Acquired Immune Deficiency Syndrome), and hepatitis C, which may lead to fatal liver cancer. The HIV spread to hundreds of Canadians, including unknown totals indirectly infected through sexual or maternal transmission from the estimated 1,200 people poisoned by blood transfusion. And when the results of an inquiry into the blood scandal were published on November 26, 1997, experts estimated that the bad blood had spread hepatitis C to more than 60,000 Canadians.

Separately, federal health records in 1997 showed that the cumulative total of AIDS diagnosed in Canada since detection of the first case in 1979 ranged from 15,100 to more than 21,000 infections. The comparable total of positive HIV tests on record exceeded 33,000.

By some measures, that made AIDS a plague. But Canadians had experienced much worse, in terms of the speed and scale of infection and death, in the Spanish flu epidemic of 1918-1919. In that scourge, which caused an estimated worldwide toll of 21 million deaths, Canadians succumbed at a rate of almost 500 a week–about 50,000 in all.

The disquiet bred by war, revolution, disease and deadly accidents during the century's second decade fostered a streak of paranoia in some psyches. A brief report in *Maclean's* in the wake of the worst of the flu epidemic injected such postwar fears with a dash of political menace.

JOY IS MIXED WITH CAUTION at this Calgary celebration of the end of the First World War. The masks worn by celebrants are intended to protect them from germs as a deadly influenza epidemic swept the world, killing an estimated 50,000 Canadians—a total approaching the number of fatal Canadian war casualties.

1920 Dread Disease Sweeping West

JUNE 1920 There is another peril, almost as menacing as Bolshevism, which is spreading westward from Russia: this is the peril of disease. Typhus and other epidemics are steadily advancing from the land of Trotsky and Lenin. In the decade preceding the war, plagues like typhus and cholera were almost unknown in Europe outside of Russia and the Balkan region. The excellent sanitary systems of Germany and Austria usually held plague incursions closely to the Russian frontiers.

The end of hostilities opened the fronts, while the general disorganization which ensued largely destroyed the sanitary organizations as well. The wholesale migrations of refugees and war prisoners spread disease. Russia remained the plague centre, conditions becoming steadily worse until every portion of that unhappy country is riddled with disease.

1962 The Unfolding Tragedy of Drug-deformed Babies

June Callwood – MAY 19, 1962 The small tablet that sold for about ten cents has precipitated the medical tragedy of this age. Across Canada, expectant mothers who used the pill containing a new drug, thalidomide, to relieve morning sickness

THIS CHILD ON A TRIKE in the 1960s is one of the victims of the drug Thalidomide, an early-1960s prescription for pregnant women suffering morning sickness that caused birth deformities.

in early pregnancy are waiting now to discover whether or not their babies will be massively deformed. Their ordeal is shared by obstetricians, who prescribed the drug in innocent faith in its advertised ability to prevent morning sickness harmlessly. It is shared by two pharmaceutical companies who manufactured the tablets under the names of Kevadon and Talimol in the belief they were bringing Canadians the safest sedative ever devised. It is also shared by government officials who were warned of the risk of the drug three months before they took any action, and four months before their decision was enforced.

The first effect of this drug is that babies may be born without arms and legs. At the time of writing, eight Canadian women have given birth to living and otherwise healthy infants suffering from varying degrees of phocomelia, a deformity so rare before thalidomide that few doctors have ever seen it. In phocomelia, the baby has crude hands joined to the shoulders, and foot-like appendages at the hip. "Seal-limbs," they have been called. Some of the deformed Canadian babies were born in this totally helpless state, others were more mildly afflicted.

The history of thalidomide will be cited by doctors, researchers, drug manufacturers and governments for years to come. It most certainly will alter attitudes, methods of testing and regulating all over the world. Canada, unhappily, has the poorest record of all. The drug had only been on the Canadian market for eight months when medical directors of both manufacturers visited Ottawa to warn that doctors in Europe suspected thalidomide of damaging embryos. More than three months later, on March 2, the Department of Health decided the drug should be withdrawn. But on April 11, it was still being sold over drug store counters.

1997 A Harsh Rebuke

John DeMont – DECEMBER 8, 1997 They still serve up doughnuts and juice afterward. Otherwise, much has changed for anyone giving blood at a Red Cross clinic in Canada. The questions are chastening. Have you ever paid for sex, a nurse asks. Has anyone ever paid you for sex? Do you have AIDS? Have you had sex with anyone who has AIDS? Have you ever taken illegal drugs? The nurse takes the potential donor's temperature and blood pressure to check for signs of infection, then examines the inside of the arms for needle tracks. The donor is asked to sign a waiver, attesting to his honesty. Only then is the blood drawn from his veins–and carried off to a laboratory to be tested for the AIDS virus.

All told, the process usually takes over an hour–a far cry from a few years ago when a donor could roll up his sleeve, have that juice and doughnut and be out in 30 minutes. That was before thousands of Canadians became infected with HIV and hepatitis C through tainted blood products in the late 1970s and 1980s. What has made tainted blood the Canadian medical scandal of the century is the undeniable fact–obvious even before Ontario Appeal Court Justice Horace Krever started his probe into the tragedy in 1994–that the blood system had failed the very people it was entrusted to protect. All of which makes Krever's final report, which became public last week and sheds new light on the institutions and individuals responsible for the tragedy, so devastating.

After 427 witnesses, 50,000 pages of testimony and more than $17 million, the report's enduring value is the way it dissects a tragedy that, according to Krever, is much more widespread than originally estimated. Many of his 50 recommendations, including an end to the role of the Red Cross, have already been embraced by the politicians, who have decided that a new blood supply system must be in place by September, 1998. The report is a horrific, haunting tale of bungling and negligence. The RCMP announced it was reviewing Krever's report to see if criminal charges were warranted. And finally, the Red Cross apologized through its new president, Gene Durnin: "To the victims and their families, while we cannot feel your pain, we hurt with you; while we cannot know your suffering, we weep with you; while we cannot feel your loss, we grieve with you."

The Years of Desperation

But the Dirty Thirties Also Spawned the Politics of Caring

CANADA survived many harsh years getting through the century. But for sustained hardship, nothing matched the Dirty Thirties–grim years of economic doldrums, Prairie drought and social disruption. The world slithered into the Great Depression from the crash of the stock markets on October 29, 1929. For Canada, fullscale recovery began only 10 years later with its declaration of war against Germany on September 10, 1939. The war provided soldiering jobs for thousands of unemployed young men and work for almost everybody else in the weaponry industry.

The impact on Canada of the global economy was heavier than in many countries because Canadians had been relying on export sales for 33 cents of every dollar earned. The western provinces, with their heavy dependence on grain and forestry exports, suffered especially severely. An eight-year drought compounded the misery on the Prairies, particularly in southern regions, even as the slowdown in international trade built a huge wheat surplus. (The Canadian Wheat Board, founded in 1935, was set up to promote sales and maintain floor prices.)

Hungry, jobless men roamed the country looking for work. In 1935, complaints in British Columbia against dire conditions in federal work camps for jobless men grew into a protest movement that became known as the On-to-Ottawa

THE WORLDWIDE ECONOMIC SLUMP ravaged Canada. For every dollar's worth of national production in 1929, the value of output had plummeted to 58 cents by the end of 1933–the year before this Toronto soup kitchen line-up was photographed.

OFTEN IT WAS A CASE OF NO WORK and then no home, but some victims of the Great Depression retained enough sinew to protest against public relief conditions.

Trek. Jobless men took over freight trains and headed east, picking up others on the way, until they numbered about 2,000 on reaching Regina. There, the railways refused to carry the protest farther but its leaders went on to Ottawa. They received short shrift from Prime Minister R.B. Bennett and returned to Regina, planning to disband the protest after a final rally on July 1. At Bennett's behest, squads of RCMP and local police turned up that day to arrest the leaders, provoking a melee reminiscent of the notorious Bloody Saturday in Winnipeg on June 21, 1919, when mounted police attacked demonstrating workers during a general strike. The Regina Riot, as it came to be known, left a policeman dead, dozens on both sides injured and 130 trekkers under arrest. (Fifteen weeks later, Bennett and his Conservative government went down to defeat in a general election.)

Nationwide, families were impoverished by an unemployment rate that peaked in 1933 at 30 per cent of the work force and never fell below 12 per cent for the rest of the decade. Average wages got whittled down to as little as half pay. One in five Canadians were "on relief"– municipal or provincial welfare. The courts outlawed a 1935 federal unemployment insurance program on constitutional grounds, and by the time Parliament overrode the judicial veto, in 1940, the Second World War was generating full employment.

IN 1932, the federal government began establishing Unemployment Relief Camps, run by the defence department, where jobless men received shelter—this Relief Project 27 hut in Ottawa was one—and got 20 cents a day for construction work. The program petered out after protests against camp conditions turned ugly in 1935.

THE ON-TO-OTTAWA TREK, initiated in British Columbia as a protest against the treatment of unemployed men in federal relief camps, ended in Regina when the railways refused to take an expanding crowd of freight-car trippers any farther.

One legacy of the Dirty Thirties was the Co-operative Commonwealth Federation and its successor in 1961, the New Democratic Party. A coalition of labor, farmer and social democratic forces formed in Calgary in 1932, the party formally launched itself into the political arena with its Regina Manifesto the following year. J.S. Woodsworth, the party's first leader and now its patron saint, is described in a *Maclean's* profile in November, 1951, nine years after his death, as "the father of the welfare state in Canada." Blair Fraser, then the magazine's Ottawa editor and later its editor-in-chief, observed that Woodsworth, through his party and as an MP from 1921 until his death in 1942, forced the pace of federal legislation that expressed a social conscience: old-age pensions, unemployment insurance, family allowances. Woodsworth's agitation for a national health care program bore fruit

JAMES SHAVER WOODSWORTH, here expounding on his "social gospel," the democratic socialist message that the Methodist minister came to view as the answer to economic injustices. His work among the disadvantaged in Winnipeg carried him to the leadership of the Co-operative Commonwealth Federation, forerunner of the New Democratic Party.

posthumously, with party leader Tommy Douglas, like Woodsworth a clergyman, then in the vanguard of the struggle.

Another inheritance from the 1930s was a lesson for prime ministers of how not to treat an economic depression. Both the Conservative Bennett and Mackenzie King, his Liberal successor in 1935, were proven sadly wrong in trying to cure the sick economy by reining in federal spending, paying down debt and counting on private business to generate employment.

It was in 1935 that *Maclean's* political writer Grattan O'Leary, a staunch Tory, chastised both leaders for their ineffectual policies. O'Leary caustically summed up King's program as propounding no more spending programs, the same old dole and reliance on "government hopes that, with world recovery and betterment of trade, unemployment will cure itself." That was a policy that post-Depression governments spurned in times of recession for 50 years. Only in the century's closing decade, as unemployment approached Depression-era rates and average incomes fell, did both Conservative and Liberal governments revert to old nostrums, dismantling social programs in the name of fiscal probity.

1932 What Stocks Did in 1931

F.B. Housser – JANUARY 15, 1932 **A**t the peak of the bull market in September, 1929, the index for a selected list of 100 industrial stocks was at 315.8 points. The first crash occurred on October 29. For the week ending October 31, 1929, the industrial stock index was at 222.4. The second crash came in November, and by the end of that month the industrial index had sunk to 205.6. At their high point of 1931, industrial stocks were 59 per cent below the peak of the bull market in September, 1929.

The lowest weekly point for industrials in 1929 was 75.9. The lowest point for industrials in 1931 was reached in the week ending October 8, when they were at 68.1 compared with a low of 112.6 in 1930. The 1931 low point was 10.2 per cent below the low of 1929.

Every class of industry has been affected. The best showing was made by telephone and telegraph companies, which, at their high for the year of 111.6, were down only 4.1 points from their high in 1930. The greatest decline has taken place in the oils, which, at their low for the year of 98, were down 198 points from their high of 1930. In no class was the high in 1931 above the high for last year. In every case the low was lower.

1933 The Challenge

Leslie Brook – NOVEMBER 15, 1933 **A**lthough most of us young unemployed people are fortunate enough to have a home where we are provided with food and shelter, there are many other demands which our parents with their depleted depression incomes cannot cope with. Many of us have not been to the dentist for the past three years. We can't afford it. When our teeth begin to ache until it is no longer possible to bear the pain, we shall have to go and pray that we may find the money on the way to the dentist. By that time it will likely mean extraction–a loss we can never replace. Our clothes are threadbare and fast approaching that state when we will hardly be presentable to apply for a job. We have had to forego many of the pleasures we have been accustomed to–not an easy thing for youth to do. But we are more concerned with a problem more far-reaching in importance and bearing greater influence on our morale–our future.

1934 The Quintland Distraction

In the depths of the Great Depression, five happy events provided a distraction from the prevailing gloom. The Dionne quintuplets, the first fivesome known to have survived birth, became almost immediate international celebrities after their arrival on May 28, 1934. They were born two months prematurely in the six-room farmhouse of Oliva and Elzire Dionne, already the parents of five children, in the hamlet of Corbeil, 10 kilometres outside North Bay, Ontario.

But the true story of the Dionne quints proved later to be less than happy. Responding to a public outcry over the family's plans to let a private promoter exhibit the quints, the provincial government made Annette, Emilie, Yvonne, Cécile and Marie wards of the province, which built the Dionnes a home but kept the girls separate from their family and on exhibition for tourists at "Quintland."

As Maclean's *reported in a cover story of November 21, 1994:*

By the time they were toddlers, those dimpled faces framed by the dark, beribboned ringlets were everywhere. They were on the covers of *Life*, *Look* and *Time*. They appeared in films and on radio. They endorsed a host of products, everything from Carnation Milk to Remington typewriters.

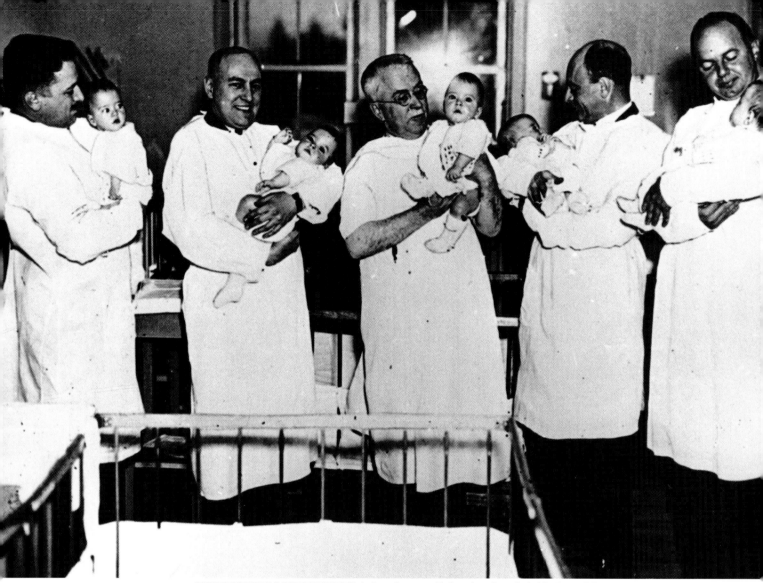

THE DIONNE QUINTUPLETS, being shown off shortly after their births on May 24, 1934, with Allan Roy Dafoe, the doctor who delivered them, in the centre and the camera-conscious Ontario premier Mitchell Hepburn second from the left.

There were quint cutout books, and quint dolls even outsold the Shirley Temple variety for a time. But there was a huge catch: the people who looked after the quints also spent a lot of the money that the girls earned. "The guardians took their fees out of the money," says Bertrand Dionne, the 33-year-old son of Cecile, who works full time doing public relations for his mother and two aunts. "They paid for the salaries of the staff at Quintland and all of the costs of the day-to-day operations of the place. It cost them $200,000 to build that ridiculous observatory. They were even charged $5,000 for the construction of a toilet for the public."

Sixty-three years after their birth, living in a Montreal suburb, pleading poverty and claiming they were cheated out of a major part of a childhood trust fund, surviving quints Yvonne, Cécile and Annette, after a legal tussle, received a multimillion-dollar settlement from the Ontario government on March 6, 1998.

1934 Mortgaged!

George Newman – NOVEMBER 1, 1934 The Prairie town banker, under instructions from his head office, was driving out to check up on a farmer who had paid nothing on a $250 chattel mortgage for over a year. Bitter thoughts went through his mind as he drove.

For two full years no rain had fallen. For three, maddening winds had raged over the prairie wheat lands–chilly and biting in the spring, blowing out the seed time and time again; hot and blistering in the summer, burning up the straggling grain plants that survived, with relentless fury. It wouldn't have been so bad had it rained. But the clouds of moisture refused to gather, and what had once been a fertile wheat belt was now nothing but a dry, yellow wilderness.

Hundreds of families were practically destitute, so people said. Government relief was being given wholesale.

DEPRESSION-ERA FAMILIES whose southern Prairie farms were destroyed by drought–such as Abraham Fehr and his family, pictured on arrival in Edmonton from Saskatchewan on July 1, 1934–fled northward or to the cities in search of productive land or work.

Then, it was reported half the livestock hadn't survived the winter. How much longer could the weary people last out under such conditions? Would there never be redress for all this suffering and want? It didn't look like it.

Late that night, the banker finished his report on the mortgage: "We visited this man's farm today and regret to report our security has been seriously impaired. Out of fourteen horses and seven cattle, only seven horses and one cow remain, the rest having died during the winter owing to shortage of feed. Our loan must be regarded therefore as doubtful. Crop prospects are poor, but the mortgagor assured us of his intention to pay up promptly this fall, if conditions improved."

1934 Remedies

Archibald J. Trotter – NOVEMBER 1, 1934 Canadians and others have fought for Canada before this; but it looks as though Canadians now have a major fight on their hands to save a large part of this country. Nearly half of the arable land in Canada is threatened.

EIGHT YEARS OF DROUGHT laid waste to vast regions of southern Alberta and Saskatchewan, destroying farms—including this one near Cadillac, Saskatchewan— and devastating families.

The menace hangs over Southern Saskatchewan and part of Southern Alberta. It is drought, the worst enemy of the farmer. Already for several successive seasons, stark famine has stared the people of this area in the face. It has not been a case of crops damaged by drought, but the total destruction of crops. Assistance by their governments has kept some of the people going. Others in thousands have "moved north," with or without assistance from the Government.

It is a pitiful sight to see these people moving away from their homes with all their personal effects piled in a wagon, their farm machinery following, and last of all the boy or boys herding those of their animals that have not already vanished in the famine.

Behind them is their abandoned home, which has taken perhaps 20 or 30 years to develop. The work of two generations. Ahead of them what? Perhaps a chance to make a new home in the Northern parts, where so far at least drought has not crept in. Where they will at least have water for their animals without having to haul it for miles.

The stricken area is a huge one, greater than all of the inhabited farming area of Ontario or of Quebec. Its loss would be a dreadful blow to the country. Hence the battle to save it. The weapons to be employed? Tree planting and directed agriculture. The first step would be to rehabilitate as such the millions of lakes and sloughs which have been dried out. Take these lakes and sloughs out of cultivation and ring them about with trees. A secondary step that will prove essential and profitable is the planting of strips of trees or hedgerows north and south across the farms at proper intervals.

There is no doubt that as time goes on, other steps can be taken to speed up the desired results. Water courses can be dammed, and the spring freshets impounded in artificial lakes. Whole areas may be flooded to create additional water surface to aid in the work. These things will cost a great deal to accomplish, however, and they are, after all, a secondary method of attack. The first thing is the tree-planting.

CANADA DURING THE DEPRESSION, especially on the Prairies, proved to be a breeding ground for the Ku Klux Klan. Pictured here is a crowd assembled to listen to Alberta Klan Leader John James Maloney in 1932.

THESE BRITISH COLUMBIANS, and many like them across the country, demonstrated in favor of government spending to generate jobs, a campaign that fell on political deaf ears for the most part.

1934 Hamstrung by Politics

H. Napier Moore, Editor – NOVEMBER 15, 1934 **C**ertain of the country's business leaders have privately expressed themselves as being worried by the growth of radical

publications in Canada. They suggest that somebody ought to start counter-propaganda journals to woo readers of the first-named sheets back to "sound thinking." They have got hold of the wrong end of the stick.

The question to be answered is why are so many people interested in radical ideas? They are not all anarchists or revolutionists. They want security, and security and revolution don't go together. The answer is that for them the old system has broken down.

They cannot get work except in relief camps. They cannot feed and clothe and educate their children. They may get state or municipal charity. But they cannot establish themselves. If they are middle-aged, they may never get a steady job again. A vast army of idle youth is waiting to take the jobs if and when they come.

WHEN POLICE INTERVENED to break up a Regina rally of unemployed men protesting against conditions in government work camps on July 1, 1935, the resulting "Regina Riot" led to the death of one policeman, dozens of injuries and scores of arrests.

Like it or not, is there any wonder that they turn a listening ear to those who promise betterment via new and untried systems, however unsound or impracticable such theories may be? Correct their situation and there is no need to worry about them seeing red.

The Seething Sixties

*Rock 'n' Roll and Other Rebellions
Defined a Decade*

I T was nearly the most terrible of times but also the most terrific of times. In the 1960s, prosperous but tumultuous, world views collided, spreading social friction in Canada and almost everywhere else. At its simplest, it was age and youth finding new ways of how not to get along. It was the three-piece suit, blow-dries and the girdle versus ripped jeans, long hair and no brassiere. It was the Beatles and The Band, Joni Mitchell and Joan Baez, Neil Young and Bob Dylan against whatever the top-20 music used to be. It was Rachel Carson's *Silent Spring* at odds with Morton Shulman's *Anyone Can Make a Million*. It was the guerrilla war of conflicting messages waged between the underground and campus press and the mass media, only to have Marshall McLuhan advise them all that the medium was the message.

Beneath the surface was a question: whether the way to improve the human condition lay with the adversary system of parliaments and courts and commerce or in the get-it-together ethos of the commune and the love-in or doing your own thing collectively. A major collision point involved the difference between the way things really were in the fearful Cold War and the way they might become in a green and peaceful world. It was a clash between nuclear armament and flower power, between the regimentation of thought and action on one side and the stimulation

CELEBRATIONS OF THE CENTENNIAL of Confederation in 1967, including Expo '67, the Montreal World's Fair, brought about a rare convergence of establishment culture and the rebellious counterculture of youth that year in Canada.

SATURDAY, JULY 1, 1967, the Canadian Confederation's 100th birthday, was a special Dominion Day (July 1 became Canada Day officially in 1983), especially on Parliament Hill in Ottawa, cake and all.

by pot and acid on the other. It was a time when it was often hard to tell whether the world was truly psychotic or simply psychedelic.

The early activists against warmongering, racism and sexism were graduates of the Beatnik Fifties, but the Boom generation was growing up and filling out the Hippie ranks. Half the Canadian population was under 25 years old on the eve of Confederation's centennial year, 1967, when the postwar baby boom began to slacken. In Canada, apart from student uprisings and sit-ins to protest a range of perceived grievances, the decade was largely terrific, with its folk festivals and rock concerts, its anti-nuke and pro-environment demos, and its promotion of Canadian nationalism. In Quebec, where Premier Jean Lesage's Quiet Revolution marched to a different beat, the manifestations later turned terrible: radical separatism's mailbox bombs led to the kidnapping crisis of October, 1970.

The power-to-the-people decade also fuelled violence in the United States, Asia and Europe. The first U.S. president born in the 20th century took office as the 1960s opened, and John F. Kennedy immediately became a global exemplar of the new and the different, the best and the brightest. But the Cold War mindset froze out his Camelot. The nearly most terrible thing of the 20th or any century happened in October, 1962, when Kennedy went to the brink of nuclear war with Russia over its placing of missiles in Cuba, a counterplay to American missiles pointed at Russia from Turkey. Thirteen months later, Kennedy died at the hands of an assassin with Russian and Cuban connections. Kennedy's successors built on his early military forays into Vietnam in pursuance of America's determination to contain communism. The Vietnam War soon became the primary target of young America's crusading. The cause spilled over the border, invigorating

Canada's counterculture movement both in sympathetic anti-war protests and with reinforcements—as many as 80,000 young Americans who ultimately moved to Canada, dodging the draft or simply disillusioned.

Not that the Canadians lacked local controversies, among them a project to base U.S. Bomarc anti-aircraft missiles with nuclear warheads outside North Bay, Ontario, and La Macaza, Quebec. In the opposition's vanguard was the anti-war Voice of Women, an organization of all ages. The VoW lost the anti-Bomarc crusade and its leader when, in 1963, the newly elected government of Lester Pearson authorized the Bomarc bases and his wife, Maryon Pearson, was obliged to resign from the organization's chair.

In counterpoint to the disputes, there were positive political and social developments, and lighter diversions, during the decade. Despite a six-year stretch when three federal elections produced three minority governments, Canada during the period gained the Maple Leaf flag and national medicare, the Canada Pension Plan, a space-based

THE WHOLE WORLD turned up to help Canada acclaim the centennial of Confederation: there were roughly 120 nations and regions represented at Montreal's Expo '67, and a total of 50,306,648 paid admissions to the six-month international party from April 27 to October 29, 1967.

telecommunications program and the nationwide centennial-year party featuring Expo '67 in Montreal.

The middle of the decade produced a spate of scandals involving politicians on the take and the country's first rousing political sex scandal—the exposure in Parliament of an earlier affair between an associate defence minister, Pierre Sevigny, and Gerda Munsinger, a German woman with a shady background. In the Cold War climate, people were thinking espionage, but an investigation determined there was no security risk.

The archetypical year of the decade was 1968, encapsulating much about the Sixties. It was a year rocked abroad by social turbulence and political violence—from the communist Viet Cong's stunning Tet offensive against American forces and the cities of South Vietnam to anti-war upheavals in the United States, a student uprising in Paris and Soviet tanks from the Soviet Union snuffing out liberal

FOR THOSE WHO BELIEVED in the vision-granting powers of hemp or LSD in the 1960s, and that, as the Beatles sang, "all you need is love" to solve problems, it made perfect sense to promote such ideas by sitting in front of Toronto City Hall.

hopes in Prague. Martin Luther King Jr., the passive-resistance leader of the American civil rights movement, was slain in Memphis, U.S. presidential candidate Bobby Kennedy shot to death in Los Angeles. Under Mao Zedong's cultural revolution, the Red Guard imposed its disciplines on almost every aspect of China's life. Pope Paul VI's rejection of his church commission's birth-control proposal fomented controversy worldwide.

But for Canadians, 1968 mainly meant keeping alive the centennial-year party spirit and indulging in a year-long political infatuation: Trudeaumania. Bachelor Trudeau's charismatic combination of erudition and athleticism captivated much of the electorate. Barely more than two years in federal politics, Trudeau, 48, was chosen Liberal leader in April and became the first Canadian prime minister born in the 20th century. Then, dedicated to the defeat of Quebec separatism, he led his party to victory at the polls on June 25. Among measures enacted in the following activist months, the new government liberalized abortion law and established French and English as offical languages of Canada.

Among the closing acts of the decade, one of the most memorable took place in the fields of southeastern New York State, near the town of Bethel. There, for three mid-August days of 1969, the Woodstock Music and Art Fair staged the first free rock-'n'-roll festival, drawing upwards of 400,000 young Americans and Canadians to the beat of unfettered fun. In another fitting finale the same year, Trudeau proclaimed a nuclear-free policy for the Canadian Armed Forces, which mothballed Canada's Bomarcs within two years.

Aspects of the spirit of the Sixties persisted beyond the decade, mutating over the years into the New Age culture and its whole-person consciousness. The boomers went into business, passing the torch of disaffection to the nihilistic punks and Generation-X. In a summing up as the Sixties drew to a close, *Maclean's* recognized the uniqueness of the period, but was at a loss when it came to labelling it.

1968 Who says Pierre Elliott Trudeau is all that hot? Writers and editors just about everywhere, that's who

SEPTEMBER 1968 Last year we had Expo. This year we've got Trudeau. If you think Canadians have flipped over our new PM, scan this sampling about what readers abroad are being told about him:

In West Germany, *Stern*, the country's largest illustrated weekly, can't get enough. "Trudeau," enthuses news director Norbert Sakowskli, "is the biggest political story ever to come from North America!"

In France, *Le Monde* editorialized: "Young, dynamic, competent, anti-conformist, M. Trudeau has literally seduced the middle-class Anglophones, who have seen in this perfectly bilingual Québecois an answer to the problem that Quebec's particularism poses."

In Britain, a lyrical tribute from the weekly *Spectator*: "It was as if Canada had come of age, as if he himself, single-handed, would catapult the country into the brilliant sunshine of the late 20th Century from the stagnant swamp of traditionalism and mediocrity in which Canadian politics had been bogged down for years."

In the United States, a *Washington Post* commentator noted: "Canada now has leadership by personality cult with all the trappings."

Scoffed *Sovetskaya Russyia*, the Soviet Russian publication: "The millionaire Trudeau is one of the ardent advocates of closer political, economic and military ties with the U.S.A."

ATHLETIC AND ERUDITE, a bilingual mixture of French and Scottish ancestry, a dashing bachelor of 48 who admitted then only to 46, Pierre Elliott Trudeau touched off a case of Trudeaumania in Ontario and Quebec during the spring of 1968 as the new Liberal leader. In the federal election on June 25, after three elections in the previous six years had failed to produce a clear winner, the electorate handed his party a parliamentary majority.

1969 The 1960s: Remember?

DECEMBER 1969 What will we call them 40 years on? The Swinging Sixties? The Sick Sixties? The Era of Excess? We don't know; but there was something about those 10 years, something that had to do with excitement and struggle for change. What was it? Here *Maclean's* recaptures a taste of the fact and folklore that will make the decade as well remembered as the Roaring Twenties or the Gay Nineties.

First, the Bad News

GI Joe, Major Matt Mason, et al.: for the first time in history, U.S. toy manufacturers had little boys playing with dolls, and paramilitary dolls at that.

Instant Breakfast: By packing enough calories in a glass to tide you over until lunch, this insidious powder speeded the decline of a civilized start to the day.

The topless bathing suit: Rudi Gernreich designed it, mostly for publicity, and contributed a memorable image of 1960s tastelessness.

Now . . . the Good News

The cassette tape recorder made portable sound accessible to almost anybody.

Montreal-London return for $165: While almost everything else went up, air fares came down through charter and group rates, giving stay-at-homes even less excuse for not seeing the world.

Ralph Nader helped start a consumers' revolution. Indirect results: safer (but not much more sensible) Detroit cars, supermarkets that poll their customers, a useful new federal government department.

Three inventions that made getting up in the morning less of a burden: stainless-steel razor blades for men; for women, panty hose that stay up without garters and electric hair curlers that do the awful job in 10 minutes or less.

The miniskirt pleased everybody by not going out of style.

THE BAND—*Robbie Robertson, Rick Danko, Garth Hudson, Richard Manuel and American expatriate Levon Helm—was born in Toronto as the decade began. They backed Rompin' Ronnie Hawkins, toured the world with Bob Dylan, made great recordings and starred in a 1976 farewell movie,* The Last Waltz, *before breaking up.*

Women are People, Too

The Barbie Doll was introduced by Mattel as the decade began. With the success of Barbie, her glossy good looks, her insatiable appetite for new clothes, somehow told a lot about how women were regarded in North America. Hugh Hefner made a fortune with live Barbie dolls: the first bunny club opened in Chicago in 1960. The go-go girl was invented, too; significantly, she usually danced in some kind of cage. The backlash started with Betty Friedan, whose pro-feminist book, *The Feminine*

Mystique, made a lot of women wonder why they weren't "fulfilled." It continued with the growth of the Women's Liberation Movement, which takes a dim view of brassieres, and, in Toronto, disrupted a bikini contest that was felt to be a prime example of male exploitation. A Canadian sociologist named Lionel Tiger had the next-to-last word: His book, *Men in Groups*, argued that men are dominant because of their biological inheritance from the animal kingdom.

Notes on Poverty

In Vancouver, city officials evicted vagrant Larry McNamara from a city works yard, where he'd been living for several years beneath some propped-up slabs of cement. In Toronto, where it was estimated that 93 per cent of the people can't afford to buy a house, police evicted Svetomir Kusmanovich from his home in a concrete pit at the bottom of a manhole.

Trivia Explosion

On a memorable night in 1966, a televised Batman walked into a discotheque wearing cape, hood, tights, etc., and told the waiter, "A corner table, please; I don't want to be conspicuous." This, from the first episode of the big hit of the 1966 TV season, launched the great boom in camp, first defined in Susan Sontag's article in *Partisan Review*, which described camp as a new, decadent sensibility that builds an elaborate aesthetic around corny trash such as *Major Bowe's Amateur Hour*. In no time at all, camp was a major social force. Comic books of the 1940s enjoyed a revival on campuses, and you weren't considered well-informed unless you knew the name of the Green Hornet's chauffeur. One of the biggest things about the 1960s, in fact, was the 1940s.

Jokes?

Why Poles? Why Italians? Why Newfies? Nobody knows, but these groups were singled out for special and unflattering attention on the smoking-room circuit. The trend burned itself out with a sprinkling of WASP jokes. (*What do you call a WASP girl who makes love once a year? A nymphomaniac.*) The elephant jokes were gentler, more mysterious, and didn't necessarily involve elephants. (*What's brown and wrinkled and hums? The electric prune.*)

    You figure it out.

The Heroines

There were great men and great moments. The New York Mets finally won the pennant. Canada produced Harry Jerome, Bill Crothers and Bruce Kidd. Bobby Hull scored 58 goals in one season. But the real phenomenon was our girls, most of them young enough for teeth braces and training bras, who did most of the big winning for Canada. Nancy Greene. Elaine Tanner. Petra Burka. And let us not forget Violetta Nesukaitis, who won the North American table-tennis championship at the age of 14.

*BRITISH COLUMBIAN SKIER Nancy Greene became all
Canada's hero in 1968, winning Olympic gold in the giant
slalom, silver in the slalom and a second World Cup. Her
royal reception in Toronto, pictured here, took place near
the same spot and almost exactly 20 years after a similar
tumult greeted figure skater Barbara Ann Scott.*

*IN STEP WITH SIXTIES-STYLE student protests,
West Indians and Canadians at Montreal's Sir George
Williams University, alleging faculty racism, destroyed
the school's mainframe computer and set fire to its data
centre on February 11, 1969.*

Perils of Technology

In the American midwest in 1962, a man electrocuted his wife by short-circuiting her
electric toothbrush.

At a medical symposium in 1963, Dr. Preston A. Wade of Cornell University
described an unforeseen hazard of space travel: "If, while in a room in weightless space, a man is unfortunate enough to pass flatus, the thrust thus produced
is enough to hurl him to the ceiling with such force as to fracture his skull."

New York doctors discovered that, nine months after the 1965 power failure that
blacked out most of the eastern U.S. and Canada for several hours, the birth rate
increased significantly.

A week after the computer riot in 1969 at Sir George Williams University in
Montreal, some data was being processed as usual. The university had duplicate
memory tapes stored off-campus and, by using remote terminals, was running
them through computers in Ottawa.

Sickies

The slogan of the U.S. Air Force team in Vietnam that specialized in defoliation raids:
"Only we can prevent forests."

Go-go girls (starting with Carol Doda in San Francisco), in the finest traditions of
competitive free enterprise, offered the customer more by having their breasts
injected with silicone.

*THE VERSION of the annual Woodstock Music and Art Fair held on a farm in upstate
New York from August 15 to August 17, 1969, was a weekend rock 'n' roll 'n' marijuana fest
attended by an estimated 400,000 young Americans and Canadians that became a defining
event of the 1960s hippie culture.*

In Montreal, two motorists ran over the body of a 12-year-old boy after he'd been killed in a traffic accident, and at least seven others drove by without stopping.

Canada, which both deplored the war in Vietnam and profited handsomely by it, donated 460,000 textbooks to the Vietnamese school system for–yes–social studies.

The Poisoned Public

North America finally realized that, as a byproduct of industrial progress, we're methodically poisoning our environment and each other. Hopeful signs: steam cars; new companies that make a profit by "mining" garbage and industrial waste; emergence of a public (and even a few governments) determined to put a stop to it.

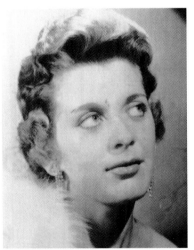

GERDA MUNSINGER, pictured here in a Montreal studio portrait, was characterized by a Liberal cabinet minister in 1966 as a possible Communist German spy who had been sexually involved with a Tory associate defence minister, Pierre Sévigny. A royal commission found nothing much wrong, but the idea of a parliamentary sex scandal made headlines in the excitable sixties.

Scandals We Have Known and Loved

A random list of juicy–but highly forgettable–scandals. We've awarded stars (5 is the highest possible) to each on the basis of significance, shock value, titillation and general interest:

Lucien Rivard: Montreal drug peddler who escaped from Bordeaux jail with a little help from his friends, thereby creating much awkwardness for the Pearson government. Now serving 20 years in a U.S. prison. ***

Christine Keeler: She slept with British cabinet member John Profumo and with the Soviet military attaché. Great consternation when Profumo lied to Parliament. She's still in London, selling her memoirs. *****

Charles Van Doren: Professor at Columbia, son of a distinguished scholar, he took part in a rigged TV quiz show and later confessed. Now in private business in Chicago. ***

Dick Clark: In the early 1960s, ran a TV deejay show for teenagers and took payola for plugging pop records. He's still under contract with ABC, emcees *American Bandstand*, moonlights in commercials for an acne remedy. **

Gerda Munsinger: Do we really have to remind you about Gerda? She was too friendly with John Diefenbaker's associate minister of defence. She's now the wife of a Munich cigar manufacturer. ***

The Prophets

At first they were just those four lovable mop-tops, a fleeting exercise in instant hysteria like Elvis, Sinatra, Valentino and all the rest. But then something unexpected happened. The Beatles not only endured; they revealed themselves as creators on the lavish scale of a Picasso, perhaps the ultimate prophets of the decade. It wasn't just their lyrics, which have entered the language as surely as Shakespeare's. It wasn't just their songs, which have been compared, favorably, with Schubert's. It was more than anything their coolness, their searching, their liberated lifestyle, the very look of Paul,

NEAR THE CLOSE of a decade when "love" was a behavioral watchword, "peace" a salutation and Hair *a hit Toronto rock musical, honeymooning Beatle John Lennon and bride Yoko Ono began a seven-day "bed-in for peace" on May 26, 1969, in Room 1742 of Montreal's Queen Elizabeth Hotel, conversing on the subject with visiting celebrities.*

George, John and Ringo, that made them the icons of the electronic age. Social historians a hundred years from now will look at our time, and conclude that the Beatles were what really happened in the 1960s. "What do you call that haircut?" a newsman inquired. "Arthur," replied the Beatle.

The Life of the Mind

A partial list of 1960s movements, chemicals, panaceas, etc., that were supposed to make you happier: Scientology; transcendental meditation; nude encounter; T-groups; sensitivity training; behaviorist psychiatry; group grope; acid; communal living; macrobiotic diets; regression therapy; organic farming.

Body Counts

Starvation: According to Oxfam, 36.5 million people died through insufficient nutrition in the 1960s.

Biafra: Two million (est.) deaths since May 1967, mostly from starvation. Death rate still running at 2,000 a day.

Traffic: About 44,000 people died on Canadian highways in the 1960s.

Vietnam: 560,308 North Vietnamese and Vietcong killed up to October 1969, according to U.S. sources, whose body counts have been known to be inflated; 38,969 U.S. troops dead; uncounted civilians killed on both sides of the border.

Sudan: 500,000 (est.) in one of those obscure little civil wars that bothers nobody.

Canada: Life expectancy of Canada's 450,000 Indians and Metis is 34 years, vs. 71 for all Canadians.

Big-Neighbor Factors

How Great-Power Pressures Shaped Canadian Policies

THE century was only six weeks old when Prime Minister Wilfrid Laurier presented Parliament with a no-progress report on a dispute with the United States over the boundary between British Columbia and the Alaska Panhandle. Argument was raging on public platforms and in the press of both countries. Laurier told the House of Commons on February 11, 1901: "The Americans have taken such an attitude and such a course, and we have also taken such an attitude, that it seems almost impossible to reconcile the two opposing views." He later warned that delay would make it difficult to recover Canadian land occupied by American settlers. The doubts proved prescient. In 1904, the sole British representative on a six-man arbitration panel sided with the three American panelists against two Canadians. Ottawa refused to sign the deal, but the boundary ran where Washington wanted it.

The total eclipse of Canada's claims in that contest heralded the kind of frustrations the country would encounter throughout the century in its fitful attempts to develop an independent foreign policy and even, at times, to pursue domestic policy free of ouside interference. Circumstances compelled Canadians to live and relive a quasi-colonial role as an economic, cultural, military and even political subsidiary. After graduating from British supervision in foreign and military affairs in the first quarter of the century, Canada perforce played junior partner to the United

IN THE SIX MONTHS of 1963 when their terms overlapped, President John F. Kennedy got along better with Prime Minister Lester Pearson—in the foreground—than he had with the prickly John Diefenbaker. Pearson later damaged relations with Lyndon B. Johnson by criticizing Washington's Vietnam War policy in a 1965 Philadelphia speech.

THROUGH MUCH OF THE FIRST HALF of the century, the need to develop farming in western Canada drove Ottawa's immigration policy. The inducement of free or cheap homesteads attracted many American settlers, such as the group that posed here at a stop in Rivers, Manitoba.

States as the mighty American neighbor developed into the dominant global power during the final half of the 1900s. If the transboundary relationship proved to be primarily benevolent and richly beneficial much of the time, political and economic realities assured the senior partner the upper hand in disagreements and the capacity to disturb the weaker neighbor without malice or even intent.

Pierre Trudeau, who ranks with John Diefenbaker among the most assertive of Canadian prime ministers on the international stage, memorably portrayed the nature of the association between the two countries in a speech to the U.S. National Press Club in Washington on March 25, 1969. "Living with you is in some ways like sleeping with an elephant," he said. "No matter how friendly and even-tempered the beast, one is affected by every twitch and grunt."

Laurier had said the Alaska boundary experience supported Canada's case for control of its foreign relations "so that if we ever have to deal with similar matters again we shall deal with them in our own way." But even Rudyard Kipling, an evangelist of the British Empire, foresaw a Canada free of British colonial restraints falling under American tutelage. The British author, during a visit to Canada, is quoted in *The Busy Man's Magazine* in November 1907: "One of the greatest questions you have to consider, I think, is the influence of the big country just south of you. Oh, it is not a question of allegiance to Great Britain; it is a question of nearness, common interests and common business."

Kipling was perceptive about the business angle. Transborder commerce came to drive diplomacy and much else in Canada as the century advanced. At the start of the 1900s, the United States accounted for 48 per cent of Canada's total trade; Britain was the partner in another 40 per cent of transactions. By mid-century, 66 per cent of trade was with the Americans, only 14 per cent with Britain. By the end of the century–after the 1959 U.S.-Canada Defence Production Sharing Program, the 1965 U.S.-Canada Auto Pact, the inauguration of the U.S.-Canada Free Trade Agreement in 1989 and the 1994 North American Free Trade Agreement–80 per cent of Canadian trade was carried on with the

United States. Britain's portion disappeared into the 7 per cent of commerce that Statistics Canada attributed to the whole European Union.

After experiencing disciplinary measures meted out by Washington in reaction to Canadian trade surpluses–a ceiling imposed on Ottawa's U.S. dollar holdings in the 1960s, the "Nixonomics" U.S. import curbs in the 1970s, periodic restrictions subsequently against an array of Canadian products, from fish to lumber–Canadian traders learned to do business the American way or no way. From time to time, Washington sought to make companies in Canada (and other countries) comply with American rules barring business with countries whose regimes found disfavor in Washington, notably Cuba. All that put crimps in Canada's political, cultural and even diplomatic freedom.

The historical irony is that Canada walked into its subservient role just as it was shedding the last vestiges of British colonialism following the Second World War and was carving out an independent role in the United Nations as a middle-power peacekeeper. But by joining NATO in 1949, Canada placed substantial elements of its land, sea and air forces under American command. When Newfoundland joined Canada in the same year, the new province brought with it U.S. military bases on what was now Canadian soil. American and jointly run radar stations were strung across arctic and subarctic Canada. In 1958, the two countries were even more tightly linked in NORAD, the North American Air Defence Command.

In the early 1960s, Prime Minister John Diefenbaker proved less accommodating to the Americans than his predecessors had been, earning him the enmity of President John F. Kennedy. During the Cuban Missile Crisis of 1962–a tense showdown between the United States and the Soviet Union over the presence of

ALTHOUGH CANADA HAD already constructed a defensive mid-Canada radar network on its own, Cold War pressures prompted the establishment of far-north Distant Early Warning radar stations manned by Americans on Canadian soil.

PUBLIC PROTESTS failed to deter Ottawa from permitting nuclear-armed American Bomarc missiles to be based in Ontario and Quebec in the early 1960s and American cruise missiles to be tested in Alberta in the 1980s.

CANADA'S DEFIANCE of American pressure to demonize Fidel Castro—expressed anew in April 1998 by Prime Minister Jean Chrétien's meeting with the Cuban president in Havana— was a rare deviation from Canada's usual pragmatic acceptance of its position as an economic dependency of the United States.

Soviet missiles in Cuba—Diefenbaker delayed responding to a U.S. request to place Canada's NORAD forces on alert. Washington was further enraged at Diefenbaker's hesitation over accepting in Canada American Bomarc missiles armed with nuclear warheads. That controversy split the cabinet and contributed to Diefenbaker's defeat in the 1963 election, which carried Lester Pearson into the prime minister's office and the nuclear-armed Bomarcs into Canada. The Bomarcs were phased out eight years later under Trudeau. His government attempted to pursue diplomatic and economic policies more independent of the United States, but did not manage it with great or lasting effect. In any case, Prime Minister Brian Mulroney zealously courted the Americans from the time he entered office in 1984 until he left in 1993. An election-campaign promise by his successor, Jean Chrétien, to renegotiate Mulroney's Free Trade Agreement turned out to be just a promise. But an American project promoting freedom of foreign ownership regardless of national boundaries—the proposed Multilateral Agreement on Invesment, or MAI—collapsed while being negotiated in 1998 under the weight of its own widespread unpopularity.

Over the years, the experience of an increasingly intrusive American presence in the life of the country became as much a permanent feature of Canada's identity as the perennial domestic quarrel between Quebec and The Rest. On matters of great debate to petty things, Canadians regarded their southern neighbors with ambivalence. For a start, there were conflicting complexes of superiority and inferiority. In tandem with envy of the American way, its energy and ingenuity, is a fear that the big neighbor will ultimately overwhelm whatever makes Canada distinct and simply absorb the country, even if by inadvertence. There are many, of course, who dispute that destiny's possibility. It is they who form a tenacious core within Canada's perennial resistance to the erosion of its own community values.

1921 Union Labor at the Cross-roads

Roland Lamberth – NOVEMBER 1, 1921 One of the greatest difficulties in the way of closer and more friendly relations between Capital and Labor in Canada is the fact that the great bulk of our organized labor has its membership in American unions. These unions are described as "international" organizations, but the term international is a misnomer. There is nothing international about them. The great majority of their membership is American, their central officers are all American, their funds are paid into, and are controlled from, American head offices, and these same American head offices control the policies of the Canadian minority members.

Such an arrangement is becoming more and more obnoxious to all thinking Canadians. American labor has no intimate knowledge of, or sympathy with, or part in, our natural schemes of nationhood and should have no voice in our industrial life.

I am not a "Red." I believe in the principle of collective bargaining. But the desired co-operation between Capital and Labor will never be realized to any appreciable degree until Canadian workers assert their right and determination to govern their own affairs.

THE VIOLENT mid-century usurping of the Canadian Seamen's Union—its members pictured picketing in 1949—by the American-led Seafarers' International Union conflicted with a prevailing pattern of secession of Canadian locals from American-based unions in the latter half of the century.

1948 If We Joined the U.S.A.

Arthur Lower – JUNE 15, 1948 If customs union led to annexation, Canada might gain a richer life at little cost–except her soul.

Every few years old Satan comes around to us Canadians, displaying the glittering rewards he has for a little easy submission: these invariably wear such labels as "Commercial Union," "Unrestricted Reciprocity" or, simply, "Reciprocity." We used to assume that Canada would be annexed and would disappear. As a result, we got used to throwing Satan out. We did this in two famous general elections, 1891 and 1911.

But it is usually forgotten that for 12 years, from 1854 to 1866, there actually was reciprocity. While the customs houses were not closed up, a wide measure of free trade existed between the two countries and Canada prospered as never before and seldom since.

The pros and cons are endless but, everything considered, Canada, I imagine, would gain materially from a continental economy. But we have never made our decisions on such a basis. We have always looked to the more indirect results, the political, constitutional, legal results, even to the cultural results.

Would this involve a currency union? At present, an American presented with a Canadian coin drops it as if it were a hornet. A currency union would at least avoid this–because there would no longer be Canadian coins. Would we miss them? I have yet to meet the Canadian who has any great objection to taking American money.

The real difficulty, of course, is the fear that commercial union would lead to political union. Disguise it as we may, it is the old bogey of annexation.

It is when we come to symbols of citizenship that we get into dangerous territory. Common heroes? Would we have to stop naming our schools "King George" or "Winston Churchill" and begin calling them "Abraham Lincoln"? There is no reason to think we would, though we would be more respected (especially in England) if we dug up a few heroes of our own and quit borrowing those of Great Britain. Would we have to rewrite our popular historical legends and, for example, depict the war of 1812 as an American triumph?

Would we have a common government? Would Ottawa cease? Anyone who has been in Edinburgh can see what an abandoned capital looks like–a city bravely trying to keep up appearances after the reality has fled. Abandoning Ottawa would be pretty hard to take.

AFTER OTTAWA CANCELLED development of Canada's highly advanced Avro Arrow jet interceptor in 1959 and then accepted American Bomarc missiles to defend Canadian skies, many Canadians lamented the resulting loss to Canadian innovation and industry along with the deepened dependency on the United States.

Provincial rights would be rearranged. The special and official place of the French language in Canada would disappear, though in Quebec there would be nothing to prevent its position remaining as strong as it is now.

The intangible advantages of union with the United States are of profound importance for the sensitive and the creative spirit, on whom the inadequacies of Canadian life weigh heavily. For such, merger in a real nation, with a genuine national spirit and tradition behind it, would flush out many of the shoddinesses of Canadian life—its imitativeness, its divided loyalties, its deep-rooted colonialism (and perhaps its parochialism), its hangdog submissiveness to the greater world beyond its borders.

Merger might get rid of our polite hypocrisies—the conceit that, somehow or other, we are more "refined," less "materialistic" than our neighbors. It might relieve our sorry subjection to another country's culture. At any rate, the American movies, such as they are, would be our movies and their popular heroines, ours. When we supplied an actress to Hollywood, she would not, as now, be lost to us. Nine-tenths of our people live, move and have their being in American popular culture anyway.

Our native culture—and it is only by its cultural creativeness that, in the long run, a country can justify its existence—is a tender plant. We have done magnificently in political and legal institutions. We have done creditably in medicine and science. We have done rather well in painting. We are beginning to make a literature of our own and even some music. We show some promise in the scholarly world. But in none of these fields, except the first, have we gone far as yet, and a distinctively Canadian culture and way of life has not yet decisively manifested itself.

A large part of the explanation for this lies in the mentality of our people. We oscillate between a touchy vanity and the servility that accompanies deep self-distrust; we have little deep pride. We sometimes seem afraid to allow anything really native to grow up: for generations, for example, the universities, admittedly among our most conservative institutions, have imported teaching talent from Great Britain and Europe, all too often turning aside their own promising young men and forcing them into exile in the United States. The result has been unreality and colonialism in one of the most vital areas, higher education.

We export our best, carelessly and casually, whether they be professors, writers or athletes, and then wonder why they so quickly forget us, out-Americaning the Americans in their scorn of the backward fringe of settlement "up north." Such attitudes do not make for a healthy community, one rejoicing in its strength, confident in its destiny.

It may be that to become American would be to have the gates of imagination and creativeness open up to us. It may be that the power, the vitality of American life would thaw this frozen northern ground and that in the end, whatever we have worthwhile about us would not be submerged, but would come out stronger, more valid than before. On the other hand, the frozen north might continue full of frozen northerners, still living on the thin gruel of unrealistic notions of superiority.

Intellectually, I am afraid the balance may not be difficult to strike, as the points I have enumerated go to suggest. But is cold logic the whole story? When you are faced with decision, there wells up within you that which renders rational argument difficult and you think of another unfortunate country whose course, so similar to our own, has been touched off by the English historian Trevelyan, in words with which this article must close:

"For two centuries and a half after Bannockburn, Scotland remained a desperately poor, savage, bloodstained land. Her democratic instincts had prevented her from being annexed to England, who would have given her wealth and civilization . . . . What then had Scotland gained by resisting? Nothing at all – except her soul, and whatsoever things might come in the end from preserving that."

1985 After the Eyes Stopped Smiling

Marci McDonald – APRIL 1, 1985   The scene had been meticulously orchestrated as the climax to a public relations triumph. Fresh from chorussing *When Irish Eyes Are Smiling* and signing a record number of bilateral accords, Ronald Reagan and

ONE THING ABOUT Brian Mulroney's performance as prime minister that rankled with many Canadians was his sometimes fawning courtship of the American president. Here, on March 17, 1985, in Quebec City, the prime minister and Mila Mulroney, with President Ronald Reagan and Nancy Reagan, perform "When Irish Eyes Are Smiling" at a gala.

Brian Mulroney wrapped up their "Shamrock Summit" talks on March 18 by strolling on the ramparts of Quebec City's Citadel. But as the President and the Prime Minister posed against the backdrop of a fortress raised to defend the country from American attack after the War of 1812, the symbolism proved fitting in a way that the summit organizers had not planned. Even before their 24-hour meeting had ended, critics had provoked a stormy Commons debate by accusing Mulroney of failing to protect Canadian interests. Charged New Democratic Party Leader Ed Broadbent: "It was a shamrock shuffle with President Reagan calling the tune and Prime Minister Mulroney eagerly dancing along."

Part of the controversy over whether Mulroney had traded away too much to demonstrate his "new partnership" with Washington arose from startling revelations of what the Reagan administration might be asking of Ottawa. U.S. Defense Secretary Caspar Weinberger said in a CTV interview that missile launchers to intercept Soviet cruise missiles and bombers could be stationed on Canadian soil in future. And Reagan himself, during a luncheon speech in which he expressed strong anti-Soviet sentiments, extended an offer to the Mulroney government to take part in research for his Strategic Defense Initiative—the space-based antimissile program popularly known as Star Wars.

To some critics, that confirmed charges that Ottawa had opened the way to participating in U.S. offensive military strategy.

Observed Colin Campbell, a Canadian professor of politics at Washington's Georgetown University: "It shows there is just incredible ignorance of the issues which raise the Canadian dander–a total lack of perception of the degree to which Canadians will not tolerate integration into the American defence grid." University of Toronto political scientist Stephen Clarkson said: "Singlehandedly, Mulroney has brought about a historic reversal of what had been a slow and difficult process of increasing Canadian autonomy."

1989 A Free Trade Anniversary

Tom Fennell – DECEMBER 18, 1989 Throughout the raucous seven-week federal election campaign in the fall of 1988, there was one dominant issue–the Canada-U.S. Free Trade Agreement. And one issue in that emotional campaign soared above all others: Would an agreement with the United States that removed all protective tariffs lead to widespread layoffs and ultimately shatter Canada's identity as a nation? On election day,

Nov. 28, the country voted decisively in favor of Brian Mulroney's Conservative government, saying yes to its free trade initiative. But now, nearly a year after the deal was implemented on Jan. 1, a *Maclean's*/Decima poll has found that the nation is deeply pessimistic about the accord, with 52 per cent of respondents saying that they believe the pact should not have been signed.

WHEN THE GOVERNMENT tried to preserve domestic periodicals against what Heritage Minister Sheila Copps and François de Gaspé Beaubien of the Canadian Magazine Publishers Association–pictured here in 1998–agreed had long been a menacing invasion of American publications, the U.S. threatened retaliation and Ottawa gave ground in a deal in May 1999.

The fear captured in the poll seemed all too close to reality as layoff notices went up in factories across Canada. Free trade critics were blaming the agreement for the loss of 33,000 jobs. In the same vein, the new free trade issues that will dominate 1990 and 1991– U.S. challenges to a range of Canadian programs, from federal subsidies for the arts to regional development funding–are just as emotionally and politically charged.

Despite the turbulent outlook for the FTA in its second year, the past year has seen one of its prime objectives fulfilled. Trade flows between the United States and Canada are up, and forecasts for 1990 growth in commerce between the two countries, the world's largest bilateral trading partnership, are bright. And many Canadian firms, such as clothing manufacturers, which analysts predicted would be killed by free trade, have forged successful survival strategies.

Still, free trade critics, led by the Canadian Labour Congress, claim that the accord is costing Canadian jobs as U.S. parent companies shut down or relocate subsidiaries to the United States. And they say that, despite the lowering of tariffs,

Canadian consumers have not benefited from free trade and, in fact, are crossing the border in record numbers to purchase cheaper U.S. products. They also charge that the sell-off of Canada's vital energy resources has increased alarmingly.

The U.S. commerce department, citing Canadian subsidies, imposed sweeping, punitive tariff action, or countervails, against a number of Canadian companies. FTA dispute-settlement panels have already failed their first major test–rulings on West Coast fishing rights that the two governments interpret differently.

AFTER THE TRADE AGREEMENTS of the 1980s and '90s, free-market apostles were pitted against advocates of the collective approach to commerce, as in a dispute between individualist grain farmers and these 1996 Regina supporters of the co-operative system run by the Canadian Wheat Board since 1935.

Ontario Premier David Peterson declared: "I have yet to be persuaded that free trade is in the national interest." Maude Barlow, chairman of the Council of Canadians, noted: "There were more foreign takeovers in the first six months of 1989 than in the three previous years put together." Trade Minister John Crosbie says that many of the council's concerns are "poppycock"–just as many factories have opened as have closed, he says, and it is impossible to determine the cause of every opening or closing.

1998 The Americanization of Emily

JANUARY 19, 1998 **M**ore than one million Canadians enthusiastically tuned in to the Jan. 4 premiere of the TV series *Emily of New Moon*–and none more so than Prince Edward Islanders. The new CBC drama, based on the novel by Island author Lucy Maud Montgomery, is set in the Prince Edward Island of the 1890s and was filmed there over the past two years. But for many viewers, interest turned to annoyance with a particular gaffe. During a schoolhouse scene, when Emily and her classmates sing an alphabet song, they pronounce the letter Z in the American style, "zee."

Not only is that pronunciation offensive to all patriotic Canadians, says Terry Pratt, a linguist at the University of Prince Edward Island in Charlottetown, but it is also an anachronism. The students of that era simply would never have heard "zee." Pratt, who is also editor of the 1997 *Gage Canadian Dictionary*, says he does not understand how the show's producers let the mistake slip in–unless they had the U.S. market in mind. "If that's true, they're pandering too much," he adds. "They should have 'zed' in there, and if Americans have to scratch their heads, that's OK."

An Attachment to the Arctic

The Burdens of the North Often Outweigh the Benefits

REPORTS from the Far North in *Maclean's* over the years usually wax ecstatic about the region's unique scenery and wildlife, its few but fascinating people, and simply the feel of being there, the spirit of the place. But the enthusiasm is hedged with doubts, even implicit guilt, about whether Canadians truly care enough about the North to warrant their stewardship of it. Explorer Vilhjalmur Stefansson remarked on the difficulty of attracting Canadians to his 1919 expedition. Thirty-five years later, Pierre Berton quotes a veteran Arctic hand lamenting that "young Canadians are damnably uninterested in the North."

But attachment to the North courses contrarily through the Canadian cultural bloodstream. Philosopher John Ralston Saul, pianist Glenn Gould and Prime Minister John Diefenbaker are three among many associated with the notion that not only are Canadians in the North, but the North is in Canadians. It is what philosopher Saul describes as the "animist integration" of place and person. Gould, who made programs for CBC Radio with a series of voices discussing northernness, highlighted what he called "The Idea of North." Diefenbaker, campaigning as prime minister in the 1958 federal election, struck such a popular chord with what he termed "the Vision" of northern development–"I see a new Canada," he

TEENAGER HANNAH UNIUQSARAQ posed with her baby son in 1998 outside Iqaluit High, where she was then a Grade 11 student, precisely one year before her Eastern Arctic home area became the new Territory of Nunavut, which started out with only about 25,000 people but boasted a higher birth rate than any other Canadian region.

THE PAINTING HERE ON show in an Apex Hill schoolroom outside Iqaluit in 1956 is a far cry from the magical-nature images in the Inuit paintings, prints and carvings that were then gaining popularity in southern Canada. This pupil-painter may have fallen under the influence of the townsite's new housing.

insisted, "a Canada of the North"—that his Progressive Conservative Party won the greatest parliamentary majority recorded in Canada.

And yet, apart from the harvests of fur, gold, oil, gas and diamonds north of the 60th parallel, and the riches of Inuit art, crafts and sculpture, the North has often seemed as much a burden as a benefit to southern Canadians, including successive federal governments. The Arctic, as in the words headlining Stefansson's reports in *Maclean's*, is a problem to be solved.

From the outset of the century, the new country of barely 5.3 million widely scattered people was faced with digesting almost unpopulated territories more than twice the combined size of its then seven provinces. The territories—bequests of the Hudson's Bay Company in 1870 and of Britain, which handed off the Arctic islands in 1880—ran from the North Pole to the 49th parallel on the Prairies and stretched from the Yukon to Labrador.

The federal government dealt away great swaths of the lands piecemeal to junior governments. To provide local administration during the Klondike Gold Rush of 1898, Ottawa had sliced the Yukon from a corner of the enormous Northwest Territories. On September 1, 1905, two southern swaths became Alberta and Saskatchewan. Three provinces to the east absorbed more of the territorial lands on May 15, 1912, the transfers more than doubling the areas of Manitoba and Quebec while expanding Ontario by over half. Eighty years later, as part of an Inuit land-claims settlement, a northern referendum led to a 1993 federal law to transform the entire eastern section of the Northwest Territories—one-fifth of Canada, with about 25,000 people, four out of five of them Inuit—into the new territory of Nunavut on April 1, 1999.

Despite those dispositions, there was much left to fret about throughout the century, as foreigners from time to time displayed altogether too keen an interest in the Canadian Arctic for Canada's liking. Stefansson, an American who had been born of Icelandic parents near Gimli, Manitoba, followed a familiar pattern in his early explorations of the Canadian North. He conducted them for moneyed American institutions. During the century's first decade, American and European navigators, whalers and cross-country explorers bustled around the Arctic. Norwegian Otto Sverdrup discovered several islands (1898-1902), claiming them for Norway. Roald Amundsen, also Norwegian, became the first to navigate the Northwest Passage in 1906.

On April 6, 1909, an expedition led by American explorer Robert Peary became the first to reach the North Pole. Twelve weeks later–on Dominion Day, 1909–Joseph-Elzéar Bernier, a Quebec mariner, sometime public servant and tireless advocate of Canada's rights in the Arctic, placed a plaque on Melville Island proclaiming sovereignty for Canada over the entire Arctic archipelago. Aboard his ship, *Arctic*, Bernier conducted a series of patrols of the eastern Arctic for the federal government. But foreign ventures testified to the fragility of Canada's grip on a hinterland that Stefansson accurately predicted would prove to hold both mineral wealth and strategic importance.

Before Stefansson set out in June 1913, on an epic journey of discovery that was to last five years (and produce a book-length *Maclean's* series in 1919), Canada reinforced its sovereignty claim over the High Arctic in a practical manner–by taking over sponsorship of his venture from the Americans. When the

THE SCULPTING ARTS *of Arctic Canadians are rooted in antiquity–the archeological evidence having turned up in the shape of stone, bone and ivory miniatures–and are as new as the creations of such Inuit carvers as Judas Ullulaq, pictured here with some of his soapstone work on a Vancouver visit in 1988.*

explorer asked Ottawa to top up his $75,000 expedition budget with a $5,000 grant, Prime Minister Robert Borden agreed. taking the view that it should be a Canadian expedition. As a result, previously unknown islands discovered by Stefansson were claimed for Canada and later named for Canadian leaders, including Borden, Arthur Meighen and Mackenzie King.

The federal government exerted sovereignty by investing sporadically in the Arctic's use, including exploration, resource development and tourism. In the 1920s, faced with challenges to Canada's claims by Denmark and other countries, Ottawa extended its practice of establishing remote RCMP sovereignty detachments. One such base, the two-man Bache Peninsula station set up in 1926 on Ellesmere Island, included postal and customs offices. Such operations seemed pointless in that uninhabited area, but they were recognized in international law as ways to prove sovereignty.

Decades after Roald Amundsen, the Mounties conquered the Northwest Passage, the dreamt-of Atlantic-Pacific link of yore, the navigational grail that for centuries lured the Cabots and Cartiers, the Frobishers and Hudsons into Canadian waters. From Vancouver on June 23, 1940, in a little RCMP patrol boat, the *St. Roch*, Staff-Sergeant H.A. Larsen and crew traversed the passage, arriving in Halifax on October 11, 1942, then retraced the trip to Vancouver two years later.

Soon afterward, the Cold War, aptly, generated interest in the North, albeit primarily among American military leaders and others mindful that the top of the world was a potential shortcut for bombers, missiles and nuclear-powered submarines. The United States, with Ottawa's permission, duly built its Distant Early Warning radar system—the DEW line—in the 1950s. It made little difference to life in the North after its construction along the Arctic Ocean shoreline, and it was rendered obsolete as time and circumstance eroded American-Soviet animosities.

By the end of the century, the Canadian presence in the Arctic was sparse and often transient. The 1996 census numbered 95,168 people in the Northwest Territories and the Yukon, together more than one-third of Canada's land. The North had registered a 25-per-cent gain in 10 years, but due to no great influx from Canada south. "The increase was the result of high fertility rates and declining mortality rates among the aboriginal population," reported the census takers.

Canada's claim to the entire Arctic Archipelago, including the waterways between the islands, was seriously undermined by the refusal of the United States to accept that claim. Washington thumbed its nose at the notion in 1985 by refusing to request Ottawa's permission to send the U.S. Coast Guard icebreaker *Polar Sea* through the Northwest Passage. That, said External Affairs Minister Joe Clark later, remained Canada's "one pure sovereignty issue of truly major proportions." The Canadian government of the day blustered about buying a fleet of 10 nuclear submarines, building a giant icebreaker and instituting warplane patrols to police the Arctic waters. But the plan and the panic, as so often on matters to do with the Canadian North, eventually melted away.

THE MACKENZIE RIVER DELTA town of Tuktoyaktuk—"Tuk" to its friends and acquaintances—is a crossroads community of the Western Arctic and the site of a Cold War radar station, visible here on the beach where Tuk children play.

1919 Solving the Problem of the Arctic

Vilhjalmur Stefansson – APRIL 1919 **T**o begin with, even among our tens of thousands of university graduates it is not easy to find a dozen or more men who combine the qualities of being young and of sound body, with an unexcitable temperament and an imagination that sees fascination in work which to other temperaments would be only hardship. The expedition being Canadian, we preferred Canadians in our choice, yet we were able to get in Canada only five out of a staff of thirteen. We turned next to other parts of the Empire, and secured three men from Scotland, one from Australia, and one from New Zealand. We had to look farther and take one man from France, one from Denmark, one from Norway, and two from the United States.

The winter of 1914-1915 found us on the coast of Alaska, 250 miles east of Point Barrow, with crippled resources and our entire task yet before us. The expedition had various subsidiary scientific aims, but its main purpose was exploration of as much as possible of that great unknown area which lies between Alaska and the Pole. This area was estimated by some to be as low as 500,000 square miles, but others, among them myself, have estimated it at over a million.

VILHJALMUR STEFANSSON (1879-1962), the Manitoba-born son of Icelandic parents, devoted the better part of the years from 1906 to 1918 to three exploratory journeys in the Canadian Arctic and expended almost as much energy extolling the North as a great place to live and work.

We had to make journeys north from Alaska comparable in mileage to, or even exceeding journeys previously made by sledge on any part of the polar sea. A stock-taking of our resources showed that we had available for our proposed journeys over the frozen sea two good sledges and two poor ones.

One of the curious errors about the North that are prevalent among those few who have any ideas about the North at all is that cold is the chief enemy. Cold is our best friend. For that reason, February is a better month than March for sledge travel, and January would be as good as February were it not for the fact that it is then too dark for safe working among broken ice, where water-holes are a danger everywhere. In April, when the temperature seldom goes lower than 30 degrees [Fahrenheit] below zero for a night, if a gale breaks up the ice, as often happens, it takes several days for the frost to form ice over the lanes, which are impassable moats while they remain unfrozen.

It was therefore heart-breaking to lose by delays in outfitting, as it proved, the whole month of March. On the 1st of April we at length had a moderate frost and were able to travel. Ten days later our party of six had made fifty miles from shore through the worst going of the whole trip.

It was known at our shore base that we had had forty days' provisions and when that forty days became eighty days, and then one hundred and twenty days, every one agreed that we had perished. In the Canadian Parliament in April, 1915, the Minister of Naval Service, the Hon. J.D. Hazen, was sorry to say that there was no hope of our being alive. On the basis of this, a great many editors in various parts of the world published kindly and (as is often the case with the dead) flattering obituaries that are now the most interesting section of my scrapbook.

While these opinions were growing, we were travelling successfully and comfortably northward, finding abundant food and fuel in these theoretically inhospitable regions, and securing them by methods which require only a moderate application of common sense, and that reasonable absence of ill luck which permits a careful man to cross Fifth Avenue with safety after the traffic policemen have gone home.

1929 Conquest at World's End

Harwood Steele – FEBRUARY 1, 1929 The loneliest and most northerly human habitation on earth is occupied by the Royal Canadian Mounted Police. It is also the most northerly and loneliest police detachment, customs house and post office. One of the most dramatic episodes in the Force's history is found in the narrative of how this

detachment came to be established, despite obstacle after obstacle, failure after failure, at the extreme limit of reliable sea communication, the World's End of Northern navigators on Bache Peninsula, Ellesmere Island, within eleven degrees of the Pole.

The trail to Bache Peninsula begins over 30 years ago, when the Mounted Police, always a frontier corps, first drew up its thin red line to assail the Last of All Great Frontiers, beyond which lay the vast and terrible mystery of the Polar zone, the Empire of Tomorrow. The trumpets sounded the onset in 1894, when Canada sent a small detachment into the Yukon. After a time, they boldly announced the extent of the Arctic dominion they meant to hold for Canada. Embracing the whole Canadian Arctic Archipelago–a land area more than the combined area of Alberta and Saskatchewan. Of this territory with all its boundless fur and mineral wealth, they said, "There! That's ours!"

Till detachments dominated the entire Far North and, above everything, till a detachment guarded the extreme limit of reliable sea communication, Canada's dominion over the Arctic was not complete nor was her rule secure.

Two men deserve more credit than anyone else for the successful establishment of the world's most northerly detachment, Inspector C.E. Wilcox and Inspector (then Staff-Sergeant) A.H. Joy. After

FOR MOST OF THE 20th century, the Mounties stood on guard against acquisitive aliens in the Canadian Arctic. Their reward at the creation of Nunavut: the right while in dress uniform—as here in Iqaluit at Nunavut's birth—to wear spiffy kamiks, the traditional Inuit sealskin or caribou hide footwear.

two fruitless attempts to establish a base on northern Ellesmere Island, the old vessel (the 600-ton *Arctic*) left Quebec harbor in the summer of 1924, fully equipped for another try. On August 11, Smith Sound was found free of ice. But Bache Peninsula, once more, was out of reach. The tiny harbor of Fram Havn offered itself as substitute. Erect a detachment there and Bache Peninsula would be only fifteen miles away.

They painted a board in Eskimo and English, "Kane Basin Detachment, Royal Canadian Mounted Police," and hung it up over that unspeakably lonely little building, at Latitude 78.46 N., Longitude 74.56 W., the World's End, for the information of passers-by. They raised the Union Jack. This done, they went south to return to civilization on leave until they had another chance–next year.

Except this time it was 1926. Out of St. John's, Newfoundland, swept a new champion–the *Beothic*, 2,700 tons, no less, a steel 10-knotter, under Captain E. Falk, well-known in the sealing profession. Off Ellesmere, no sooner had the ship turned her back on Bache Peninsula than she was caught in a jam which cracked her open, and from which she escaped only by the use of explosives. But by that time all was well. Perseverance and determination had conquered. On August 6, 1926, Inspector Wilcox and Staff-Sergeant Joy stood on Bache Peninsula.

Hear what Inspector Wilcox says of the site, Latitude 79.04 N., Longitude 76.18 W., which, at long last, on August 9, 1926, witnessed the opening of the world's most northerly police detachment: "This is by far the most pleasant and attractive place in the Eastern Arctic."

1954 The Mysterious North

Pierre Berton – November 15, 1954 **I** am writing these opening words on the deck of a stubby little tugboat bobbing along down the great water highway of the Mackenzie River system on its sixteen-day journey from northern Alberta to Aklavik on the Arctic delta. It is a good place to begin a report on the North–that vague, unspecific term we Canadians apply to more than half our country–for the North lies all around me. Behind is the Athabaska country: tarsands that won't give up their oil, salt too expensive to mine and the biggest uranium production on the continent. To the west lie the fierce limestone crags of the South Nahanni valley where six companies are seeking oil, and beyond that the Yukon River, which in the next generation will yield up twice as much power as the St. Lawrence Seaway. Over to the east, on the rim of the great Pre-Cambrian shield, sits the gold country of Yellowknife, and beyond that the tundra stretches off five hundred miles to Hudson Bay. And to the north the broad cold Mackenzie rolls endlessly on, a thousand miles or more to the Arctic sea. Here is the heart of the North–a land empty of road and rail and this enormous watercourse draining one fifth of Canada is its only highway. Yellowknife came down this river. So did Port Radium and Norman Wells. The new town of Aklavik is coming down it now– 265,000 board feet of it on the barge up ahead.

The name of our tug has the ring of the North. She is the *Radium Yellowknife* and the cargo aboard her five barges reads like a northern roll call: sulphur for the leaching plant at Port Radium, whisky for the oilmen at Norman Wells, a tractor for

PHOTOGRAPHER FRED BRUEMMER caught this happy-looking Arctic lineup in apparent tug-of-war mode.

the reindeer station on the delta, speedboats for the Mounties at Arctic Red, fertilizer for the Oblate's potato patch at Good Hope, and—though this is only August—a crate of Christmas parcels for the Gilbey family, who run the experimental farm at Simpson.

No one who has not seen it can fully comprehend the size and emptiness of this country. The Yukon and Northwest Territories encompass a million and a half square miles and less than one per cent of Canada's population. Only five years ago an air-force flyer discovered three new islands in Hudson Bay, one twice the size of Prince Edward Island. Where else in the world could a river, 190 miles long, be lost for almost a century? This happened to the Hornaday, which flows into the Arctic north of Great Bear Lake. A missionary reported it in 1868. It wasn't seen again until 1948.

All through the Canadian North there is unmapped land still waiting to feel the white man's moccasins. The idea tantalizes everybody but Canadians. The Roman Catholic missionaries are largely French. The Protestants are largely English. The Hudson's Bay clerks are Scottish. The tourists are nearly all Americans. "Young Canadians are damnably uninterested in the North," says Lt.-Col. Pat Baird, the eagle-faced English explorer who has just retired as head of the Arctic Institute, a society dedicated to exploring the North. Few apply for Institute's grants for northern research. Ninety percent of these go to Englishmen and Americans. Our neglect of the North, besides bequeathing us a native problem that will take generations to untangle, has on occasions all but cost us sovereignty of the Arctic.

THE 1950s-VINTAGE single-engined de Havilland Otter pictured here in 1981 and its two-engined successor, the Twin Otter (1965)—products of Toronto-based de Havilland Aircraft of Canada—served for decades as the airborne workhorses of the Canadian North and in many other parts of the world.

Now once again a Canadian prime minister has talked about "the active occupation and exercise of our sovereignty right up to the Pole." The result is the new Department of Northern Affairs, a new deal for the North and a slowly growing interest among Canadians in the unknown frontier across the top of the world.

This western North is the land of big rivers, thick forests, airports, gold mines, tugboats, prospectors and mining and fur towns. Almost all the white population of the Canadian North lives in the western half of it. All the great mineral discoveries, except the nickel of Rankin Inlet and the iron of Labrador, have been made here. If the North has a banana belt, this is it.

But on the other side of Canada, lies another, entirely different north. The vast wastes of Keewatin and Franklin stretch off to the east and northeast, still largely unmapped and unpopulated, devoid of any hope of agriculture and forestry, scarcely scratched by the prospector's pick. Except for tiny isolated communities, this eastern land in the Hudson Bay area is much as it was in the days before the white man.

These are lands that still know starvation and tragedy. On Boothia Peninsula not long go, an Eskimo youth named Beriykoot complied with custom by garroting his 45-year-old mother at her own request. She was in an advanced state of TB. On Foxe Basin, in the winter of 1948, a man and two boys starved to death slowly and painfully while searching for a meat cache. The wife and daughter survived by eating the cadavers.

Flying over the grey twilight land that skirts Henry Hudson's huge inland sea, a ragged monochrome of grey-green lichen, broken by patches of black stunted spruce and thousands of round little ponds runs back from the shore line for three hundred miles, flat and uninspiring.

As we flew northwest, summer vanished and the lakes below us were frozen white. Below us lay Churchill, the oldest civilized settlement in the north, stark as the rock on which it is built. Churchill was founded three centuries ago by Jens Munk, the son of a Danish nobleman. Sixty of his shipmates died there of scurvy, exposure, frostbite and gangrene.

Northeast across the bleak bay, Baffin Island loomed out of the horizon, an enormous expanse of jagged mountains and swirling glaciers. Ours was only the sixth aircraft to land at Pond Inlet. Soon they were upon us, a hundred or so Eskimos and as many animals. They came racing up on long wooden sleighs jammed with parka-clad passengers of all sizes and shapes, each grinning broadly, and pulled by a dozen or so dogs fanning out in a wide arc, their lines inexorably tangled and confused. These eastern Arctic Eskimos are quite different from their western Arctic cousins. They live in snowhouses, eating meat raw or cooked over a blubber lamp, and they seem to smile almost all the time, possibly because they have had so little contact with the white man.

It is only the Eskimo that keeps any whites in settlements like Pond. The Hudson's Bay is here to trade for fox furs. The police are not here to keep law and order for it is a crimeless community. Their tasks consist chiefly of distributing family allowances. These aren't given in cash but in vouchers for certain staples that can be bought at the trading post. In fact there is little or no cash at Pond Inlet. Life runs on the ancient barter system.

In the winter the police go on thousand-mile patrols for fifty days at a time. They live in snowhouses each night but keep on paying board and lodging to the government. Like everybody else in the north they are here by choice and the life on this treeless, lonely beach, visited once a year by a supply ship and occasionally by an aircraft, fascinates them. Constable Doug Moodie, a neat good-looking Montrealer, had just finished his three-year tour at Pond when I arrived and had promptly signed up for three years more.

Every desert has its oasis, and the Thelon country is the oasis of the barrens. Out of the harsh dry tundra a deep-green valley suddenly appears. Here two rivers meet, the Thelon and the Hanbury, and here are fat clumps of spruce, wide grassy meadows, green copses of willows, all growing on the bottom of an ancient inland fresh-water sea. The Thelon Game Sanctuary has the toughest restrictive laws in the world. No one is allowed within its 15,000 square miles without a permit, and permits are rare. Since its establishment in 1926 until recently, hardly a soul ventured here. Now the door has opened a crack and a few scientific parties have gained access. The Thelon is a scientific oddity, unique in the world, a land where tundra and tree line merge. Here robins nest alongside Lapland larkspurs and marten, and wolverine mingle with musk ox, bear and caribou. Fish lie thick in the waters.

If the North has a soul, it is here in this empty land which, harsh though it is, has a beauty that no man who has not lived here a lifetime can really understand. But an eloquent old Indian put it into words one day when talking with an Oblate priest. "My father," the old man said, "you have told me of the beauties of heaven. Tell me one thing more. Is it more beautiful than the country of the musk ox in summertime, where the mists roll over the hills and the waters are very blue and the loons cry? That is beautiful and if heaven is still more beautiful, then I will be content to rest there until I am very old."

1969 The 'Black Gold' Rush of '69

Pat Carney – NOVEMBER 1969 **R**ea Point is a collection of red shacks shimmering like a mirage on Melville's frozen sand. The north coast of the Canadian mainland is 400 miles to the south, the North Pole only 800 miles away. In summer the island is a brown desert of waddies and eroding ridges and the polar sunshine shivers on the offshore pack-ice. In winter the ice fog creeps across the snow crust and the cold spreads through your clothes like a blue dye. They shot a wolf near Rea Point not long ago. It froze rigid with the snarl still on its face.

Question: Since this glacial wilderness is clearly unfit for man or beast, why bother with it?

Answer: Oil. This is the major supply centre for the greatest oil search Canada has ever known. Panarctic Oil Limited is gambling between $35 million and $45 million that the western hemisphere's largest untapped oil basin lies beneath these islands. In Arctic exploration, no other country—not even Russia—has attempted anything so bold. There has been nothing like it in the Canadian experience since the railway opened the West. This is Canada's moon shot.

1984 A Brutal Passage Yields to Tourists

David Lees – SEPTEMBER 24, 1984 **T**he cape, located 900 km northwest of Fairbanks, Alaska, on the northwestern tip of the continent, marked the end of the MS *Lindblad Explorer*'s journey through the twisting ice-clogged straits of the Northwest Passage and the beginning of its open-ocean cruising. It was the first time a cruise ship had ever attempted the notorious passage. For the ship's 96 passengers, who had paid from $16,000 to $22,000 to make the voyage, the sight of the promontory brought the thrill of making history. And for the owners of the vessel, New York-based Salen Lindblad Cruising Inc., and its insurers, it meant that

TO EXPANDING BANDS of adventurous tourists in the last quarter of the century, the Canadian Arctic's attraction lay in such situations as the pictured encounter between touring humans and an oblivious ice-behemoth of the North.

they would not have to honor a guarantee to refund 40 per cent of the passengers' fares in the event of an unsuccessful passage. The journey began in St. John's on Aug. 20 and will end on Sept. 29 at Yokohama, Japan.

Capt. Hasse Nilsson insisted that his double-hulled ship, at 2,350 tons and 250 feet long, was never in any real danger. She was built for northern waters but cannot break ice by herself and once the Canadian Coast Guard icebreaker *Camsell*, which kept a watchful eye during the voyage, had to clear the way.

The arrival of the *Explorer* looming out of the ice caused a stir in the three small communities it visited along its way. On Sept. 1 the ship stopped in Spence Bay, N.W.T., and local RCMP constables rushed to don their scarlet dress uniforms to greet the passengers as they disembarked. The grateful passengers responded by spending $44,000 in the local Hudson's Bay store and Paleajook Eskimo Co-op within four hours. At Gjoa Haven the Inuit demonstrated Arctic games and dances, and most of the community of 640 turned out for a feast of Arctic char and caribou at the local co-op hotel. The visitors from the south again depleted the stock of the local craft store, spending almost $45,000 on duffel mitts and socks, and appliquéd wall hangings with Inuit motifs. Then they wandered through the community buying soapstone carvings from the local craftsmen. At Cambridge Bay the passengers took time for fishing and a bus tour to a nearby DEW Line station before spending another $10,000 on local crafts.

Accompanying the voyage as icemaster was Thomas Pullen, 66, a veteran of several northern voyages. Before retiring in 1965, Pullen, a retired veteran of 30 years in the Royal Canadian Navy, served as Canada's official representative on the American ice-breaking oil tanker Manhattan during its Northwest Passage sailing in 1969. Pullen warned that changing ice conditions mean the route can never be used for regular excursions. "If you assume you are going to be able to make the crossing year after year," he said, "you are just asking for trouble. You are insulting the Arctic."

1987 An Epic Arctic Journey

Bruce Wallace – MAY 11, 1987 **P**itched alongside a sheltering cliff, the tiny campsite on the frozen sea of Maxwell Bay in the Canadian Arctic was only a speck in the seemingly endless expanse of polar ice. Inside a pair of tents on the southern edge of Devon Island, five Canadian adventurers paused at the halfway mark of an 1,800-mile northern trek to await the arrival of a Twin Otter aircraft with seal meat for their 44 sled dogs. The purpose of the gruelling journey: to retrace the route followed by an Inuit shaman, Qitdlarssuaq–Qitdlak the Great in the Inuktitut tongue–who led the last recorded migration of Baffin Island Inuit to the northern coast of Greenland 125 years ago. The group planned to complete in three months a dogsled journey that took Qitdlak six years.

WHILE MOUNTIES MAINTAINED Arctic outposts on land, a crew of RCMP colleagues conquered the Northwest Passage in the little patrol boat St. Roch—*now on permanent exhibition at the Vancouver Maritime Museum—which journeyed from Vancouver to Halifax in 1942, then back west in 1944.*

The campsite provided a respite from the -20 degrees C temperatures and the physical strain of driving dogsleds across heavily ridged ice. But the delay in late April was still in some ways an unwelcome interruption. With each passing day, the breakup of winter ice in Smith Sound, separating Canada from Greenland, potentially forces the group ever farther north to seek solid sea ice for a safe crossing.

For expedition organizer Renée Wissink, 28, and his four companions, the dangers of the trek were obscured by its challenge and symbolic value. Setting out from Igloolik on March 6, the group arrived at the beginning of May in Grise Fiord, at the southern end of Ellesmere Island, Canada's northernmost Inuit community. They travelled at night—the night sky in spring is almost as bright as in the daytime, but the snow underfoot is firmer. "It is also a more beautiful time to travel because of the changing light," said Ottawa photographer Michael Beedell, 30, a member of the expedition.

The team is rounded out by three Inuit residents of Igloolilk—Theo Ikummaq, 32, a former arctic wildlife officer and a great-great-great-nephew of Qitdlak; Paul Apak, 32, another descendant and an Inuit Broadcasting Corp. TV cameraman who is recording the journey on videotape, and Mike Immaroitok, 18, a nephew of Ikummaq's and a dog driver.

By recreating Qitdlak's epic journey, the expedition members hoped to draw attention to the achievement of a little-known northern pathfinder and also to

THE INUIT MOTHER AND child and the tea kettle is one of the Far North compositions of peripatetic photographer Fred Bruemmer, who has gained worldwide fame for his Arctic pictures.

reinforce Canadian sovereignty, underlining the fact that northern routes across the frozen sea have been travelled for centuries. That supports Canada's contention that the arctic waterways—frozen and used like land for much of the year—should have special territorial status in international law. "We are not rich kids out for a lark," said Wissink, a former high school social sciences teacher from St. Thomas, Ont., who fell

in love with the Arctic from afar as a child and became a schoolteacher, first in Frobisher Bay and then in Igloolik. Now he is a tour outfitter in Igloolik. "We are explorers dedicated to traditional ways of travel in the Arctic who are proud to be Canadians and believe in asserting a Canadian presence up here."

Since August 1985, when the U.S. Coast Guard icebreaker *Polar Sea* sailed the Northwest Passage without Canada's permission, Ottawa has sought to strengthen its claim to sovereignty over the region. Faced with suspected incursions by Soviet and U.S. nuclear submarines in arctic waters, Prime Minister Brian Mulroney's government now is considering the acquisition of as many as 10 nuclear-powered submarines for the navy.

Qitdlak's journey from the Canadian Arctic to Greenland lives in oral legend. In one tradition, a bloody intertribal feud near Pond Inlet on northern Baffin Island in the middle 1850s forced Qitdlak to flee. Another theory: as a shaman, a religious leader, he had brought about deaths and had to leave. He rallied 38 followers, but after two years of hardship 24 turned back. In the early 1860s, Qitdlak led the rest across Smith Sound to Greenland. There, near Etah, they met hunters from a tribe of Polar Inuit. After six years there, Qitdlak decided to return home, set out with followers but died during the first winter. The survivors returned to Greenland.

Qitdlak's descendant Ikummaq claims to feel no special spiritual affinity with his ancestor. But he is equipped to pass on to younger Inuit some of the skills that are fading from his people's cultural memory. As a boy of 11, he left his native Igloolik to live in a wilderness encampment where his brother Emile's and two other families survived by hunting and fishing. Ikummaq learned how to build igloos and travel by dogsled. But he says he is worried that many young Inuit may not be interested. "In the last 30 years," he said, "we have gone from the Stone Age to the middle ages to the space age. Now the younger people are introduced to the school system at an early age. That is good, but they don't have a feel for the culture that my generation does. And there are going to be fewer and fewer young people who care. That is how cultures are lost."

Still, Ikummaq and the other trekkers say they hope that their expedition may remind Canadians of the importance of their northern heritage. One month into their journey, expedition members symbolically planted a Canadian flag in the heavily ridged ice of Lancaster Sound, at the eastern entrance to the disputed Northwest Passage. Said Wissink: "It was our way of saying that this is a pretty important piece of real estate, and we have to stand up for it."

SUCH NORTHERN INSTITUTIONS as the high school in Iqaluit have played a key role in the urbanization of the Arctic by congregating students and families from a wide area. The federal government aimed to have aboriginal people making up half the teaching staffs in the northern territories by the year 2000.

1998 Letter from Iqaluit

Brian Bergman – February 19, 1998 Inside Iqaluit's Navigator Inn, delegates to a northern telecommunications conference are taking a spin on the information highway. The room is buzzing with talk of accessing the Internet, videoconferencing and otherwise "wiring" the Arctic. Outside it is -30. C, with a bracing wind that makes it feel more like -50.C, and the sun is already setting even though it's only 3 p.m. The climate is a constant reminder–like the jet-black ravens circling overhead and the caribou roaming the cliffs above town–of the harsh, beautiful land surrounding this modern community of 4,000 on the southern tip of Baffin Island.

And while the contrasts may seem jarring to an outsider–the primordial Arctic meeting the global village–to people like Iqaluit Mayor Joe Kunuk, who participated in the daylong high-tech conference, it is all part of an inexorable march to the future. "The leap we've made from hunting and gathering to the life we have now, it's amazing," says the 36-year-old Kunuk. "The key is that we've kept adapting."

Adapting. It's a buzzword among the Inuit, and for good reason. When the whalers came, the Inuit joined their crews; when the missionaries arrived, they adopted their religion; and when, over the past four decades, the government bureaucrats moved in, the Inuit abandoned their hunting posts for tiny Arctic settlements like Iqaluit and began to live to the rhythms of the wage economy. Now, they are preparing to make perhaps their biggest leap yet: the establishment, on April 1, 1999, of the new Inuit-dominated territory of Nunavut ("our land" in Inuktitut), almost one million square miles of tundra and sea ice–roughly a fifth of Canada's landmass–carved out of the Northwest Territories. At the centre of the action is Iqaluit, which in an Arctic-wide plebiscite in December was chosen by a 60-40 margin over Rankin Inlet to become the new territory's capital.

Until recently, Iqaluit was known to the outside world (if known at all) as Frobisher Bay, named for the British explorer Sir Martin Frobisher, who landed in the area in 1576 mistakenly thinking he had discovered the Northwest Passage to the Orient. Among Frobisher's exploits was the abduction of several Inuit, whom he took to England to parade before the Royal Family–and then left to die of disease. Unimpressed by the legacy, the town opted in 1987 to adopt the community's traditional Inuit name, which means "many fish." For southern-based journalists, the name change proved problematic: following the norms of English grammar, they tended to insert an extra "u" and spell it "Iqualuit." That is a source of some consternation among residents since, in that spelling, the town's name is transformed into a vulgar term that roughly translates as "big rear end."

The choice of Iqaluit as capital of Nunavut–which brings prestige but the prospect of only about 100 new government jobs–was not without its critics. In northern circles, Iqaluit has long had a reputation as a hard-drinking, sometimes violent, town. Linked to Montreal, 1,205 air miles to the south, by daily jet flights, and to the smaller Baffin Island communities through a number of regional carriers, the town is a distribution point not only for food and other staples, but also for smuggled booze and drugs. And compared with the smaller settlements, where alcohol is tightly restricted, the drinks flow fast in Iqaluit's bars and licensed restaurants.

That reputation, the cold and its high costs aside, Iqaluit is a place that many transplanted Canadians are happy to call home. They contribute to the ethnic diversity of Iqaluit, the Arctic's least Inuit place–60 per cent of the population, compared with 85 per cent in Nunavut as a whole. In some ways, it is also the most Canadian. A meeting place for the races and cultures, Iqaluit has attracted Inuit from across the Arctic, as well as Quebec francophones, Newfoundlanders and expatriate Scots. And the town has a nationalist streak. On the day that 150,000 people rallied last October in Montreal to plead with Quebecers to stay in Canada, more than 100 people in Iqaluit braved Arctic winds for a similar pro-unity rally, and to sing *O Canada* in English, French and Inuktitut.

From Torments to Triumphs

The Century Produced Mixed Results for Canada's Native Peoples

M ANY of the citizens of Canada's First Nations have proved themselves creatively constructive in the arts, business, sports and war, the professions and politics—their numbers too great to list beyond a sampling: actors Graham Greene and Tantoo Cardinal; architect Douglas Cardinal and entrepreneur Walter Twinn; painter Roy Henry Vickers and sculptor Bill Reid; musician-conductor Kim Bell and playwright Tomson Highway; political activists and leaders Matthew Coon Come, George Erasmus, Phil Fontaine, Elijah Harper, Kahn-Tineta Horn and Mary Two-Axe.

The underside of the aboriginal experience—the maltreatment of Canada's first citizens, the broken promises, breached treaties and rebuffed rights—is partly told in the federal statistics collected during the 1980s and charted in *Maclean's*, October 8, 1990. For status Indians, compared with the total population, average adult yearly income is barely over half as much; the proportion of adults with more than a Grade 9 education is only three-quarters as great; ten times as many homes have more than one person per room; and the infant mortality and suicide rates are each more than double, while the violent-death rate is almost triple.

WHEN SOLDIERS ADVANCED on the Kanesatake reserve at Oka, Quebec, on September 1, 1990, the staredown between the young Canadian Armed Forces infantry man and the masked member of the Mohawk Warriors Society became a symbol of the Mohawks' defiance of governmental authority.

THE POTLATCH—the ceremonial giving away or destruction of goods and chattels to establish prestige and assert power—was outlawed by the federal government from 1884 to 1951. Daniel Cranmer held the last big potlatch in 1921 at Alert Bay, British Columbia, and federal agents afterwards seized the goods given away.

Throughout the century, people of the First Nations knew both abuse and applause, condescension and celebration. In the early years, common wisdom held that assimilation to white ways was the solution to "the Indian problem." To that end, Ottawa established farming settlements on reserves and organized the removal of aboriginal children from their homes to attend Christian residential schools. There, as it became widely public only late in the century with a series of Indian lawsuits against churches and the federal government, the pupils were often abused physically, mentally and sexually. Native women who married non-natives lost their Indian status, as did their children. The official discrimination persisted until 1983, when the first ministers of Canada and the provinces jointly declared that aboriginal rights are guaranteed equally to both sexes under the Constitution.

By that time, an activist aboriginal leadership was in the thick of a campaign to regain rights to elements of self-government and to the ownership of vast

DOUGLAS CARDINAL, the internationally acclaimed architect born to a half-Blackfoot father in Red Deer, Alberta, built his fame into the design of St. Mary's Church at Red Deer, the Edmonton Space Sciences Centre and the Canadian Museum of Civilization in Hull, Quebec, among other structures.

BRITISH COLUMBIA'S Bill Reid, in expressing the Haida imagination inherited from his mother through both finely wrought jewelry and massive sculptures, is widely viewed as a primary contributor to the revitalization of aboriginal Canadian art during the last several decades of the century.

regions never ceded to Canada. Although much of Central Canada and the Prairies had been transferred to the Crown for cash and the promise of future social aid under 11 treaties negotiated between 1871 and 1921, most of the rest of the land had never been legally yielded. The year 1973 marked a turning point. Following a strong minority opinion in the Supreme Court of Canada favoring a land claim by the Nisga'a people of British Columbia, and under pressure from native leaders and supportive arguments in Parliament, the government of Pierre Trudeau abandoned a policy of assimilation that would have erased special rights for Indians. Jean Chrétien, then Indian Affairs minister, established an Office of Native Claims to resolve land disputes between aboriginal bands and governments. Within a decade, compensation settlements had been agreed with the Quebec Cree and Inuit in the James Bay region and the Inuvialuit along the Beaufort Sea in the Northwest Territories. But progress elsewhere was snail-like, notably in British Columbia, home to one in five of Canada's Indians (the 1996 census showed about 113,000 of the total 550,000 Canadian Indians of Canada living in the westernmost province). Appropriately, the breakthrough in British Columbia was a federal-provincial compensation agreement in the summer of 1998 with the Nisga'a, the people who had helped get things moving with their court case in Ottawa 25 years earlier.

1913 The Indian is Not Dying Out

John MacCormac – MAY 1913 **"T**he Indian problem? Yes, that will solve itself in a few years, you know. The Indian is dying out." How many Canadians, one wonders, would so express themselves in regard to the first citizens of this North American continent? Assuredly a large percentage, for certainly few questions have been made the subject of so much vague misinformation as the problem presented by the aboriginal races of Canada and the United States. Popular opinion places the Indian in the same category as the great auk, and it is prone to link him with the fast vanishing buffalo–to whose extermination, by the way, he himself has largely contributed–but popular opinion is wrong. Any Canadian Indian department official would proclaim it so.

True, he would admit, the Indian has passed through a period of exhaustion consequent upon the first contact with civilization, but this once behind him, he either remains stable or begins to increase and multiply again. How to help him to do so is one of the things the governments of two great nations are yearly spending millions on. What is to become of him ultimately is another question.

AFTER CONFEDERATION, CANADIAN Indian agents encouraged the native people to give up their traditional way of life and rely on agriculture for subsistence. By the 1920s, when this photo was taken on a reserve in the West, conditions had improved considerably. However, the Depression of the 1930s would force many native people to leave the land for the cities.

The red man's health must be preserved, the stamina of the race in general improved, through education he must be brought to a higher mental level, and Christianity must benefit him ethically.

Canada's system has always kept the red man in tutelage to a certain degree, but it has finally succeeded in inspiring him with a wholesome respect for civilization, and for the white man's intentions toward him.

The basis of the Canadian system, established by law as far back into history as the 17th century, has been that no Indian should be dispossessed without his consent. You cannot in Canada today buy a foot of land from an Indian without a legal surrender from the Crown and from the Indian himself. The result of this policy has been evident. The Riel Rebellion has been Canada's only serious trouble with the Indians, and even then only the Crees went out while the rest of the red men turned a deaf ear to the call of blood and remained loyal.

The Indian is not dying out. His recuperative force is remarkable. The total Indian population of this country is 103,661 Indians, with some 4,600 Eskimos, British Columbia boasting the greatest number and Ontario following close.

Public opinion has never rated the Indian very high as a producer, unless it be of

GREY OWL, AN ENGLISH IMMIGRANT NAMED Archibald Belaney without a drop of the Apache blood he claimed to possess from mixed parentage, waged an influential campaign through books, lectures and lessons for schoolchildren—as shown here—promoting the preservation of nature.

THE WIDE POPULARITY early in the century of Pauline Johnson's verse and its invocation of her Mohawk heritage—she was the child of a chief at Brantford, Ontario—did not long outlast her death in 1913, as public recitation faded out of practice.

furs. It comes rather as a surprise then, to learn on glancing over the statistics covering the total production of the Indian population of Canada during the last year, that their total amount is $1,460,462.46, an increase over the preceding year of $85,647.46. The whole industry is the direct result of the promotion of farming and the assistance which has been given to ex-pupils of boarding and industrial schools to establish themselves on the soil immediately after graduation.

The difficulty is perhaps not so much in changing the Indian as in keeping him changed. The aboriginal character is always more or less in a condition of flux, and ever ready to flow back into the old mold. Lacking sympathy from the better class of white people, they find association with the lowest type, and then begins the easy journey along the downward path of degradation. Laws to the contrary, someone may always be found who will sell liquor to the Indian, and thus the sot is bred, while the girls, too "smart" for the Indian villages and unfitted because of hereditary tendencies for city environment, swell the ranks of the white slaves.

The white man of Canada and the United States is slowly, steadily and surely absorbing his red brother. In time there will be no more Indians. But there will be a new strain in this new world blood of ours, and a new writing on the palimpsest of national character. We believe nowadays in the survival of the fittest. Let it be our hope, therefore, that, gradually freeing ourselves from the inherent weaknesses that were the Indian's, we may retain, in this North American breed of men, some of the stoic virtues of his race.

1914 The Last of the Indian 'Potlatch'

J. Sedgwick Cowper – NOVEMBER 1914 **T**here is mourning now among the Coast Indians of British Columbia for the Government has put its foot down on the last of the old tribal customs, the "potlatch." Forty years ago on the shore at Port Simpson, the last of the cannibal feasts was held by the Tsimpseans. Here and there still linger a few shamans or medicine men, but the coast missionaries and the hospitals have made a dent in their practice. Nowadays the Siwash buys a bottle of painkiller when he goes to town, and the would-be shaman finds it scarcely worth while to starve himself into madness, until he "sees things" in the bush that a normal healthy man can-

EACH OF THE MANY ABORIGINAL nations across Canada possesses a rich tradition of tribal arts and mythic images. On the West Coast, the influences of the sea, the forest, the climate and the tribal legends come together in the creation of the totem pole.

not. In the practice of chasing the bad medicine out of sick Indians, the game is not worth the candle nowadays.

Forty years ago the cannibal feasts ended. Then dog eating became unfashionable. After that, the war dances were stopped. Last New Year's night, five ancient Haidas in the old Masset village on Queen Charlotte Island, danced for the last time, by consent of the tribe, the old devil-doctor dance. The Haidas are the Norsemen of the Pacific Coast. Fiercest of all the tribes in war when in the olden days their huge sea canoes led the raids on the mainland tribes, they have since become the most enlightened and progressive tribe on the coast. It was by request of the younger educated members of the tribe that the old devil-doctor dance has been abolished.

But with the potlatch it was different. "Potlatch is a good thing for poor Indian. He gets blankets and presents of good things and is not expected to give potlatch in return like rich Indian," said Chief Jimmy Okus of the Cape Mudge Indians to me with indignation a few weeks ago, when he saw Chief Ned Harris and Chief George Bagwany being tried in a criminal court on a charge of holding a potlatch. Chief Jimmy had been planning to hold a potlatch himself this year. Now, alas, he has no way of going down to fame as a man who was rich, but who gave away all his belongings to his neighbors in one big potlatch.

1967 The Lonely Death of Charlie Wenjack

Ian Adams – FEBRUARY 1967 Charlie Wenjack would have been 13 years old on January 19, and it's possible that during his short and disturbed life someone may have taken a snapshot of him—one of those laughing, open-faced, blurred little pictures one so often sees of children. But if a snap was taken, nobody knows where it is now. There are five police pictures of Charlie, though. They are large 8-by-10 prints, grey and underexposed, showing the thin, crumpled little body of a 12-year-old boy with a sharp-featured face. He is lying on his back and his thin cotton clothing is obviously soaked. His feet, encased in ankle-high leather boots, are oddly turned inward. In one of the photographs, an Ontario Provincial Police sergeant is pointing down at Charlie's body, where it lies beside the CNR track. It is the exact spot where on the night of October 22 Charlie collapsed and died from exposure and hunger, just four-and-a-half feet from the trains that carry the white world by in warm and well-fed comfort.

When they found Charlie, he didn't have any identification. All they got out of his pockets was a little glass jar with a screw top. Inside were half a dozen wooden matches. They were all dry. And that's all he had. Charlie Wenjack was an Ojibway Indian attending Cecilia Jeffrey Indian Residential School in Kenora, Ont. He became lonely and ran away. He died trying to walk 400 miles home to his father, who lives and works on an isolated reserve in Northern Ontario. It is unlikely that Charlie ever understood why he had to go to school and why it had to be such a long way from home. It is even doubtful if his father really understood either.

1990 Starting Over

Anthony Wilson-Smith – OCTOBER 8, 1990   **A**fter 78 days of anger, threats and misunderstandings, the armed standoff ended with one last burst of violence. At 6:55 p.m. on Oct. 26, about 50 Mohawk warriors, women and children emerged from the drug and alcohol rehabilitation centre in the Kanesatake community near Oka, Que., that had been their headquarters and final redoubt during their summer-long conflict with the federal and Quebec governments.

Several hundred metres away, behind a razor-wire boundary, soldiers from the Royal 22nd Regiment, the renowned Van Doos, watched them approach. The evening before, Mohawk and government representatives had negotiated the terms under which the Mohawks would put down their weapons and surrender. But as the

A LAND DISPUTE produced a crisis in the summer of 1990 between the local establishment at Oka, Quebec, and native militants on the next-door Kanesatake Mohawk reserve. Here, a Mohawk observes the approach of armored vehicles from a golf cart on the disputed land.

Indians began to approach the army lines, some of them suddenly veered to the right. In the subsequent confusion, scuffles and fistfights broke out and soldiers wrestled individual Mohawks, including women and children, to the ground. The soldiers herded the hooting, chanting Indians into a circle, surrounded them and finally put them onto waiting buses that took them into army custody.

The chaos ended a drama that opened on July 11 with the death of Quebec provincial policeman Marcel Lemay, shot in an abortive police assault on Mohawk barricades. What began last spring as a dispute over the town of Oka's plan to expand an existing golf course onto land claimed by the Mohawks developed into a nation-wide crisis over Indian land claims. And, more than any other incident involving natives in recent Canadian history, it sharply underscored the frustration among Canada's first people over the perceived unwillingness of governments to deal with their grievances.

1994 The Fight of a Lifetime

John DeMont – JANUARY 17, 1994 **E**ven now, decades later, the memories return to her like the fragments of a long-ago dream: the crunch of snow beneath the dog sled, the eternal silence of the landscape that stretched as far as the young Innu girl could see. Katie Rich remembers the fragrance of the tree boughs laid on the tent floor, the welcoming heat from the small portable stove where her family cooked their meals, the voices of her mother and the other women as they told the old tales of Tshakapesh (man in the moon) and Kueuatsheu (wolverine) in their tent after dinner each evening. These are the best memories for Katie Rich: the hard, good life her family once lived on the Labrador Barrens.

Then, there is the reality of Davis Inlet, her home for the past 26 years. Tonight, it is five children out on the snow-covered ice, rambling in their Innu tongue and reeking with the smell of the gasoline fumes they had inhaled. The oldest is nine, the youngest five. But if anything, their colorful stocking caps, boots and snowsuits make them look

AMERICAN-BORN and raised on the Odanak reserve near Sorel, Quebec, and in Trois-Rivières, Alanis Obomsawin later made Montreal her base as a singer and storyteller and then established herself on the staff of the National Film Board as a sensitive chronicler of Canada's First Nations.

even younger as a social worker and two Innu teens bundle them into the community's makeshift clinic.

They are coherent and in good spirits by the time Rich, the solemn-looking chief of the immensely troubled community, arrives. She stays anyway, serving glasses of water and ketchup-slathered hotdogs to the children. By now, she has seen the awful ritual repeated countless times in her community, where the fumes of a gasoline tank are the refuge from the pain of life. But this scene, on a bitter December night, left her reeling. "What can we do to stop this?" she asked wearily. "It just breaks your heart to see this happening to our children."

By anyone's definition, the Davis Inlet community of 500 is a frozen hell on earth where drug abuse, alcoholism, sexual abuse of children, suicide and domestic violence run unchecked. Its future, if it depends on any single person, hangs on Rich's shoulders. The burden is immense: in November, she resigned as chief under pressure from her family and out of frustration with intractable governments in Ottawa and St. John's, Nfld. Even she was surprised by the outpouring of support from across the country that followed. But the ultimate decision to stay on to lead the stricken community was rooted in something deeper than ego or obligation. "I was a nasty person, a bad person," she told *Maclean's*, "and I guess I've tried to make up for how I lived." She–like Davis Inlet–is searching for redemption.

Rich, 33, reacts to both good news and bad with sphinx-like detachment. She seems an unlikely savior, sitting in her hooded parka, sweatshirt and snowboots. She is a short, squarely built woman with shoulder-length dark hair parted in the middle. Although she didn't speak any English until she was 13, Rich is known throughout Canada mainly as her band's articulate spokesman. But she also calls shots from behind the scenes, where she has emerged as a tough negotiator with the various levels of government.

The jurisdictional lines are sometimes confusing. The province funds a host of services in Davis Inlet, including schools, a health clinic and general store. At the same time, under a five-year, federal-provincial agreement signed in 1991, Ottawa pays 90 per cent of a $19.5-million program that covers budgetary shortfalls and water and sewer systems in both Davis Inlet and Sheshatshiu, a settlement about 400 km south, where the rest of Labrador's 800 Innu live. Last year alone, the federal government responded with $7.8 million for, among other things, new housing and drug and alcohol counselling. Still, most of the core Innu demands have gone unheeded–including relocation to the mainland Labrador site of Sango Bay, 11 km west, which provides the water and sewage systems that Davis Inlet sorely lacks as well as better hunting.

THIS 1994 PHOTO of a group of lively youngsters from the Innu First Nation of Quebec and Labrador belies the often bleak truth about the Innu, whose lives were marred by a gas-sniffing epidemic and disputes over land claims in the 1990s. Happier news centred on the artistic life of this vibrant community.

Davis Inlet burst into the world's consciousness last January when six gasoline-sniffing children were pulled from an unheated shack on a frigid night, screaming that they wanted to die. The army of reporters that descended on the settlement told of a place where the sense of hopelessness is so profound that many young people see death as the only alternative. Now, conditions are no better. "We still live like animals," explains George Rich, 31, a huskily built vice-president of the Innu Nation. "Nothing has changed."

1994 Kanehsatake: 270 Years of Resistance

Barry Came – JANUARY 31, 1994 There is a moment of pure farce in Alanis Obomsawin's film about the Oka crisis. It occurs near the end of *Kanehsatake*, a two-hour National Film Board documentary about the 1990 Mohawk uprising in the pine forest on the outskirts of the little Quebec town of Oka. The filmmaker, an award-winning 61-year-old Abenaki native from Quebec, captures a bizarre encounter between a Canadian army major and a clutch of besieged Mohawk warriors. The major is indignant and the Mohawks bemused as they trade insults and accusations, facing each other across rolls of gleaming razor wire. Despite the setting, the argument is banal. It concerns eggs–or rather, the precise identity of the culprit who hurled a few against the heavily armored flank of an armed forces personnel carrier. It is an epiphany of sorts, a glimpse of the essential absurdity of the whole sorry affair that seized the attention of Canada, and the world, for 78 days in the summer and early fall of 1990. Obomsawin was present for most of that time, living with the Mohawks behind the barricades, sleeping in the sand under the pines, and often working without a crew and shooting her own footage on a video camera. The resulting documentary has picked up several international and domestic awards.

The viewpoint is what distinguishes the production. Written, directed and narrated by Obomsawin herself, an NFB filmmaker for 25 years, the film draws its strength from her intimate knowledge of her subject. Born in New Hampshire, she grew up on the Odanak Reserve, northeast of Montreal. When she was nine, her parents moved to Trois-Rivieres, where they were the only native family in town. Speaking little English and no French, Obomsawin learned the hard lessons about cultural isolation and racial discrimination at a very early age.

That experience illuminates the film. In one scene, cabinet minister John Ciaccia, then in charge of Indian Affairs, repeatedly assures journalists that the authorities have guaranteed the natives unrestricted access to food and medical supplies. Obomsawin's camera tells a different story. It tracks the progress of a Red Cross truck as it is held up for hours at a police roadblock and finally rerouted to a puzzled non-native farmer, who is told to hold the truck in his barn until further notice.

From the title on, the film is a reminder that the conflict did not begin in the summer of 1990 but, rather, centuries ago. There is a detailed recapitulation of the betrayals and double-dealing that gradually robbed the Mohawks of the land they once controlled in and around Montreal.

Obomsawin says that she made the film "to show what the Mohawk people were like and why they took the stand they did." In that, at least, she has succeeded. But whether her efforts will have any lasting effect remains in doubt. The Mohawks at Kanehsatake are no closer to control over the pine forest than they were in 1990.

1997 The Professional Frontier

Brian Bergman – OCTOBER 6, 1997   From his law practice on the Opawakoscikan Cree reserve in Prince Albert, Sask., Gerry Morin has been involved in some of Canada's most controversial legal cases. In the early 1990s, Morin represented the family of Leo LaChance, a Cree trapper who had been shot and killed by Carney Nerland, a Prince Albert gun-shop owner with links to neo-Nazi groups. Morin spoke before a public inquiry into whether Nerland, who had received four years for manslaughter, had gotten off too lightly. The inquiry upheld the verdict–but raised fundamental questions about whether the original decision had been influenced by racism.

Then there was the case of Billy Taylor, a Cree from La Ronge, Sask. In 1995, after being convicted of raping his former common-law wife, Taylor asked that his punishment be determined by a native sentencing circle, which banished him to an uninhabited island for six months. But Crown lawyers thought Taylor deserved more–four years in prison–and appealed the ruling last year. Morin says it is high time to let native Canadians have a greater say in determining their own rules of justice and punishment. "We always look towards punitive measures," he says. "Is it not better to get some input from the community, and start the healing process?"

As Morin works to place those questions in the public eye, Toronto-based lawyer Jean Teillet is putting related issues before the courts. The great-grandniece of 19th-century Métis leader Louis Riel is an impassioned advocate of her people's rights. Among Teillet's recent cases is one concerning fishing rights of Métis in northwestern Saskatchewan. Two Métis from the isolated community of Turner Lake were charged with fisheries violations, among them fishing without a licence. Teillet maintained that, because such rules do not apply to natives, they should likewise not apply to Métis, who also rely on the fish for food. The trial judge agreed. " I see aboriginal people who really are in great despair," says Teillet. "I don't think I'm going to be the answer to their problems, but I think I can help."

1998 Ottawa Says It is Sorry

John DeMont – JANUARY 19, 1998 **A** few sentences into his historic speech in Ottawa on Jan. 7, Phil Fontaine's eyes began to well with tears. The silver-haired grand chief of the Assembly of First Nations tried to carry on. But as his voice faltered, it was apparent that the long-awaited apology for the brutal treatment of native children in residential schools–delivered moments earlier by Indian Affairs Minister Jane Stewart–had awakened painful memories. In the four decades since leaving a residential school in Fort Alexander, Man., Fontaine has spent countless hours with counsellors, trying to come to terms with the physical and sexual abuse he suffered at the hands of priests after being taken from his family at age 7. Clutching a sacred eagle feather, he spoke of the moment as a new beginning for thousands of similar victims. "We honor you," he said, "and pray that the creator guide your healing process."

THE LAST OF AS MANY AS 80 CHURCH-RUN, federally financed residential schools for aboriginal children–such as this typical example from Lebret, Saskatchewan, in the early 1900s–finally closed in the early 1980s. By the late 1990s, Ottawa was calculating the cost of compensating former pupils and their families in the hundreds of millions of dollars.

As the most influential spokesman for native Canadians, Fontaine must deal with a growing chorus of unmet demands from the aboriginal community. The $350-million healing fund that Stewart announced during the same ceremony, for instance, fell far short of the billions in new spending recommended by the Royal Commission on Aboriginal Peoples in its report of November, 1996. And some aboriginal leaders were quick to dismiss the government's new action plan for natives—arrived at in consultation with the AFN– as simply more vague promises. But wringing a statement of atonement from Ottawa for the residential schools at least gives the grand chief, who was elected last August, something concrete with which to prove that his conciliatory approach works.

ACTING ON ROYAL COMMISSION findings on January 7, 1998, federal Indian Affairs minister Jane Stewart—here greeting Phil Fontaine, National Chief of the Assembly of First Nations—publicly apologized at a Parliament Hill ceremony for past government actions that damaged native people.

Fontaine, by nature, is a consensus-seeker and deal-maker. That makes him far different from his uncompromising predecessor, Ovide Mercredi, whose all-or-nothing approach to native sovereignty alienated the government. In contrast, Fontaine and Stewart—an up-and-comer in the Chrétien cabinet with well-tuned political antennae—have a personal rapport. Not all native groups are happy with that relationship, preferring Mercredi's up-front style.

Certainly, the problems facing aboriginal peoples seem overwhelming–and the solutions far from easy. Chief among the commissioners' concerns are the stunningly high rates of poverty, family breakdown, suicide and substance abuse. If such problems are not fully addressed, the report says, Canada's native peoples will be consigned to a bleak future little different from their recent past.

1998 History in the Making

Chris Wood – JULY 27, 1998   **A** mere 111 years after a group of northwestern B.C. natives first asked Ottawa and Victoria for a treaty confirming their title to hundreds of square kilometres of the remote and lovely Nass River valley, their descendants may finally be on the verge of satisfaction. Negotiators acting for 5,500 Nisga'a and the federal and provincial governments shook hands on July 15 on a draft treaty that would confirm the band's right to a measure of self-government and nearly 2,000

JOSEPH GOSNELL, *the tribal chief of the Nisga'a people of British Columbia, in the centre of this picture, calculated that it had taken more than a century to negotiate the agreement on land rights he had just signed, on August 4, 1998, with federal Indian Affairs minister Jane Stewart and B.C. premier Glen Clark.*

square kilometres of land, while paying the Nisga'a $190 million in compensation for the release of the rest of their traditional territory. Band spokesmen welcomed the agreement as righting a historic wrong. "Many of our elders died fighting for our land," said chief tribal negotiator Joe Gosnell after the agreement. "I'm happy some of our elders could be here today."

Officials of both the federal and provincial governments lauded last week's tentative settlement. It would, they said, pave the way for similar deals with other natives, most of whom never signed treaties with the Crown and whose combined land claims actually exceed the total area of British Columbia. But any celebration on that score was clearly premature. Far from bringing new momentum to the bogged-down negotiations with more than 50 other native groups in British Columbia, the draft deal with the Nisga'a faces intense hostility from other aboriginals and from the province's political opposition.

For the Nisga'a, though, it was a victory–at long last. Their leaders first travelled to Victoria in 1887 to plead for a treaty giving them assured access to land they had occupied for millennia. But British Columbia's premier at the time, William Smith, rejected their plea with the caustic observation: "When whites first came among you, you were little better than wild beasts." It was not until a mid-1970s series of court decisions favoring aboriginal rights that Ottawa agreed to enter treaty talks with the band. It took more than a decade for the province to join the negotiations. An agreement in principle reached in 1996 has taken another two years to nail down in legal form. Now, in addition to land and cash, the draft treaty would see the Nisga'a–only 40 per cent of whom still live on their ancestral lands 800 km north of Vancouver–give up their tax-exempt status and receive self-government over culture and many social areas.

Once finalized, the treaty must be ratified first by the Nisga'a in a referendum, then by Parliament and the B.C. legislature. But that process promises to be stormy. The opposition Liberals, who have promised to vote against the deal in the B.C. legislature, charge that it will grant powers to the Nisga'a that, in some areas, will exceed those of either the federal or provincial governments. And, indeed, part of Section 27 of the draft agreement reads: "In the event of an inconsistency between Nisga'a laws and federal and provincial laws of general application, Nisga'a laws will prevail." (The section applies to only a handful of areas, including Nisga'a culture and language.) As well, the Liberals say, the agreement will restrict voting rights on native territory to people of Nisga'a descent. "It is clearly a racist argument," declares leader Gordon Campbell.

If critics oppose the Nisga'a deal for giving natives too much, other aboriginal groups object that it gives too little. Their position, moreover, has hardened since a landmark decision last December by the Supreme Court of Canada. That ruling, in a case brought by the Gitxsan and Wet'suwet'en hereditary chiefs (including the head of the Delgamuukw clan), whose traditional territory adjoins the Nisga'a's, confirmed the existence in principle of aboriginal title to traditional territories. In a decision penned by Chief Justice Antonio Lamer, the court also ruled that while aboriginal title does exist, specific claims remain to be proven on a "case-by-case" basis. But that qualification has largely been lost in the debate, with most native leaders insisting that the court simply confirmed their outright ownership of most of British Columbia's land mass.

Fifty-one native groups have been participating since 1993 with Ottawa and Victoria in settlement talks choreographed by the B.C. Treaty Commission. In a January response to the court ruling, the First Nations Summit, which represents the participating native groups, declared: "Aboriginal title is a legal and proprietary interest in land. We assert our aboriginal title to all of B.C." The summit demanded that governments immediately stop granting third parties any rights over provincial resources, including timber-cutting permits and grazing licences on Crown land, "until our informed consent is obtained." Dale Lovick, aboriginal affairs minister in Premier Glen Clark's provincial government, says that "the provincial Crown is still asserting its right to manage the land of this province."

With the Nisga'a pact certain to become the test-case for every opposing view, the people of the Nass may be forced to wait a little longer still before they can truly celebrate their long-sought treaty.

Color Canada Dusty Green

A Sense of Urgency Spurred Efforts to Repair the Environment

THE environmental movement and the 20th Century made a perfect fit. Neither was likely to have lasted without the other. The century got dirty, dirtier, and then the dirtiest of them all. That gave the crusaders for a clean earth an ever-expanding reason for being. A natural symbiosis often developed between the offensive and defensive parties. On some battle fronts, co-operation supplanted confrontation. But the war raged on in the rain forests and where chemical cauldrons bubbled as well as in public argument over such scary matters as biogenetics.

In a sense, the 1900s possessed an inborn impulse to play fast and loose with the planet. Canada, among many countries, was emerging from the better part of three centuries when mere survival entailed a constant struggle against nature– clearing land, building cities and creating lines of communication, battling the extremes of geography, terrain and the seasons. And right off the bat in the new century arrived the automobile, its engine waste destined to be a toxic scourge of the air, the rain, the lakes and the land. Periods of plenty, of too much stuff, left millions of tons of waste. There were all the new contaminants, from asbestos to PCBs to pesticides. And looming over all from the 1940s was the big one–the bomb, destroyer of two Japanese cities and at least 240,000 lives on August 6 (Hiroshima)

THE GREENPEACE MOVEMENT, a Canadian invention whose activist operations in defence of nature and people proved to be globally contagious, seized every opportunity, often spectacularly—as here in Toronto—to promote its causes.

and August 9, 1945 (Nagasaki). The bomb's threat lived on, its much deadlier descendants poisonously test-exploded for decades afterward, and its peaceful applications humming with menace in the nuclear power plants.

It was anti-bomb activists in the 1950s who planted the seeds of the environmentalist movement. The Quakers who sailed to Bikini Atoll in 1958 in a vain effort to stop nuclear tests in the South Pacific were models for the birthing voyage of Greenpeace, an environmental group organized in Canada, out of Vancouver on September 15, 1971, to oppose nuclear tests in the Aleutians. Reinforcing suspicions about the nuclear menace, even when used for peaceful purposes, was a near-disaster on March 28, 1979, at Three Mile Island, a Pennsylvania nuclear power plant. A full disaster took place at Chernobyl in the Ukraine on April 26, 1986, when explosions and fire in a nuclear power plant spread radioactive gas, death and lasting damage far and wide.

Warnings of hidden hazards also mobilized activists. In the 1960s, American biologist Rachel Carson's hugely influential book, *Silent Spring*, served notice of the damage wrought by chemical pesticides–air and water poisoned, animal and human health endangered. Manufacturers of the chemical cocktails often played down the dangers. But the deadliest industrial accident on record occurred at a Union Carbide pesticide plant in Bhopal, India, on December 3, 1984, when a poison gas leak from the factory caused at least 2,500 deaths.

The growing pressures to protect the environment made headway on some fronts, including clear-air and clean-water laws and, in 1977, the postponement of a gas pipeline project along the Mackenzie River Valley in Canada's North. But new dangers, which developed without wide attention, became devastatingly apparent–the disappearance of the cod off eastern Canada and warnings of the same fate for salmon off the west coast.

The questions raised by the scarcity of fish and other wildlife echoed anxiety in the first half of the century. Scientists then expressed concern that excessive exploitation would exhaust resources. As early as the 1930s, there were fears for the future of Pacific salmon. Conservation persisted as a strong element in the environmentalist causes. And in the face of humankind's capacity to develop ever more efficient ways of despoiling the earth, there were matching expansions in such organizations as Greenpeace which, 25 years after its Vancouver beginnings, listed more than 40 offices and a worldwide membership exceeding five million.

Environmental groups thus globalized in step with the major business corporations–sometimes thanks in part to corporate donations. For a time, no goods-producing company seeking status on the cutting edge of commerce could do without an environmental expert in its executive offices. But by the 1990s, with both corporations and governments in Canada bent on cutting costs and governments relaxing the enforcement of regulations and the protection of natural assets, the environment appeared to face rough treatment and its advocates tough times in the new century.

1908 What Will the World Do When Coal is Gone?

Brand Whitlock – JULY 1908 **W**ith the domestic coal supply dwindling at the rate of 400,000,000 tons per year and the foreign supply disappearing at an equivalent rate, the problem of fuel supply takes on more than an academic interest. It is all very well profanely to inquire what posterity has done for us that we should forbear

POVERTY DROVE THESE people in 1909 to a so-called cinder colliery to glean unburned coal from smoldering ash heaps. But wider anxieties about wasting the world's natural resources gave rise to the conservationist and environmental movements.

skinning the earth's resources on this account, but from the present outlook this matter has ceased to involve waiting for posterity. It has reached a point where there may be trouble within the lifetime of children now alive.

If the coal consumption of the country increases at anything like the present rate it will probably not be more than a quarter of a century before the calamity of far dearer fuel will be upon us. Heating is a terribly serious matter in our climate, and if one relies on electrical heating the outlook is bad, since the whole power of Niagara could not keep even New York City from freezing to death. The outlook is grave.

1938 **Our Future**

C.M. Campbell – MAY 15, 1938 **D**iamond Jenness, chief of the Anthropological Division of the National Museum, estimates that in all Canada there are only 150 million acres that it will be profitable to cultivate. Though this acreage might produce enough food for 100 million people we will never boast that population, for, says Jenness: "No amount of food will ever banish the cold or turn the wheels of industry, and in resources apart from food the country is very limited."

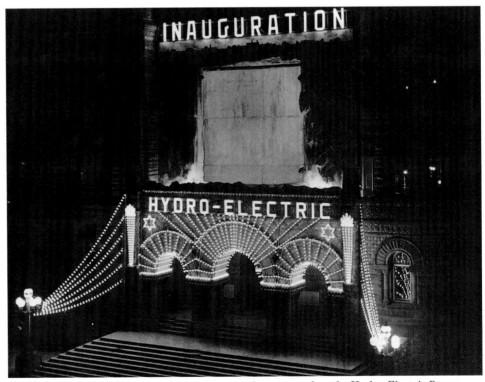

IN THE GOOD YOUNG years of the century, such as 1910, when the Hydro-Electric Power Commission of Ontario began transmitting bulk energy to the cities, electricity was created by water power. By the dirty and dangerous 1990s, water's share was down to 60 per cent, with nuclear energy, coal, gas and oil supplying the rest.

This will seem strange in view of the publicity in regard to our mineral and forest resources. One of the world's great silver camps, Cobalt, produced about 400 million ounces. Yet depletion in Canada is now such that the equivalent of one entire Cobalt is exhausted every six months.

The course of timber depletion takes its way. Half a century ago, the harbor of Saint John, N.B., was surrounded by lumber mills, and lumber rafts were characteristic of the Ottawa River. Those days are long past. Today, the Pacific Coast leads in timber depletion. Canadians, in short, are nothing more than butchers–butchers of their natural resources.

The salmon pack on the Fraser River dropped from five million cases in the decade ended 1905 to three million cases in the decade ended 1935, and there is the threat of foreign floating canneries beyond the three-mile limit. We must realize the gravity of the situation.

1976 What Goes Up Must Come Down and What Comes Down Can Be Deadly

Gloria Menard – NOVEMBER 29, 1976 In the argot of ecologists, it is known as acid precipitation. More colloquially, it is called acid rain. But by any name, the formation of acids in the atmosphere is causing serious damage to fragile environments on several continents. Falling back to earth in rain and snow, the acids settle into soils and lakes, changing the delicate chemistry of ecosystems and affecting forest growth and fisheries. The acids form by the interaction of industrial pollutants.

According to McMaster University geologist James R. Kramer, "recent estimates suggest that, given our continued industrial growth, all the lakes in Canada's susceptible areas will become acidic." The susceptible areas constitute much of Canada: most of Quebec, significant portions of Ontario, British Columbia, Newfoundland and the Northwest Territories.

1977 Now the Scheming Starts

Ian Urquhart – MAY 30, 1977 The report of Mr. Justice Thomas Berger on the Mackenzie Valley gas pipeline proposal, released on May 9, is not the end but the beginning of a furious struggle. It will take place over the next three months as the country crashes toward a decision on a northern gas pipeline after nearly nine years of debate, starting with the first discoveries of oil and gas in abundance at Prudhoe Bay on the northern Alaska coast in 1968. The pipeline decision by the Canadian

COMMERCIAL WHALING, once a thriving business off all three Canadian coasts, petered out in the Arctic by 1914 because the industry had virtually killed off the prey. Later, Ottawa outlawed commercial whaling from Canadian ports in 1972 and in Canadian waters generally in the 1980s.

EAGLES, BALD and otherwise, were among numerous wildlife species that began disappearing in the 1950s and 1960s as a result of pesticide poisoning. After 25 years of governmental restrictions on the use of DDT and other such chemicals, the birds have made a spectacular comeback.

government will, in a fundamental way, shape not only Canada's energy policy but also its economic direction over the next decade.

It is not just a fight pitting the survival of the caribou in the northern Yukon against the comfort of the 2.5 million Canadian homes heated by natural gas. It is, as well, a clash between the consumerist, industrial society and the no-growth environmentalist movement. For the northern natives, the debate and the Berger report are watersheds in their battle to preserve something of what they once were before the white man came.

Berger has helped sharpen the focus of the debate with his blitzkrieg-like attack on Canadian Arctic Gas Pipeline Ltd. (CAGPL), the consortium of 16 companies proposing to build a $10-billion, 2,625-mile pipeline from Prudhoe Bay and the Mackenzie River Delta, along the Mackenzie Valley to the U.S. and Canadian south. In his 213-page report, written in the first person, Berger recommends a 10-year postponement of any Mackenzie pipeline construction–and rules out the CAGPL project absolutely.

As recently as 1974, Jean Chrétien, then Minister of Indian Affairs and Northern Development, stated: "This government, after weighing all the factors involved very carefully, has come to the conclusion that a gas pipeline down the Mackenzie Valley is in the national interest." Now, after Berger, it may never happen.

1990 Clearing the Air

James Deacon – NOVEMBER 5, 1990 Through the early hours of Oct. 22, 1990, in Washington, D.C., 33 senators and congressmen argued bitterly in a Capitol Hill conference room, the latest round in 15 weeks of struggle to agree on conflicting proposals for a clean-air bill. Finally, just before dawn, the negotiators struck a deal that was later passed by Congress and is expected to lead to a substantial reduction in sulphur dioxide and nitrogen oxide emissions from American electrical utilities and factories. Agreement on the bill ended years of impasse between Washington and Ottawa.

Under the new law, electrical power utilities that use coal or oil as fuel will have 10 years to sharply reduce sulphur dioxide and nitrogen oxide emissions. And in an effort to reduce the smog that chokes many cities, the law requires reduced automobile

CLEAN-AIR REGULATIONS in the 1970s and 1980s helped to slow down the acid-rain poisoning of lakes and rivers in northeastern North America—mainly because of tougher American anti-pollution standards. Scientists monitored the persistent 20th-century blight, as in this Nova Scotian water-sampling procedure by Dalhousie University biologist Tony Blouin in 1985.

THE CANADIAN FORESTRY industry encountered growing hostility to such practices as clearcutting and logging old-growth trees. In British Columbia—where these workers graded and trimmed timber in 1993—both the industry and the hostility operated on bigger scales than elsewhere in the country.

tail-pipe emissions of nitrogen oxide by 60 per cent and hydrocarbons by 40 per cent by 1997.

Environmentalists on both sides of the border called the new bill a victory for Canada's anti–acid rain lobby, led by the Canadian Coalition on Acid Rain, which for years worked in Washington for tougher action against the pollution. But some environmentalists said that the new U.S. clean-air measures expose weaknesses in Canada's own attack on acid rain.

PROTEST MARCHES SUCH as this one in 1990 expressed rising anxiety over the prospect that air pollution from power plants, factories and motor vehicles would permanently damage the earth's atmosphere and climate.

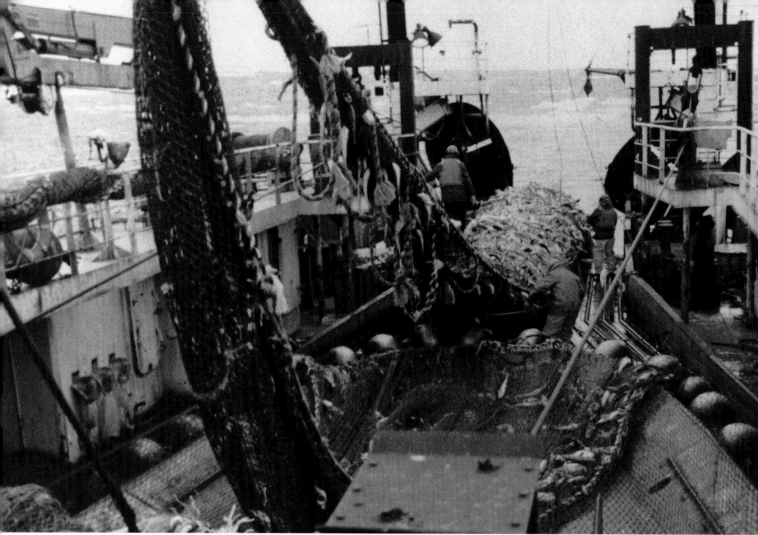

WITH A DRASTIC DECLINE in cod stocks, Ottawa in mid-1992 imposed a two-year ban on catches in a major portion of the East Coast fishery. Before the end of that moratorium, there was daunting news for fishing operations, such as this one in Newfoundland: recovery of the cod was far in the future, if ever.

1992 When the Future Died

John DeMont – JULY 13, 1992 **R**oy Anderson's family has fished off eastern Newfoundland since 1840, when his ancestors first arrived in Chance Cove, a tiny village nestled in a curved inlet 120 km northwest of St. John's. Usually, the cold waters of Trinity Bay have provided a comfortable living. But as he looked out on the choppy sea last week, the 49-year-old fisherman also stared into an uncertain future: the schools of cod that have filled his nets reliably since 1959 have almost disappeared. Indeed, the two-year ban on cod fishing announced by federal Fisheries Minister John Crosbie on July 2 was largely academic for Anderson. He had not taken his boat out regularly for months. "I never thought I would see the day when the cod stopped coming," Anderson lamented. "Now, we are all wondering whether they will ever come back."

Many of the fishermen and plant workers along the bay say that emergency federal aid may not be enough to see them through the winter.

Theories abound to explain what has happened to the fish that have brought fishermen to the waters off Newfoundland for nearly 500 years. Some fishermen blame abnormally cold weather and persistent ice, which may have affected fish migratory habits. Others say cod stocks have been depleted by the population explosion of seals in Newfoundland since the 1987 abolition of the annual seal hunt. Many fault domestic and foreign boats that have operated just beyond the 200-mile limit of Canada's offshore jurisdiction. But Anderson said that small-scale inshore fishermen like himself must also shoulder some of the blame because of excessive fishing. "This did not happen overnight," he said. "We are as guilty as anyone."

1993 The World is Watching

Mark Nichols – AUGUST 16, 1993 **A**t 5:40 a.m., on a logging road near the west coast of Vancouver Island, about 100 demonstrators, mostly under 30 and wearing jeans, sweaters, serapes and windbreakers, stand in a wide circle before a bridge that spans the Kennedy River. They chant and sing and listen as Tzeporah Berman, a 24-year-old blockade co-ordinator, explains what is about to happen. She warns that when an official acting for the MacMillan Bloedel Ltd. forestry company, which is logging in the woods nearby, arrives and reads a court injunction banning protests, they should remain quiet. "The courts will be tougher," she says, "if there is noise and disrespect." At 6 a.m., a cavalcade of logging vehicles appears and halts several hundred metres away. Now, the demonstrators form a phalanx in front of the bridge, holding up signs: "We must take care of her–the Earth is our mother."

A 1993 BRITISH COLUMBIA government logging plan that protected only one-third of Crown forest in Clayoquot Sound on Vancouver Island provoked non-violent protest–blocking logging trucks. Pictured is one of the 859 people arrested and convicted of criminal contempt for a court desist order.

What follows is scrupulously non-violent and very Canadian. The vehicles begin moving down the dirt road. As they approach the bridge, Richard Bourne, a Vancouver process server, informs the protesters that they should be "off the road before this vehicle has stopped." When some stay put, eight RCMP officers approach, politely explain that the protesters are breaking the law and begin arresting them. Many refuse to be escorted away and have to be carried. The

Mounties work their way across the bridge and, by 6:30 a.m., the vehicles—including an explosives truck and four huge logging rigs—rumble across and into the forest.

So goes the almost daily ritual. This is the third straight summer of protests against logging the old-growth rain forest of Clayoquot Sound, located about 200 km northwest of Victoria. The debate—to cut and sell for cash or preserve for posterity—has been building for nearly a decade, growing from a local quarrel into a national and, increasingly, an international issue.

1998 Score One for the Ecologists

MAY 11, 1998 **F**or decades, eco-activists have criticized the logging industry's traditional practice of clear-cutting the B.C. rainforest—felling every hemlock, cedar and fir in the logging area, disfiguring pristine landscapes. The industry says it is the safest method available and the soundest way to allow second-growth forest to generate.

But at the annual meeting of MacMillan Bloedel Ltd. on April 23, chief executive officer Tom Stephens stated: "We are hearing more and more from our customers that they, and their customers, don't want wood from old-growth clear-cuts. More and more we are asking ourselves if clear-cutting old growth is the best economic harvesting method." At International Forest Products Ltd. (Interfor), senior vice-president Fred Lowenberger commented: "We think this is a good thing—in many ways, it follows what we have been thinking of doing in this company."

1998 Turning the Tide

John DeMont – JULY 20, 1998 **A** week after Federal Fisheries Minister David Anderson negotiated a short-term salmon conservation deal with Washington state, talks with the Alaskan government—which strongly disagrees with Canadian scientific reports that the northern salmon are endangered—broke down over Ottawa's insistence on strict conservation measures. But Anderson still left the impression that, while success on the international front was a mixed bag, his willingness to break with the past practice by the department of fisheries and oceans of stressing jobs over conservation is at least scoring points in British Columbia.

The undeniable logic of his "fish-first" policy seems to be catching on with environmentalists, newspaper editorialists and even non-experts, who increasingly support his argument that fishing any species to extinction is environmental genocide and economic idiocy. A recent poll showed that the vast majority of British Columbians support his decision last month to effectively shut down the province's fragile coho fishery because the fish are endangered.

A SHRINKING POPULATION of some salmon species off the West Coast, and unresolved differences between Canada and the United States in 1997 over catch limits, prompted the idled fishing fleet of Prince Rupert, pictured here, to block the passage of an Alaskan ferry in that port for three days.

Since taking over the job 13 months ago, Anderson has shut the Labrador commercial salmon fishery, resisted calls to fully reopen the East Coast northern cod fishery (shut down in 1992), and found himself demonized in Prince Edward Island after his department increased the minimum size for landed lobsters—all in the name of conserving stocks.

Drains and Gains in Brain Power

Immigrants Take Leading Roles in Scientific Research

G IVEN the record of achievement in Canadian science and the honors bestowed on the country's scientists, it may seem that the centres of learning and research have somehow surmounted Canada's notorious brain drain. There is a history of important Canadian work in medical research, most recently in genetics, as well as in botanical science, which contributed in major ways to the green revolution of the 1960s and its enrichment of Third World agriculture with new, high-yield, high-protein grains. Nevertheless, a few minutes with any practising scientist will usually produce an alarmist view about the brain drain, thin funding—and penny-squeezers in the federal and provincial governments.

Supporting evidence for the brain drain may be noted on the lists of Nobel Prize winners in scientific disciplines. Six Nobel laureates in science won for work in Canada. But there are eight Canadian-born laureates whose prize-winning work was done in laboratories abroad.

On the other hand, offsetting brain gains have worked greatly to the benefit of Canadian science. An example is the preponderance of immigrants among researchers cited in the *Maclean's* annual honor roll during the 1980s and 1990s. Eight out of 10–all but astronomer Ian Shelton, discoverer of the first clearly

CHARLES BEST AND FREDERICK BANTING, right, discovered their lifesaving insulin treatment for human diabetes by injecting diabetic dogs with extracts of dog pancreas. University of Toronto physiologist J.J.R. Macleod, who provided laboratory space and the help of physiology student Best, shared Banting's 1923 Nobel Prize.

observable exploding star in more than three centuries, and biochemist Kelvin Ogilvie, the first to synthesize the human cell's genetic ribonucleic acid–had moved to Canada from elsewhere. The immigrant scientists cited:

Pathologist Adolfo de Bold, discoverer of a heart function that regulates blood pressure; pediatrician Ranjit Chandra, whose laboratory work established a direct link between nutritional deficiencies and immune system responses; psychologist Max Cynader, who demonstrated how and when the brain absorbs information; physicist Ursula Franklin, teacher and pioneering expert in metallurgy and materials science; immunologist Tak Mak, who helped decipher the human mechanism that identifies viruses and cancer cells; geneticist Peter St. George-Hyslop, a leader in pinpointing a pair of genes believed to generate the symptoms of Alzheimer's disease; biologist Tissa Senaratna, who developed a technique for transferring beneficial genetic information into plant seeds, and molecular biologist Lap-Chee Tsui, leader of a Toronto team who discovered the gene defect responsible for cystic fibrosis.

METALLURGIST URSULA FRANKLIN is not only a pioneer in applying materials analysis to archeology and in developing science policy; she also blazed a trail by being appointed, in 1984, a University Professor at the University of Toronto— the first woman to achieve that title.

UNIVERSITY OF BRITISH Columbia biochemist Michael Smith, displaying the 1993 Nobel medal for chemistry after its presentation in Stockholm, won renown for a range of work, from studies in salmon growth to systems for examining genetic codes in DNA.

Despite those records, a recurring theme among Canadian scientists remains the need for more financial support to nourish more and better work in Canada. That common cry has received a positive response from the likes of biochemist Fraser Mustard, a pioneer in stroke therapy and founding president of the Canadian Institute for Advanced Research (CIAR), whose work includes fund-raising efforts to dissuade promising scientists from emigrating. But as gauged by Canada's scientific community itself, much more interest and encouragement is needed.

GERHARD HERZBERG is second from the right in this 1984 photo of an Ottawa gathering of Nobel laureates in science—the others are Americans Charles Townes, physics, 1964; Melvin Calvin, chemistry, 1961; and Henry Taube, chemistry, 1983—to honor Herzberg, winner of the 1971 physics Nobel, in advance of his 80th birthday.

1924 Canada's Record in Research

Frederick G. Banting, M.B. – NOVEMBER 15, 1924

Editor's Note: Canada is taking a conspicuously prominent and useful place in the world of scientific research. To Dr. Banting, co-winner of the Nobel prize in 1923 with Prof. J.J.R. Macleod, a great deal of this prominence is due.

During the last few years, the attention of Canadians has been drawn to some of the results of scientific work carried out in Canadian universities, which have been recognized throughout the world. The wide recognition of these discoveries has cheered and inspired many patient, quiet workers in our great universities whose less-known discoveries have not attracted the public interest because they are aware that it is only through the hard work of the many that success comes to the few. It was my good fortune to be one of the group of workers in Toronto which has produced a practical culmination to a long series of studies on diabetes.

Sufferers from this disease had an excess of sugar in their systems. For a great many years physicians have believed that a diseased condition of the pancreas was responsible for diabetes mellitus. With the benefit of this accumulated knowledge, the work on insulin was commenced about the middle of April, 1921, with Mr. Charles H. Best, in the department of physiology, University of Toronto.

We first succeeded in showing that the blood sugar of diabetic dogs could be reduced to its normal level by the administration of extracts made from the pancreas of dogs. Furthermore, the administration of these extracts rendered the diabetic animals sugar free, and caused a marked improvement in their condition. Another type of extract was obtained from the pancreas of fetal calves of under four months' development. The work progressed more rapidly, and led to such an increase in our knowledge that we were soon able to extract the active principle from the whole adult beef pancreas. This extract was tried with favorable results on three patients in the wards of the Toronto General Hospital.

The early extracts undoubtedly contained protein, and it was recognized that these must be removed before the extract could be used on man. Prof. J.J.R. Macleod turned almost his whole laboratory staff on the investigation of insulin. The final purification of this product was a very long and tedious process and was only possible by the knowledge that had been gained by all those numberless investigators which had been studying protein. The use of insulin has spread rapidly throughout the world. It is now being manufactured in at least ten different countries. Diabetes has been robbed of its horrors.

The fields of research for the development of our vast country are manifold. For the health of our peoples many medical problems must be solved. The man of business will suggest that for our pleasure and wellbeing many economic difficulties must be overcome, but he does not always stop to think to how great an extent economic possibilities are dependent on the advance of fundamental problems of science and of medicine.

The Panama canal was not built by the French, because the cost in lives was too great owing to the lack of medical knowledge that then existed. The Americans built the canal because they knew how to control disease. The discovery of Marquis wheat is said to have added $100,000,000 annually to the value of the wheat crops of Canada: certainly enough to have justified the government in adequately providing for its discoverer during his lifetime, instead of giving him merely a pittance when he retired.

Research gives us health, wealth and happiness, but too often we do not realize from where these good things come.

1928 Grains of Destiny

Grant Dexter – NOVEMBER 15, 1928 The development of Canada as a producer of wheat is a romance unparalleled in the story of human achievement. The brain of the scientist, the thrift and strong arm of the grower, have succeeded where either one without the other must inevitably have failed. There was a time the fate of Canadian wheat fields depended upon the growth of a single kernel.

The romance of wheat in Canada dates back to 1842, when the western prairies were a wilderness known only to a few explorers and fur traders. There lived then near Peterborough a farmer of an inquiring turn of mind–one David Fife–who, to the great amusement of his neighbors, was forever experimenting with new varieties of wheat. A friend visiting Europe shipped him a bushel of good-looking European wheat. It was meant for fall planting but Fife, not knowing that, mistakenly planted it in the spring. Only a single grain grew. He harvested the crop by hand–three heavily laden ears, about forty grains all told–and stored it in a teacup. Next year he planted these seeds and at second harvest he had one pint of grain. Its early maturing virtue remained and he began to feel the strange inward excitement of one who has stumbled upon a great discovery. The third year produced half a bushel and Fife now sent small samples to his neighbors. He had no idea of the variety of wheat he had discovered and finally named it after himself with the descriptive word "red" to indicate its beautiful coloring–Red Fife, the parent of Marquis, Garnet and Reward and nearly every successful variety now produced in this Dominion.

Red Fife made Ontario a wheat producing province and in 1876 the first seed was shipped west. Its arrival turned the southern areas of the Prairies into a wheat belt. Yet it required 110 days to mature and could not be depended upon to escape frosts, particularly in the central and northern areas. Furthermore, it was susceptible to smut and inclined to be short in the stem. These defects were observed by William Saunders, head of the new Experimental Farms of the Dominion government in Ottawa and he addressed himself to the task of discovering or evolving a variety of wheat which would yield heavily, mill up to the standard of Red Fife and mature at least 10 days earlier.

Mr. Saunders was a true scientist. He must find other varieties. The far places of the earth must be searched. When he died in 1903, his son, Dr. Charles Saunders, who succeeded him, decided to test out all those samples which cluttered up the shelves in his office. Among the samples was seed grown from a cross between Hard Red Calcutta, an early maturing variety obtained in India, and Red Fife. This seed was sown and the crop looked so promising that it was carefully harvested and sifted so that only the finest grains were retained. Finally this new variety was named Marquis.

While Marquis proved to be an exceedingly valuable variety, the search for still earlier maturing wheats was continued. Why seek to improve on Marquis? The present wheat-growing area, except the Peace River valley, is a strip of land about 120 miles in width stretching along the international boundary. To the north the soil is

THE FAMOUS MARQUIS wheat, developed in stages by Canadian agronomist William Saunders and two sons, first Percy and then Charles (above), was initially distributed to farmers in 1909, and by 1920 was growing on about nine-tenths of total Prairie wheat acreage.

excellent but the growing season is shorter. It is estimated that the season shortens as one proceeds north by about one day for each 15 miles. Marquis ripens in 100 days. Clip six days off and you have added a strip about seventy-five miles in width and 1,000 miles in length to the wheat belt, or 75,000 square miles, 48,000,000 acres. This is more than twice the present wheat acreage.

So runs the romance of wheat. It should never be forgotten that without the skill of the scientist, without his tireless effort, all the achievement of the past half century would have been impossible.

1986 Laurels for a Scientist

Nora Underwood – OCTOBER 27, 1986 It was 9 a.m., and John Polanyi was still in his pyjamas when he received the most astonishing telephone call of his life on Oct. 15. It came from a reporter requesting an interview with the co-winner of this year's Nobel Prize in chemistry. Recalling his surprise, the University of Toronto professor said later, "I didn't even know I was nominated." But Polanyi, 57, learned officially that afternoon that he shared the $406,000 award with U.S. scientists Dudley

JOHN POLANYI, THE UNIVERSITY of Toronto professor and a 1986 winner of a Nobel Prize in chemistry, is one of numerous examples of brain gains by Canada—born in Berlin, schooled mainly in Britain. Here, he is interviewed in the garden of his Toronto home on the day his Nobel was announced.

Herschback of Harvard University and Yuan Lee of the University of California in Berkeley. He quickly capitalized on the attention that his award brought him to complain about cutbacks in funding for Ontario universities. Speaking at a Toronto rally, he noted that Britain, with twice Canada's population, has won 20 times as many Nobel prizes. Declared Polanyi: "We must conclude that it is the institutional environment that differs."

Indeed, on the very day that Polanyi became a Nobel laureate, the National Research Council announced further budget cuts to comply with federal austerity imposed by the government of Brian Mulroney. Cuts would be achieved in part by scrapping its photochemistry and kinetics sections—precisely where, in 1952, Polanyi began his prize-winning research on the molecular changes that occur during chemical reactions. The Berlin-born son of a Hungarian scientist and philosopher who left Nazi-ruled Germany in 1933, Polanyi and his experiments have paved the way for the development of infrared ray lasers used in medicine and industry. His laser research has also had military applications, which Polanyi, an activist for arms control and nuclear disarmament, says he regrets.

1994 The Neutron Man

Rae Corelli – OCTOBER 24, 1994 **B**ertram Brockhouse received the 1994 Nobel Prize in physics for work he had done more than 35 years ago. "It was completely out of the blue," said the 76-year-old retired scientist, "and I had no such expectation."

The academy said Brockhouse and 79-year-old Clifford Shull of the Massachusetts Institute of Technology in Cambridge, Mass., who never worked together, would share the physics award of more than $1 million for their pioneer-ing work in the use of neutrons to study the way atoms arrange them-selves and move in various solids. "In simple terms," the academy said, "Clifford G. Shull has helped answer the question of where atoms 'are' and Bertram N. Brockhouse, the question of what atoms 'do.'" Their discoveries have played a role in developments ranging from ceramic superconduc-tors to exhaust-cleaning systems employed in automobiles.

In an interview, Brockhouse said that even though nuclear physics was in its infancy in the 1940s, "I knew from the beginning that this was a field wait-ing to be developed." He probed the

PHYSICIST BERTRAM BROCKHOUSE, a professor at McMaster University in Hamilton, Ontario, who pioneered the use of thermal neutrons to study the behavior of matter, here shows his wife his 1994 Nobel physics citation after receiving it in Stockholm. Brockhouse shares with Frederick Banting the distinction of being the only native-born Canadian Nobel winners for work done in Canada.

structure of materials by showering them with neutrons given off by a nuclear reac-tor. The way the neutrons bounced off atoms at different velocities revealed how the atoms were arranged, and how they moved within the structure of a substance.

Canadian scientists applauded the selection of Brockhouse, a native of Lethbridge, Alta., and a graduate of the universities of British Columbia and Toronto. He did his early work at the Chalk River, Ont., nuclear reactor of Atomic Energy of Canada Ltd. and later taught at McMaster University in Hamilton. "A 100-per-cent Canadian product won the prize," said Rashmi Desai, associate chairman of the University of Toronto physics department.

The award to Brockhouse is the 14th Nobel received by Canadian or Canadian-born scientists working abroad. He is the sixth honored for work done in Canada.

The Real Stuff
à la Canuck

Canadian Men, Women and Hardware Get Up Front in Space

IN December 1983, Steve MacLean is keenly geared up for the astronautical era (post-grad astrophysics and laser physics) when he is plucked from more than 4,300 applicants by the Canadian Space Agency to be one of the lucky few candidates to conduct scientific research in the American shuttle program. A flier, hiker, gymnast, canoeist and married with children, Ottawa-born MacLean is a young man, 28 years old, with the right stuff for hero status.

But the better part of nine years go by without the real stuff. The U.S. National Aeronautics and Space Administration takes time to get over the explosion of the *Challenger* on January 28, 1986, the 25th shuttle mission, a tragedy that NASA, years later on its website, describes laconically as "Loss of vehicle and crew of seven." It is not until October 1992, when MacLean, by now 37, finally lifts off aboard the shuttle *Columbia* on a mission that involves a series of experiments in space vision, sensing and materials physics.

Fellow candidate and naval officer Marc Garneau had long since been the trailblazer—aboard *Challenger* for environmental research in October 1984—barely 10 months after he and MacLean, Roberta Bondar, Bob Thirsk and Bjarni Tryggvason became designated astronauts. (Garneau was to draw a second mission in May 1996, aboard *Endeavour*.) Bondar was the second of the team in space, on *Discovery* in January, 1992, engaged in weightlessness experiments—a field of

OTTAWA-BORN STEVE MACLEAN, after nine years of training and delays, aboard the American space shuttle Columbia *at last, in October 1992.*

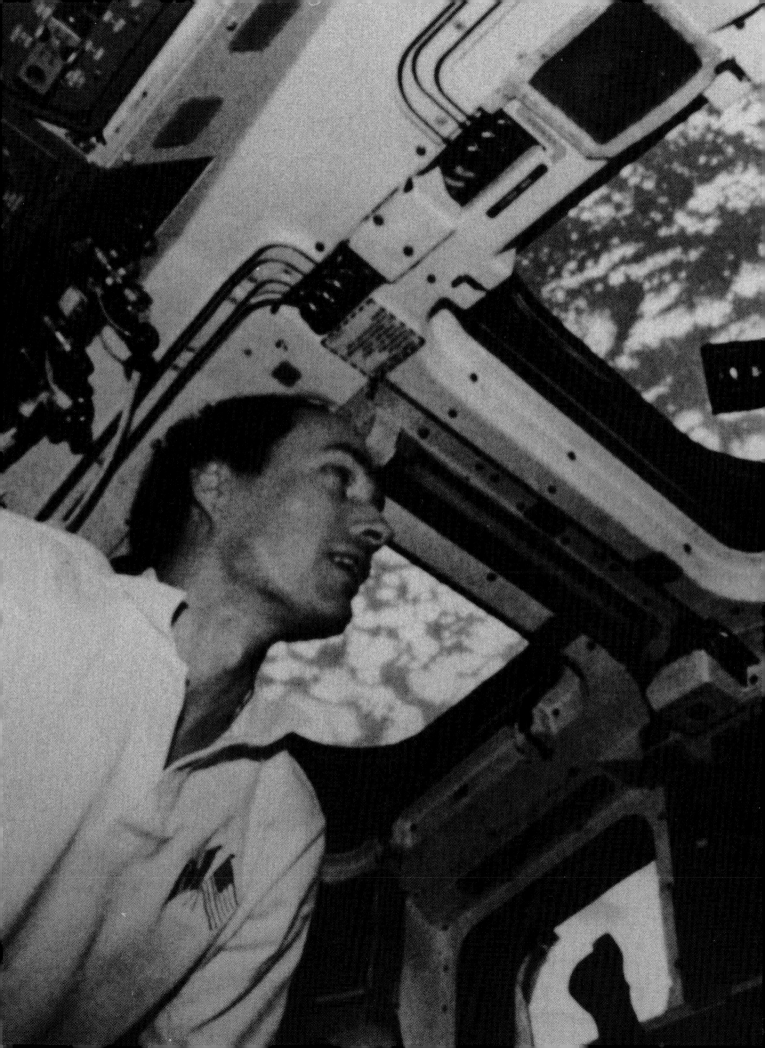

SEPTEMBER 29, 1962: At Vandenberg Air Force Base in California, an American rocket carried aloft Canadian-designed Alouette I and thus launched Canada's program of operating earth satellites for speeding TV and other communications signals across Canada and abroad.

research pursued later by Thirsk on *Columbia* in June and July 1996, and by physician Dafydd (Dave) Williams, one of a second contingent of Canadian astronauts recruited in 1992, also on *Columbia*, in April and May 1998. Then, on May 27, 1999, Montrealer Julie Payette went aloft in *Discovery* to work on the space station project – to the plaudits of Canada, especially in Quebec.

Apart from the protracted wait experienced by MacLean and others in his group, the timing of his voyage was not good back home. When MacLean began his 10-day mission on October 22, 1992, Canadian news media were transfixed by the national referendum four days later on the constitutional Charlottetown Accord. Such a matter of earthly immediacy shunted mere space travel off the agenda.

Other Canadian astronauts generally received more attention, as did such made-in-Canada material contributions to space-age activity as the Canadarm, the federally subsidized remote-controlled manipulator that became an indispensable tool for space-station work and in launching and retrieving satellites. Canada was also an early player in the construction and operation of communications satellites. The launch of Canadian satellite *Alouette I* on September 29, 1962, (on a NASA rocket) was, in Ottawa's words, "a landmark event which made Canada only the third nation in the world to have a satellite in orbit"–following the Soviet Union (*Sputnik I* launched the space age, October 4, 1957), and the United States (*Explorer I*, became the American pioneer on January 31, 1958). A flotilla of Canadian Anik satellites followed the Alouette program.

The "space race" that *Sputnik* spawned eventually gave way to co-operation between the United States and Russia. Canada, Europe, Japan and Brazil joined the two main players in NASA's program to construct a successor space station to Mir, the decrepit Russian structure that Canadian air force whiz Chris Hadfield, the only Canadian recruited and trained to crew the American shuttles, visited on a working mission in 1995. After that, Hadfield was assigned to hit space again in 1999, this time to work on the new station.

CONDUCTING EXPERIMENTS or simply doing the daily things of earthly life in outer space requires being used to weightlessness—if only for 30 seconds at a time, as Canadians Ken Money and Roberta Bondar demonstrate in 1984 aboard an American airplane on a roll.

1979 Bettering the Odds for Survival

Julianne Labreche – SEPTEMBER 24, 1979 **S**oon after the explosion, skipper Doug Larden and his five-man crew were bailing salt water from their rubber dinghy and murmuring prayers. Three days earlier, they had pointed their fishing vessel, *Mother III*, toward herring catches off the coast of Vancouver Island. The explosion, a fire and their boat was transformed into an inferno. They drifted. Rescue crews were without clues. The fishermen were prisoners of the Pacific.

Today, Larden's mishap is a year-old memory. Later that third day an Argus aircraft spotted his emergency flare and soon the survivors were scrambling for a helicopter's safety. But Ottawa's search and rescue team still use the story in telling of the frustrations of trying to track down missing ships and aircraft. In 1978–the same year Larden was lost at sea–1,592 other Canadians also waited for rescue. Of those, 181 died and 84 were never found.

It was with great expectations, therefore, that Canadian officials last month signed an agreement with France and the United States for a four-year, $13-million experimental satellite system. Called SARSAT, it has the potential to alert authorities within three hours of an air or sea accident, and narrow the search to within 13 miles.

1983 Spar's Soaring Success in Space

Peter C. Newman – AUGUST 22, 1983 Most Canadians think that buying a ticket to *The Return of the Jedi* may be their only admission to the space age. In fact, 18 Canadian companies, eight universities and five government departments maintain world-class space research facilities, and the Maple Leaf is about to go into even more impressive orbit.

The organization leading the way to the stars is Spar Aerospace Ltd., which won world attention for constructing the 50-foot-long artificial arm that lifted out of the U.S. space shuttle in November, 1981. At the moment, Spar is building a third space arm for the Americans as well as the revolutionary solar panels, stretching to half the length of a football field, that will drive Olympus, the powerful communications satellite to be launched by the European Space Agency in 1986. Those and other activities have turned Spar into a profitable growth stock, with a 1982 net income of $8.6 million–up nearly 300 per cent from the year before.

Spar has contributed to every Anik in Canada's own satellite program. Spar chairman Larry Clarke estimates that between now and the end of the century the free world will launch about 250 communications satellites and that during the next decade $23 billion will be spent in space. It intends to grab at least five per cent of this market and is counting on continued support from Ottawa to make it happen. "The government," he says, "has an extremely powerful and positive role to play–not in business but in support of business." It was the initiative (and $110 million) from the National Research Council that first got Spar into the shuttle program. Spar has also received $25 million in government grants.

NAVAL OFFICER MARC GARNEAU, the first Canadian to fly in space, aboard the shuttle Challenger *in 1984 and subsequently on* Endeavour, *in May 1996.*

COLIN WATSON (LEFT), PRESIDENT of Toronto-based Spar Aerospace, shows a model of the Special Purpose Dextrous Manipulator, a space-station successor to Spar's famous Canadarm, to Public Works Minister Alfonso Gagliano and Industry Minister John Manley in Ottawa in 1997.

1995 The Ride of His Life

NOVEMBER 27, 1995 ┃It was what he had been dreaming of and planning for nearly all his life—flight into deep space. Chris Hadfield, 36, became the first Canadian to be part of a shuttle flight crew—and a special one, assigned to the NASA shuttle Atlantis linkup with the Russian space station Mir. Hadfield, 36, whose career dream began at age nine when he watched TV coverage of Neil Armstrong walking on the moon on July 20, 1969, had a prime assignment. His main duty was to manoeuvre the docking tunnel connecting Atlantis to Mir. That made him the first Canadian to operate the Canadarm, the made-in-Canada remote-controlled manipulator.

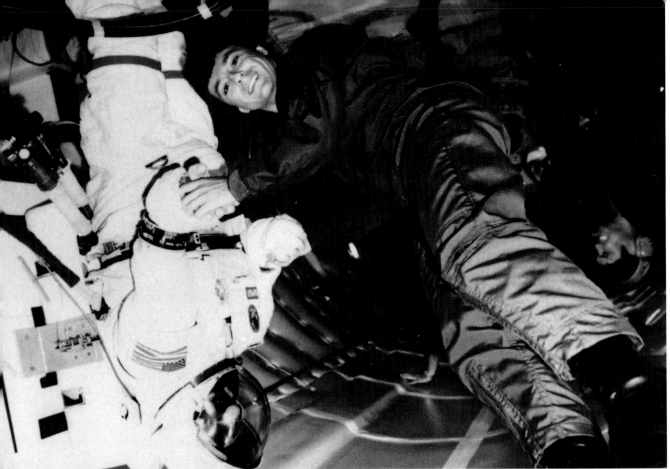

BOB THIRSK, IN A WEIGHTLESS *moment aboard an American training plane in 1984, encountered an empty suit used for spacewalking, along with its attached gear.*

A NETWORK OF RECEIVING *stations similar to this terminal near Ottawa form links across Canada in a worldwide program, inaugurated in 1982, called SARSAT, a satellite-aided search and rescue network.*

A TEAM OF ROOKIE CANADIAN *astronauts—from the left, Bob Thirsk, Bjarni Tryggvason, Roberta Bondar, Steve MacLean, Marc Garneau and Ken Money—tried some hockey in a wind tunnel at the National Research Council in Ottawa early in 1984.*

WHEN PART-TIME GUITARIST Chris Hadfield heard that a cosmonaut aboard the Russian space station Mir *had broken his guitar, the Canadian astronaut took along a replacement on a working mission to* Mir *in 1995. Here, Hadfield performs in the same year for earthlings in Toronto.*

In an interview from space during the eight-day venture (Nov. 12-20), Hadfield was gleeful about how the mission was going. Rhapsodizing on weightlessness, he said: "Suddenly I realized I'm floating around–you know, just cruising along like a paper airplane through Mir, and it's almost a surreal experience."

Canada's Expositors

How the Artists Explain the Country to Its People

FIRST come the explorers and the builders, then the expositors, the artists who describe and explain the country to its people. In Canada early in the century, the discoverers and developers were still at work when the writers and the painters began to examine what it is about the land and its inhabitants that make them unique. Gradually, the artists worked out for Canada its sense of identity, shaping their various understandings and images of the country in words and pictures.

Among the pioneers in the exploration of the Canadian psyche were two immigrants–Louis Hémon, a journalist from France who arrived in Quebec in 1911, and Frederick Philip Grove, a poet and translator from Germany who settled in Manitoba in 1912. Both men spent time working on back-country farms. They wrote novels–Hémon in French, Grove in English–that critics regard as Canada's first modern fiction. They were realists rather than romantics in relating their stories of the physical and psychological hazards of trying to survive in an unyielding land, an unforgiving climate and a sometimes unfriendly human environment. Their writings–Hémon's *Maria Chapdelaine* (published posthumously in 1916) and Grove's *Settlers of the Marsh* (1925)–proved to be literary pathfinders for the prolific ranks of writers that flourished in later years, in both languages and across the regions.

WILLIAM ROBERTSON DAVIES, Ontario man of genius and spinner of tales, and William Ormond (W.O.) Mitchell, the plain-speaking Prairie wise man and literary raconteur, with younger writers Margaret Atwood and Timothy Findley in the fall of 1990.

FROM HIS BIRTHPLACE IN Brantford, Ontario, to his final home in New York City, Thomas Costain, pictured here at age 70 in 1955, developed his literary talents as a newspaper reporter, as editor of Maclean's *from 1914 until 1920, in several American media jobs, and then as the author of hugely best-selling historical novels.*

STEPHEN LEACOCK, economist by profession, conservative by nature, at times offended women and others—often in Maclean's *in the 1915-1925 era—with his old-fashioned opinions about gender and race. But he gained acclaim for his humorous essays, which often reflected a developing Canadian ethos that favored community ahead of individualism.*

Not that all the artists, and notably not the painters, regarded the nature of the country as entirely hostile to humans. Against the view of the northern environment as an enemy of people stands the existential idea of humans in harmony with nature. Both views appear in Canadian literature.

The sense of nature as a menacing force finds expression near the beginning of Grove's *Settlers of the Marsh* :

"The wind came in fits and starts out of the hollow north-west; and with the engulfing dark an ever thickening granular shower of snow blew from the low-hanging clouds. As the trail became less and less visible, the very ground underneath seemed to slide to the south-east. . . . A merciless force was slowly numbing them by ceaseless pounding."

By contrast, Tomson Highway's similar wintry scene in his 1998 novel, *Kiss of the Fur Queen*, is cast in a more beneficent light:

"He could hear the endless stands of spruce groaning within their shrouds of

MORLEY CALLAGHAN, shown here at age 57 in 1960, studied to be a lawyer, but luckily for literature he went to Paris in the Roaring Twenties and established a foothold in fiction writing. Back in Canada, he moved from the sophisticated short story to the novel, often examining how spirit and flesh collide in human behavior.

*GABRIELLE ROY was a catalyst in Canadian literature's ascent following the Second World War, a writer whose first novel—*Bonheur d'occasion *in French,* The Tin Flute *in English—brought her numerous honors. She wrote about life on the Prairies and among impoverished Montrealers with equal insight.*

snow, the air so clean it sparkled: silver, then rose, then mauve. Four-year-old Champion knelt at the front of his father's dogsled. . . . The eight grey huskies were flying through the sky, past the sun, to the heaven of Champion's way of thinking. The trail curved unpredictably; who knew what surprises lay around the next bend, which creature might be feeding on spruce cones or pine needles, a rabbit, a weasel, five ptarmigans fluttering off in their winter coats of Holy Ghost white?"

But the importance that Hémon and Grove placed on the relationship between humans and nature may be traced throughout the century, even as literary themes became more urban, in the writings of a host of creative people—Morley Callaghan and Hugh MacLennan and Gabrielle Roy; Thomas Raddall and Farley Mowat and David Adams Richards in the East; W.O. Mitchell and W.P. Kinsella and Guy Vanderhaeghe in the West; Yves Beauchemin and Marie-Claire Blais and Roch Carrier and Roger Lemelin in Quebec, with Antonine Maillet and her Acadian peers also writing in French. Many other artists drew encouragement and example

FARLEY MOWAT AWAKENED Canadians to injustices in the treatment of Native people, particularly in northern Canada, with his 1952 classic People of the Deer, *a virtual textbook in many schools. In a novel for juvenile readers,* Lost in the Barrens, *Mowat provides an interracial Canadian parable within an adventure story.*

FOR THOUSANDS OF WOMEN FROM around the world, the prime Prince Edward Island mecca is Green Gables, the home of Anne Shirley, the spirited early feminist introduced to readers in 1908 by novelist Lucy Maud Montgomery, herself an Islander, and an inspiration to girls of the world ever after.

AS THE HEART HOPES

Lucy Maud Montgomery, whose Anne of Green Gables *was a best-seller upon publication in 1908 and ever after, wrote mainly gushy romances for* Maclean's *but provided one of a pageful of rhymes in January 1915 that were inspired by the First World War.*

It is a year, dear one, since you afar
Went out beyond my yearning mortal sight—
A wondrous year! Perchance in many a star
You have sojourned, or basked within the light
Of mightier suns; it may be you have trod
The glittering pathways of the Pleiades,
And through the Milky Way's white mysteries
Have walked at will, fire-shod.

Can any exquisite, unearthly morn,
Silverly breaking o'er a starry plain,
Give to your soul the poignant pleasure born
Of virgin moon and sunset's lustrous stain
When we together watch them? Oh apart
A hundred universes you may roam,
But still I know—I know—your only home
Is here, within my heart!

CASUALTY

Robert Service, known for his narrative Songs of a Sourdough *from the Klondike gold rush of 1898-1899, was 40 when the First World War broke out in 1914. As an ambulance driver in the combat zones, he filed his impressions to* Maclean's *in verse, including this piece, published in March 1918.*

The lad I took in the car last night,
With the body that awfully sagged away,
And the lips blood-crisped, and the eyes flame-bright,
And the poor hands folded and cold as clay—
Oh, I've thought and thought of him all the day!
For the weary old Doctor says to me:
"He'll only last for an hour or so.
Both of his legs below the knee
Blown off by a bomb . . . So please go slow,
And bear in mind, lad, he doesn't know."

So I tried to drive with never a jar;
And there was I cursing the road like mad,
When I hears a ghost of a voice from the car:
"Tell me, old chap, have I 'copped it' bad?"
So I answers "No," and he says: "I'm glad."
"Glad," says he, "for at twenty-two
Life's so splendid, I'd hate to go.
There's so much that a chap might do,
And I've fought from the start, and I've suffered so.
T'would be hard to get 'done in' now, you know."

"Forget it," says I; then I drove a while,
And I passed him a cheery word or two;
But he didn't answer for many a mile.
So just as the hospital hove in view,
Says I: "Is there nothing that I can do?"
Then he opens his eyes and smiles at me;
And he takes my hand in his trembling hold:
"Thank you—you're far too kind," says he;
"I'm awfully comfy—stay . . . let's see:
I fancy my blanket's come unrolled—
My feet, please wrap 'em—they're cold . . . they're cold . . ."

IT TOOK AN ADVENTURING English migrant, posted to the Yukon early in the century by the Canadian Bank of Commerce, to turn yarns about the Klondike gold rush of the late 1890s into verse, starting with Songs of a Sourdough *in 1907. Here, Robert Service is canoeing somewhere north of 60 in 1911.*

MICHAEL ONDAATJE (right), who moved to Canada as a youth from his native Sri Lanka by way of a boyhood in England, is one of a number of talented immigrants from southern Asia who enriched the literary life of Canada. His novel The English Patient (1992), made into a movie in 1996, delivered a global, multi-media impact.

FROM DIFFERENT backgrounds and in variant ways, painter Alex Colville, a Nova Scotian from boyhood, and Manitoba-born novelist Margaret Laurence (above)—here together at an awards ceremony—performed similar services in their expositions on lives in a Canadian setting.

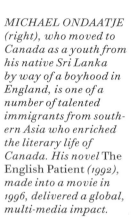

ANNE HÉBERT (left), although well into her forties during Quebec's Quiet Revolution of the 1960s, had already become an unofficial poet laureate of modern Quebec. Her role was reinforced—from her base in Paris after the middle 1960s—with her powerful novel Kamouraska (1970), which became a Claude Jutra film, and later works.

ARMENIAN CANADIAN Yousuf Karsh (below)—the photographer photographed here on January 3, 1947, in his Ottawa home town at a ceremony swearing in new citizens as Canadians for the first time (Canadians previously had been British subjects)—made his name synonymous worldwide with celebrity portrait photography.

JEAN-PAUL RIOPELLE (above) and his teacher, Paul-Émile Borduas, led a mid-century Montreal movement of abstract painters that supplanted the Group of Seven. Riopelle—here in a characteristic establishment-defying pose—went on to gain international attention as a painter influenced by both surrealism and resistance to the capitalist status quo.

NOVA SCOTIA-BORN Montrealer Hugh MacLennan (above)—here on a boat returning from Britain, where he had studied as a Rhodes Scholar—was regarded by some as a nationalist pioneer among Canada's English-language writers for exploring distinctively Canadian experiences in Barometer Rising and Two Solitudes.

EMILY CARR pursued her career as a painter at a time and in a place—early in the century in Victoria, B.C.— that gave her slight encouragement. After receiving the support of the Group of Seven in 1928, she tackled her work with invigorated freedom and success.

TRINIDAD NATIVE DIONNE BRAND resisted the notion that her work was a category of CanLit. "I don't consider myself on any margin, on the margin of Canadian literature," she said. "I'm sitting right in the middle of Black literature. . . ."

also from Margaret Laurence and Robertson Davies and Timothy Findley, Margaret Atwood and Mavis Gallant, Alice Munro and Michael Ondaatje and Mordecai Richler.

The graphic artists pursued a similar course, developing in both their stream-of-vision styles and naturalist subjects, a uniquely Canadian school of art. J.E.H. MacDonald, a founder of the Group of Seven painters in Ontario, observed that what dictated how they worked was not artistic method but nature–"that mystic north around which we all revolve." Elsewhere and over the years, others found inspiration from the same source, however different their painting styles might be–Emily Carr, W.J. Phillips, Dorothy Knowles, James Nicoll and Roy Vickers in the West; Jean Paul Lemieux and Paul-Emile Borduas in Quebec; Alex Colville and Mary Pratt and Christopher Pratt in the East. The first nations of Canada, the Inuit and Indians expressed visions of their lands and people by transforming rocks, wood, metals and paper into potent works of art.

That the first flowering of creative writing and art in Canada coincided with the early days of *Maclean's* proved fortuitous for both. The magazine made regular

AROUND THE TIME IN 1920 WHEN the Group of Seven painters shocked mainstream Canada with their then-brash portrayals of the Canadian scene, six of them (Franklin Carmichael absent) were photographed at the Arts and Letters Club in Toronto with literary critic and painter Barker Fairley (here with a pipe). Clockwise from the left foreground: A.Y. Jackson, Frederick Varley, Lawren Harris, Franz Johnston, Arthur Lismer and J.E.H. MacDonald.

3 MOONS

In August 1969, Margaret Atwood was known as a poet but not yet as an acclaimed novelist when she contributed to a page of verse in Maclean's *marking the American moon landing the previous month.*

(I)

The moon we imagined as children
has glass trees with seaweed fronds
on which grew huge blueberries;

our superhuman kings
walked to it through the sky
when they wanted to rest or explore

(wearing their Sunday crowns, although
they always took their guns)
in the short intervals between wars.

(II)

They know what it looks like:
that crystalline
lady of growth & ocean

whose disc glinted / reflected centuries
deep in our night skulls, the
eye of a prehistoric monster

is barren, a place of cinders
(slagheaps & dead rocks I saw,
black arctic)

(III)

No one can go there
now, without swords inside
his fingers, a fool's mask, a metal
plated mind.

Flying man, open another
canned song, plug your eyes
with familiar words, it is your
only weapon:

if you forget and look directly
at that bleak medusa head, that
goddess body,

she will destroy you.

THE TRUE NORTH

In a special issue of Maclean's *for the 125th anniversary of Confederation, dated July 6, 1992, the Alberta-born, West Coast poet Leona Gom contributed one of her works for the occasion.*

We are drawing the maple leaf,
we copy it from a book,
it's our national emblem,
when Laura says,
what is a maple leaf,
and we all giggle,
imagine asking that,
why we all know it's—
and teacher says,
why it's—
the maple tree leaf,
and Laura says,
how come
I never seen one,
and we all gasp,
crayons cringing
over maple leaves,
but teacher looks—
not mad, something else,

she looks—
out the window,
at the thick hair
of poplar and spruce
braided across the sky,
and she says,
you're right,
it doesn't grow here,
and we wait,
there must be something more,
but she only says,
finish your coloring,
and outside
the wind accuses
the unknown forest.

features of verse (some of which appears in this chapter) and fiction, short stories and serialized novellas. Owner-publisher John Bayne Maclean, applauding his contributors on "Publisher's Page" in February 1916, boasted that "no other magazine in the world contains in combination the names of these fine Canadian writers–Arthur Stringer, Stephen Leacock, Robert W. Service, Agnes C. Laut, Nellie McClung, Arthur MacFarlane, Alan Sullivan and L. M. Montgomery."

Augmenting the verbal images of the writers were the artists and illustrators. Franklin Arbuckle was a leader among the painters who enlivened magazine covers with vignettes of Canadiana. The etchings of the likes of Rex Woods, Duncan Macpherson and Roy Peterson, wielding trenchant wit along with sharp pens and pointed brushes, served to illuminate texts and express their own comments on Canadian life.

Maclean's enlisted many of the artists and creative writers across Canada to display samples of their works or–before as well as after the magazine changed direction toward news in the 1970s–to comment on current events. And even after the magazine's transition, the occasional poem appeared.

A Presence on the Silver Screen

Success in the Movies Means Playing the Hollywood Way

W HEN the motion picture began to catch on as popular entertainment during the first decade of the century, hopes were high in Canada that the country would develop its own movie industry and profit culturally and financially from the exciting new mode of communication. Ottawa, with the establishment of the Canadian Government Motion Picture Bureau in 1923, encouraged development of what was to become a Canadian specialty, the documentary film. But by the time the talkies began to supplant silent movies at the end of the 1920s, the early promise had all but evaporated. American distributors of American movies exercised almost total control over the feature films Canadians would get to see. And any Canadian wanting a career in filmdom—be it on screen, like Mary Pickford, or in production, like Mack Sennett—was obliged to leave home and head south.

Government initiatives designed to provide a presence in the film business for Canadians in Canada generally proved too puny to reverse American domination. The National Film Board, inspired by founding commissioner John Grierson from its beginning in May, 1939, produced a sparkling array of documentaries and, later, feature films of high quality. But Hollywood's grip on distribution meant that NFB films—or even features made with help from Telefilm Canada, the

OTTAWA RECRUITED JOHN GRIERSON, the brilliant, Scottish-born film producer who coined the term "documentary" for movies about real lives, first for his advice and then—just as the Second World War was beginning—to run the agency he had suggested, the National Film Board, which quickly became a highly creative film agency.

FILMMAKER DAVID CRONENBERG, a Torontonian like so many other Canadians prominent in the movie world, established himself in Hollywood with such productions as The Fly *and went on to further plumb the dark in* Crash *in 1996, which* Maclean's *critic Brian D. Johnson characterized as "an utterly bizarre movie." Here, the cast of* Crash *flanks Cronenberg, in the middle.*

federal film development agency established in 1967–rarely reached a wide audience at home.

Repeated proposals to correct the situation, including plans to redirect a small share of screening profits into the Canadian industry, got nowhere in Ottawa. And by the closing years of the century even the modest incentives provided by tax breaks for financing films were among the Canadian cultural measures under threat from free-trade agreements with the United States. Federal spending cuts further threatened the programs of Telefilm Canada and the NFB.

Against the odds, Canadian filmmakers created a string of critically successful feature movies during the century's later years, usually with governmental help and, in some cases, CBC and NFB co-production assistance.

BY THE 1920s, the federal government was into the movie business, its Canadian Government Motion Picture Bureau—whose staff is at work here in an Ottawa studio—turning out films lauding Canada to potential immigrants. The bureau was absorbed by the National Film Board after its establishment in 1939.

ATOM EGOYAN, ONE OF A number of young Canadians who won attention at home in the 1980s as novice makers of movies, went on to win plaudits abroad in the 1990s. His powerful and acclaimed The Sweet Hereafter *won him a best-director Oscar nomination in 1998, but Canadian-born James Cameron took the prize for his super-spectacle* Titanic.

Among the makers of films acclaimed by critics at home and abroad: Denys Arcand (*Jésus de Montréal*); Donald Brittain (*Volcano*); Gilles Carle (*Les Plouffe*); David Cronenberg (*Dead Ringers*); Atom Egoyan (*The Sweet Hereafter*); Claude Jutra (*Mon Oncle Antoine*); Bruce McDonald and Don McKellar (*Highway 61*); Patricia Rozema (*I've Heard the Mermaids Singing*); Cynthia Scott (*The Company of Strangers*); John N. Smith and Sam Grana (*The Boys of St. Vincent*).

Otherwise, as for the pressures on Canadian artistes and auteurs to move south, and on the film fans of Canada to make do with little more than American fare most of the time, not a great deal has changed since pictures first began moving on Canadian theatre screens.

1915 The Queen of the Movies

Margaret Bell – APRIL 1915 **A**bout seventeen years ago, a certain Toronto audience witnessed a certain play, which still holds its audiences spellbound. There was shooting and smacking of whips, there was weeping and laughing. In the midst of all that tripped a beautiful child, with flaxen hair and all the rest of it. Unfortunately, she floated away, right before the tearful eyes of the audience, leaving only the remembrance of her sweetness and goodness to cheer their aching hearts. Little Eva was the name of the pathetic heroine. She who played it was called Gladys Smith.

MARY PICKFORD, BORN GLADYS SMITH in Toronto and billed as Baby Gladys after going on the stage there at age five, grew up to become America's Sweetheart. She was among the first of the glamorous Hollywood movie stars, along with Douglas Fairbanks, her bridegroom in 1920 and pictured with her here in 1924.

Gladys Smith was later to be known to the world as Mary Pickford. It was in a little house at 211 University Avenue, Toronto, where her father, John C. Smith, lived with his young wife, who had been an actress, that Gladys Marie was born a little over twenty years ago, on April 8, 1893. Before she had reached the age of ten, Gladys Smith had covered more miles than many people during their whole lives.

She was soon talking business to New York's greatest theatrical magnate, David Belasco! It was then that Belasco persuaded our infantile heroine to adopt the name by which she has since become famous.

Nowadays, she may be seen tripping daintily on a screen, now as a regal personage in fine robes and ermine, now as a sobbing Cinderella, whose sobs are quickly melted in smiles, now a petted favorite in a luxurious home. It would be impossible to name all of Mary Pickford's cinema successes. Mary Pickford has become the acknowledged "star of stars" in the movie firmament.

1916 Our Newest Industry: The 'Movies'

Hugh S. Eayrs – APRIL 1916 **O**ne is inclined to think of the "Movies" only as our latest pleasure, the innovation which has tickled the jaded taste of the amusement-loving public. But the "Movies" mean much more to Canada than merely that.

THE MOVIE HOUSE EVOLVED from town halls, community centres and theatres such as the Opera House of Innisfail, Alberta (top), in 1910; through the extravagant movie palaces of the 1920s and 1930s and mid-century neighborhood cinemas, like the Glendale in Toronto (middle); to the mini-screened, multi-roomed mass movie marketplaces of the 1980s, and in the 1990s, the mega-cinema entertainment centres like this one in Mississauga, Ontario (bottom), in 1997.

They signify, among other things, our newest industry and an increasingly important means of revenue.

Roughly, there are from thirteen to fifteen hundred licensed moving picture theatres in Canada. Toronto has seven theatres, but sixty-nine "Movie" theatres. The total of "Movie" houses is an astonishing number when you figure that the first licensed motion picture theatre in Canada did not open for business till 1909. Of course, motion pictures, or rather animated pictures, for so they were then more generally known, had been shown before that in big halls, heralded with a fanfare of trumpets as something novel. But it was only in 1909 that the first theatre used exclusively for showing "Movies"–in Sudbury, Ont.–opened for business.

And what is our newest industry contributing to the coffers of the Dominion? Here again the figures are amazing. The licence fee paid by the "movie" theatre to the province in which it is located is $150 per annum–an aggregate of $210,000. In many cities (Toronto is one), there is a licence fee paid to municipal authorities of $50. There is duty payable on projectors, advertising and every reel of film coming into the country. Including licences and censors fees paid to the provinces, the various duties and fees which the "Movies" contribute to Canada per year would be almost one million dollars.

The time has not yet come in Canada when large companies are formed to build moving picture theatres or to produce the pictures themselves; but it is coming. When the stage of producing pictures is reached, it will mean that a larger percentage of the Canadian public's dime will remain in Canada. There is no limit to the possibilities of the future.

1930 **The Battle for Canadian Film Control**

James A. Cowan – OCTOBER 1, 1930 **E**very Saturday night, nearly a million Canadians fill the pews of the film temples. They are being entertained by Hollywood and they pay from a quarter to half a million dollars for the evening. But any night in the week fortunes flow through the box offices.

As these synthetic dramas have unrolled by the thousands of feet, another one has been staged behind the screens. It has no love interest. It is the battle of the box offices and the stakes run to millions. The prize is control of Canadian theatres, domination of a rich industry. But it is much more than business, as it influences public opinion and even sets styles in thinking.

Nationwide control of the film business in Canada has for some time been vested in a single organization, Famous Players. Control of this organization, in turn, has just passed into the hands of Paramount-Publix, the giant of the U.S. motion picture industry and the "Big Boss" of Canadian Filmdom.

SCOTTISH CANADIAN NORMAN MCLAREN, recruited to the NFB in 1941 by founder John Grierson, was a global ground-breaker in the production of animated films. Perhaps the highlight of his prolific ouput, issued as Cold War hostilities gripped the world in 1952, was Neighbours, *two scenes from which are pictured here, a parable about the futility of using violence to resolve conflict; it used an innovative technique of stop-motion cinematography.*

The ruling group in Canada, Famous Players Canadian Corporation, does not operate a majority of the country's cinemas centres, so outcries about monopoly are incorrect. But it does hold the key houses from Halifax to Vancouver and takes the cream of the returns. In cities such as London, Hamilton, Kingston, Brantford, Guelph, Fort William, Regina, Saskatoon, Edmonton, Calgary and Victoria, its sway is virtually complete. In Toronto and Montreal, one first-run house remains outside the fold.

This rule extends to the legitimate stage. For several seasons, no producer of spoken drama, musical comedy or operetta has been able to operate without the permission of the film moguls and the use of their theatres.

There have been resolutions galore, committees of investigation, complaints in Parliament, angry comments, solemn addresses and letters to the editor. Out of the melee, Paramount-Publix has emerged as the owner of Famous Players. The paternal Adolph Zukor, who came from tiny Ricse, in Hungary, to scale the flickering heights and sit in the seats of the celluloid mighty, rules Canadian filmdom.

Oratorical flurries about American monopoly marked discussion of the matter in the dying moments of Parliament's last session. Investigation was suggested. But the deal went through.

1953 An Ex-king Returns to Power

James Dugan – APRIL 15, 1953   In the remarkable new world of 3-D, nothing is more remarkable than the story of Louis B. Mayer, an immigrant boy who rose from cutting up sunken ships with a blowtorch in Saint John, N.B., to become King of Hollywood; lost his sceptre, his power and all but twenty million dollars of his fortune; and then, at sixty-seven, started out to make good all over again.

Mayer abdicated two years ago as production chief of Metro-Goldwyn-Mayer, largest and most legendary of all the studios. His subjects—even the not inconsiderable

number who had feared, hated or ridiculed him—knew that so mighty a fall closed an age and might be followed by anarchy.

Everybody feels better now. L.B. has returned in a suit of three-dimensional ermine as chairman of the board and production chief of the biggest did-ya-see-it in show business, Cinerama.

Mayer arrived in Saint John in 1888, at the age of three, with his Russian parents and, at fourteen, was bossing divers and salvage gangs in his father's ship-breaking business. At seventeen, the sturdy, ambitious youth went to Boston to sell junk metal. He found a wife, Margaret Shenberg, and he found the movies. It was 1902, only six years after Edison had projected the first American program: *Sea Waves*, *Venice Showing Gondolas*, *Butterfly Dance*, and *Kaiser Wilhelm Reviewing his Troops*. (Cinerama's first bill, more than half a century later, includes water-skiing, Venetian gondolas, a ballet, and a clan gathering in Scotland.)

In 1907, Mayer paid six hundred dollars for a Haverhill, Mass., flicker palace named the Gem, known to its public as "the Germ." The boy scrubbed the joint out and rechristened it the Orpheum. "Within two years," he said, "I had all the other theatres in town." By 1914, he offered the unprecedented sum of twenty-five thousand dollars for the New England rights to a film still in production, *The Birth of a Nation*. He netted one hundred thousand dollars.

Mayer headed west in 1916 with his wife, two young daughters, and an actress, Anita Stewart, to enter movie-making. He founded a factory in 1918 to make films for Metro Pictures, owned by Loew's Inc., the theatre chain. In 1924, Nicholas M. Schenck, Mayer and J. Robert Rubin, Loew's lawyer, formed the first and still the largest major movie factory, Metro-Goldwyn-Mayer, by consolidating their plants with that of Samuel Goldwyn. Mayer became plant manager, in charge of production.

He discovered Greta Garbo, Greer Garson, Mickey Rooney, and Leo the Lion. The stars he is credited with developing make up a glittering company: Lon Chaney, Lillian Gish, Lionel Barrymore, Marie Dressler, Joan Crawford, Clark Gable, Robert Taylor, Spencer Tracy, Norma Shearer, John Gilbert, Maurice Chevalier, Luise Rainer, William Powell, Freddie Bartholomew, Jean Harlow, Hedy Lamarr, Grace Moore, Esther Williams and Van Johnson.

Mayer is a wilful, overpowering man. He punched people, including the smaller Charlie Chaplin in a Los Angeles hotel lobby in 1920. Mayer sometimes resorted to the salty lingo of the Maritimes waterfront. But he made fiercely loyal lieutenants.

Mayer's star, Walter Pidgeon, was born a few blocks from the boss's humble home in New Brunswick. Mayer's fondness for Canadians in pictures extended to

LOUIS B. MAYER, THE SON OF A SCRAP dealer in Saint John, New Brunswick, began his ascent to movie mogul status when, at age 22 in 1907, he purchased a theatre in suburban Boston and began showing movies. In 1924 he joined the Metro and Goldwyn companies to form MGM. Mayer is pictured testifying before the U.S. House Un-American Activities Committee during its anti-Communist investigation of the entertainment industry in 1947.

such notables as Marie Dressler, whom he claimed as a personal discovery, to Walter Huston and Raymond Massey and, of course, to Norma Shearer.

The odd thing about his Cinerama venture is that L.B. never went for novelties. When the first part-talkie, *The Jazz Singer*, astonished the fans in 1927, Mayer predicted sound films would never hurt silent pictures. Other studios innovated color and cartoons, and some are now buying into television rather than perish in empty cinemas. Mayer has been the stand-patter. Now he is in charge of the big doo-hickey, the first man on the giant roller coaster. You will do well to fasten seat belts and hold onto your hats. There is a lot of showmanship in the old boy yet.

1987 Heroics of an Antihero

Brian D. Johnson – AUGUST 10, 1987   **B**ent over the operating table, he deftly cuts away at a special-effect wound with a pair of scissors. As he works, he describes each manoeuvre to his listeners, Chinese actors, with convincing authority: "Wash it out with saline solution, remove the devitalized muscle tissue, ligate the blood vessels." The actor wears a blood-stained apron and rubber gloves sticky with synthetic gore. As he glances up, rimless spectacles refract a piercing, blue-eyed gaze. Only a pair of yellow high-topped sneakers–safely out of the camera's frame–mar the illusion for the onlooker. Otherwise, Donald Sutherland, with his head shaved to look almost bald, bears an uncanny resemblance to Dr. Norman Bethune. The Canadian surgeon who died a hero on the front lines of the Chinese Revolution seems eerily resurrected by the actor, who has immersed himself in archival memories of Bethune's life. "Sutherland is not just acting Bethune," suggest Nicolas Clermont, coproducer of *Bethune: The Making of a Hero*. "He walks like him, thinks like him, even lives like him. I'm convinced that he is Bethune."

The 53-year-old Canadian actor has not made a habit of portraying heroes. Instead, he has bent his natural elegance into roles that few image-conscious stars would touch, from the leering child-killer in *The Dirty Dozen* (1967) to the awkward and vulnerable father in *Ordinary People* (1980). Because Hollywood tends to favor heroes, it is not surprising that Sutherland has never received an Oscar nomination, despite the fact he is a star of international stature. A veteran of more than 50 films, he has won the respect of the world's top directors. With a salary rumored to be almost $1 million a movie, he clearly ranks as the most successful Canadian actor of his generation.

Working against the grain of Hollywood glamor, Sutherland has created his own unconventional style, both on-screen and off. He crusades passionately for

ACTOR DONALD SUTHERLAND became world famous, but the native of Saint John, New Brunswick, remained steadfastly Canadian and twice played a Canadian hero he admired, the socialist doctor Norman Bethune, first in a CBC-TV production in 1977–as depicted here– and later in a Canada–China coproduction, Bethune: The Making of a Hero.

public causes that include Canadian nationalism, disarmament—and the Montreal Expos' quest for the baseball World Series title. He has been romantically involved with such outspoken actresses as Jane Fonda and Shirley Douglas, daughter of former federal NDP leader Tommy Douglas. Sutherland's eyes project a discomfiting aura of intelligence, as if he were constantly subjecting the world—and himself—to intense scrutiny. "Donald is a perfectionist who adores detail," said Bethune director Phillip Borsos. "He is able to compute many different possibilities of performance very quickly. And even though he works in a very structured way, he's one of the very great improvisational actors."

In three of his more recent films—*Ordinary People*, *Eye of the Needle*, *Threshold*—Sutherland says that he has at last found a degree of equilibrium. "It was like working from the same palette," he recalled. "The characters were all smart guys who didn't burst out or blow up."

Sutherland's Bethune is another "smart guy," but his eyes burn with missionary zeal. The role has obsessed him since he encountered the surgeon's writings in the early 1970s. He made several abortive attempts to launch a production. Now that he is finally making *Bethune*, it has turned into one of the most arduous experiences of his career. "It's like having your leg cut off," he told *Maclean's*. "I had to do it, but I'll miss the leg."

Sutherland accepted the five-month Bethune assignment for less than half his usual fee. During the third week of the shoot, he fell off a camel in Pin Yao and injured his back. For the rest of the filming, he wore a rigid corset under his clothes to relieve the pain. And the physical hardships of working in

ALTHOUGH TORONTO-BORN NORMAN JEWISON spent most of his career as a director and producer in the United States, and was honored there for such productions as In the Heat of the Night, *an Oscar winner for best movie in 1967, he moved back to Canada and in 1986 played a leading role in the establishment of the Canadian Centre for Advanced Film Studies in his home town.*

remote Chinese locations increased the strain on his health. But the actor seemed most irritated by problems that he considered endemic to Canadian film production—insufficient money, crew and organization. Defying common sense, he said he went ahead with the movie "because I'm Canadian—because I've got a maple leaf stuck up my ass. Like Bethune I feel resentfully and proudly Canadian."

For Sutherland, birthright is fundamental. Born in Saint John, N.B., he grew up on a farm, then moved to Bridgewater, N.S., at age 10. His father was an avid gambler who earned his living as a salesman. His maternal grandfather was a Presbyterian missionary. "He had that same Scots fire and brimstone as Tommy Douglas—a need to be right." The Scots ancestry oddly parallels that of Bethune, whose mother was an evangelical missionary. And, like the doctor, the actor combines a sensual flamboyance with a stubborn streak of missionary morality.

After an awkward adolescence, Sutherland entered the University of Toronto, enrolling in engineering to please his father—but concentrating on drama. He settled on an acting career after a small role in a campus production of *The Tempest* drew notice from *The Globe and Mail*'s influential drama critic. Wrote Herbert Whittaker: "Donald Sutherland has a spark that illuminates the stage."

But like many Canadian actors of his generation, Sutherland had to leave the country to confirm his talents—to England to study at the London Academy of Music and Dramatic Art at 23. Two years later he dropped out to act in British television and repertory theatre. In 1964, he landed his first major movie role: *Castle of the Living Dead*, a horror picture in which he played both a witch and an idiot soldier. Shot in Italy, the film also featured a young actress, Shirley Douglas. After divorcing his first wife, a former fellow student, in 1966, Sutherland married Douglas, who bore him twins Kiefer and Rachel. "I was pretty overwhelmed by Shirley," said Sutherland. "It was like flagging a bus and getting run over." [He married a third time, in 1972, to actress Francine Racette, a Quebecer.]

In the Wutai Mountains, Sutherland is living a spartan life. It is hard to picture him as the same man who keeps a sailboat in Los Angeles and a Rolls-Royce in London—the high roller who once bought a Ferrari in Italy with a paper bag full of poker winnings. The actor seems to relish his proximity to the past. On location, he has steeped himself in histories of Bethune and the Chinese Revolution.

It is late evening at the guesthouse. Sutherland sits slumped in a screening room watching rushes of a scene shot in Yenan—the now legendary meeting between Bethune and Mao. "Bethune was not a very relaxed person," notes Sutherland. "Hopefully, by the end of the film, he will be as serene as Mao." Meanwhile, on the screen, Bethune informs Mao that he is the son of a woman who was a missionary. Mao smiles. "Aren't we all," he says.

Television: Almost All American

'With All Its Imperfections, a Tremendous Social Force'

WRITER Robert Collins, in a *Maclean's* recollection, remembers Canadian television in its early days as "a hypnotic new toy," so contagiously habit forming that "within two years, the nation sat silent and bug-eyed in front of one million sets." What the nation watched most of the time was lightweight American fare. The new toy thus differed little from such earlier conduits of information and entertainment as radio, which chiefly delivered Americana.

Before radio in Canada was a decade old (it began in Montreal in 1919, and Canadian National Railways ran a network from 1923 to 1931), American broadcasts were drowning out Canada's sparse and underpowered stations. In response, the federal government founded the Canadian Radio Broadcasting Commission on May 26, 1932, to develop a national system. The CRBC, underfunded and subject to political meddling, was replaced in 1936 by the Canadian Broadcasting Corporation, which was given a similar mandate, with more money and less interference. But Canadian content remained virtually non-existent on private radio and even the CBC featured a lineup of American fluff on top of its original drama and music programs.

At the beginning of 1949, when American television was just over three years old and Canadian-made TV almost four years away (CBC-TV launched itself

IN THE 1930s AND 1940s, the upright radio competed with the piano in the middle-class living rooms of the nation, until the television set upstaged both in the 1950s.

on September 6, 1952, in Montreal and two days later in Toronto), *Maclean's* Ottawa editor Blair Fraser noted that the American programs picked up in Canada were "pretty deadly drivel," by and large. "But with all its imperfections and imbecilities," he added, "here is a tremendous social force, its potential impact greater than radio, telephone or movies."

Media magnate Roy Thomson, in common with others who came to own TV rights (a federal permit in 1960 to operate a station in North Bay, Ontario), cast the medium's importance in another light: "A TV licence is a licence to print money."

Newton Minow, addressing American broadcasters on May 9, 1961, as the new chairman of the U.S. Federal Communications Commission (FCC), railed against their screenfare as "a vast wasteland." The broadcasters–their output to become the mainstay of cross-Canada private television established that same year–then heard their chief regulator denounce their offerings in devastating detail: "You will see a procession of game shows, violence, audience-participation shows, formula comedies about totally unbelievable families, blood and thunder, mayhem, violence, sadism, murder, western bad men, western good men, private eyes, gangsters, more violence and cartoons. And, endlessly, commercials–many screaming, cajoling and offending. And most of all, boredom."

Communications guru Marshall McLuhan, in his 1964 work *Understanding Media*, states that "TV is a cool, participant medium," and "TV has changed our sense-lives and our mental processes. It has created a taste for all experience in depth." But Toronto-born broadcaster Mark Fowler, the 1980s FCC chairman who largely erased broadcasting regulations, pooh-poohed notions of TV's social and personal importance–including predecessor Newton Minow's admonition that "the power of instantaneous sight and sound is without prece-

BEFORE TELEVISION SIGNALS were transported via satellite in the 1960s and the advance of home delivery via cable, TV required armies of soaring microwave towers and tall home antennae to avoid interference and reduce scrambled pictures or blizzards of "snow" on the screen.

JUST AS TELEVISION was conquering the world, Marshall McLuhan, a professor of English at the University of Toronto, achieved international guru status in communication theory. He argued in such works as Understanding Media *(1964) that the electronic media were reducing the earth to a "global village."*

dent in mankind's history—an awesome power [that] carries with it awesome responsibilities." Fowler dismissed all that with the declaration: "Television is just another appliance—a toaster with pictures."

They may well all be correct, in their various ways, those viewers and owners, gurus and overseers. But, toy or toaster, TV did alter lifestyles and mindsets. It has replaced the hearth, abbreviated attention spans, forced the print media to comply with thought-truncation trends, destroyed the political careers of the untelegenic, promoted glitz over substance and passion over reason. Whether any of that is for good or ill depends on the circumstance, and the observer.

In any case, according to the statistics in the late 1990s, Canadians on average spent the equivalent of almost an entire day a week (22.7 hours) with the TV turned on—and tuned three-quarters or more of the time to American fare.

Late in the century, television offered the Canadian viewer much more quantity, and even more quality, than when the box was young. But the couch-potato viewing manner seemed little changed in the 1990s from the way that Robert Collins described early attitudes in *Maclean's*: "We wallowed in Jackie Gleason, *I Love Lucy* and Milton Berle—the fledgling CBC TV depended largely on American imports—but we would have happily watched the test pattern."

Over the years, TV has proven to be enduringly siren-like in its seductions, wooing the viewer to "taste experience"—if not "in depth," as McLuhan claimed, on the surface is surely sufficient. Don't worry, the tube advises. Be happy.

1951   What TV Will Do to You

Don Magill – MARCH 1, 1951   There's no doubt that when television finally does come to Canada—the first station is due to open this fall—it is going to make changes in your way of life. Whether the changes will be swift and sweeping (as in the U.S.) or mild and moderate (as in Britain) depends largely on what kind of TV we get. At the time of writing it seems that the CBC will okay a compromise between the two systems.

Perhaps 35,000 Canadian homes near the U.S. border already have TV sets, with their owners and their families getting dizzy staring at blurry images from distant transmitters. There's even a set in Alberta (cost: $470) where reception would be limited to about 15 minutes every two months. But if the growth of TV in Canada parallelled that of the U.S., two out of every three homes might have a TV set by 1956.

The growth and power of the new industry is either fine or horrible. Boston University President Daniel Marsh states that "if the television craze continues with the present level of programs, we are destined to have a nation of morons." But a Maryland school principal says that TV has knit families closer together, reduced street accidents to children, improved adolescent behavior and cut down on "idle conversation."

1965 How to Survive in the CBC Jungle

FEBRUARY 6, 1965 **P**ercy Saltzman interviews two young men who live in the eye of a showbusiness hurricane–Pat Watson and Douglas Leiterman, creators of *This Hour Has Seven Days*. [The program ran from October 4, 1964, to May 8, 1966.]

Saltzman: The program *This Hour Has Seven Days* has been possibly the most publicized the CBC ever had. What kind of an audience are you trying to reach?

Watson: A very broad audience, the kind that comes to television primarily for entertainment.

Saltzman: *Bonanza*, for example, and *The Ed Sullivan Show*? You expect to draw people away from them?

Watson: Well, not quite. We come after *Ed Sullivan* and *Bonanza* and it's our great hope that we can hold many of the viewers.

Leiterman: We have obligations to serve the people with certain kinds of information–generating conversation, provoking interest.

Saltzman: Well, that's spending a lot of money just to get people to talk. What kind of conversation do you think was provoked by the interview with the American Nazi, Lincoln Rockwell?

Leiterman: Conversation in many areas: concerning freedom of speech, concerning sensationalism, antisemitism, and the rights and responsibilities of the CBC.

Saltzman: You had a Lévesque interview which you didn't use.

Leiterman: When we came to do René Lévesque, we videotaped another interview in our Montreal studios. We intended to update the first one, but in the end we ran the first one, which was better.

Saltzman: The first one by Larry Zolf and Pierre Elliott Trudeau, with René Lévesque in the hotseat?

Leiterman: That's right, and the exciting things in this encounter did not recur because by the time of the second interview, the three men had the measure of one another and simply could not repeat the vitality.

Saltzman: Do I take it that I'm correctly quoting you that there is no CBC policy to play down any Canadian star system? The great names in Canadian TV are the ones that have gone to the States and England and made it and come back.

Watson: It may be that Canadians only believe they've got something good when another country, particularly the United States, puts its stamp of approval on it.

ALTHOUGH SHORT-LIVED, *the 19-month run from 1964 to 1966 of CBC-TV's weekly public affairs program* This Hour Has Seven Days *set a standard seldom matched afterward for crusading and compelling television. Absent from the panel pictured here—Robert Hoyt, Ken Lefolii, Douglas Leiterman and Patrick Watson—are three participants who accounted for much of the show's appeal: Laurier LaPierre, John Drainie and Dinah Christie. Political controversy killed the program.*

Saltzman: I have been told by a high CBC official that the greatest single factor in the Americanization of Canada over the last ten years is the CBC.

Leiterman: I think that the CBC in fact has been the agency which has been more responsible than any other for this country *remaining* Canadian.

Saltzman: What about all the film stuff they buy from Hollywood, like *The Beverly Hillbillies*?

Leiterman: Public affairs does not as a rule buy American packaged public affairs shows.

Watson: On the other hand, we share the continent with the U.S., producer of some first-rate entertainment, and I think that the corporation has an obligation to convey some of this entertainment.

1965 Everybody Loves Charlie Chamberlain

Susan Dexter – SEPTEMBER 18, 1965   Carping critics claim he can't sing, dance or act. But when this rough-cut, trouble-prone, carefree bear of a man steps before

FOR 40 YEARS, old-time, down-East music was synonymous with Don Messer and The Islanders, pictured here in 1948. The New Brunswick fiddler formed The Islanders in 1939 with bass player Julius (Duke) Nielsen, clarinetist and announcer Ray Simmons, drummer Warren MacRae and pianist Waldo Munro. Singers Charlie Chamberlain and Marg Osburne joined in 1934 and 1947.

BARBARA FRUM, who pioneered the nightly phone-out current-affairs interview show on CBC Radio's As It Happens from 1971 to 1981, went on to host CBC-TV's The Journal, a news-related show that followed the nightly TV newscast, until her death in 1992.

the TV cameras on *Don Messer's Jubilee* show and sings "Danny Boy" or "Trees," he tears the heart out of a million and a half contented Canadians, who hope he'll never change.

The whole world, seemingly, was built for Charlie Chamberlain to get emotional about. And it's this quality, more than anything else that first made him a favorite in the lumber camps and has kept him a pillar of the Messer company since 1934. This country-music show has a top rating, but very plain ingredients—old-time eastern-seacoast reels, quadrilles, polkas and toe-tapping tunes, complemented each week with popular ballads.

Charlie's role through those years has been to sing the sentimental Irish, sweetheart, mother, father and religious songs so many love to hear. The viewer has only to look at his moonlike lugubrious countenance to realize that Charlie means every word of those songs. Charlie, at fifty-four, is the same man who walked eighty miles into the lumberwoods and built roads in the relief camps near his northern New Brunswick birthplace of Bathurst in the hungry 1930s.

In 1937, Don Messer's New Brunswick Lumberjacks went on the CBC network for twenty-five dollars a week each. But in 1939 their contract expired and Don and Charlie set out for radio station CFCY in Charlottetown. There they became Don Messer and His Islanders, and their show rejoined the national network in the late 1940s.

Then in 1956 came local television. The show, produced in Halifax, was carried on the Maritimes network for two years, and in the summer of 1959 the big break came—the national network. The show has been rated in the top-ten Canadian TV shows ever since. This last year it was second only to hockey in Canadian-produced shows and ranked fifth after *Bonanza*, *The Beverly Hillbillies* and *The Ed Sullivan Show*.

1980 Screen Wars

Bill MacVicar – AUGUST 18, 1980

Since its introduction in the United States in the late 1940s and the creation of CBC-TV in 1952, TV stayed pretty much the same–until 1977. That is the year the viewing public declined for the first time.

No longer was television the mass hypnotist that developed its own loony sociology (movie houses closing down on Tuesday nights when Milton Berle's Texaco Star Theater was aired; hydraulic engineers adjusting to the precipitous drops in water pressure as thousands of toilets flushed simultaneously during football game commercials).

But nothing was destined to change the archetypal structure of TV so much as the spread of cable during the 1970s. With cable and a converter box, a Toronto home can receive 11 Canadian and five U.S. stations plus cable-originated shows and services. The closest Canadian rival is Vancouver, where a converter will bring in about half as many channels.

OTTAWA-BORN LORNE GREENE became a broadcasting legend, his stentorian basso voice and theatre training lending drama to his news reading on CBC Radio during the Second World War. After a spell on Broadway, he played Ben Cartwright on the American TV series Bonanza *for 14 years.*

Now, cable television giants and telecommunications networks are in a race to determine who will be first to introduce fibre-optics technology into Canadian homes, bringing with it the capability of offering 50, 100, perhaps an unlimited choice of channels. Sets will be able to offer as many channels as satellites can beam their way.

1997 Knights of the News

Marci McDonald – MAY 26, 1997 **T**he CBC's Peter Mansbridge and CTV's Lloyd Robertson are the country's reigning media superstars. "TV news anchors are our version of Canadian celebrities," says Peter Swain, president of Toronto's Media

FRONT PAGE CHALLENGE, *the touring CBC-TV program where a panel tried to guess the identity of news-related guests and then interviewed them, was on the air from 1957 to 1995. Here, panelists Betty Kennedy, Allan Fotheringham, Pierre Berton and Jack Webster, with moderator Fred Davis, celebrate the show's 35th anniversary.*

MOSES ZNAIMER, an innovative broadcaster, received high praise within the industry in the 1990s for stimulating the spirit and verve of a Toronto operation he directed, CITY-TV.

Buying Services Ltd., one of the country's leading purchasers of commercial airtime.

At a time when polls show that 80 per cent of North Americans get their news from television, network anchors have become the arbiters of what is deemed worthy for the population to know. In a world of dizzying information overload, network anchors frame reality into a 22-minute sampler of digestible sound bites, unsullied by passion or discernible opinion. And while anchors have never appeared more powerful, they have also never been scrutinized with such jaundiced eyes.

Media pundits have pronounced the network news anchor an endangered species. In the crowded 500-channel cablescape of the future—with a proliferation of all-news channels—they predict that the notion of waiting each night for an Olympian summary of events will become a quaint anachronism.

Broadcast executives agonize about their shrinking—and greying—audience. "It's clear a generational change is due," says Canadian-born Robert MacNeil, former half of the U.S. Public Broadcasting System's *MacNeil/Lehrer Newshour*, who retired in 1995 after 20 years as co-anchor. "You can see there's a problem with age just by the kinds of things they advertise."

Stephen Marshall, the 29-year-old force behind the radical "videozine" Channel Zero, now finds himself courted by the world's top broadcasting wizards for insights into why his peers–anybody under 35–are no longer tuning in. One of his solutions: eliminate anchors altogether and give Generation Xers around the globe video cameras to create slice-of-life news. "Anchors are only making television more alienating for young people," Marshall says. He points to a fundamental sense of disconnectedness between the world outside the window and what they see on the screen. "Ever since we were kids, we've heard the planet was in crisis," he says. "Then, Peter Mansbridge comes on the air and says, 'This happened today and it's fine. Good night.'"

Robertson retorts: "The research shows that people will need us around for a while." MacNeil says the need may, in fact, be all the greater: "In the multichannel universe, people may want the comfort and solidity of someone they know in all that anonymity."

1997 The National Music Man

NOVEMBER 17, 1997 **B**roadcaster Clyde Gilmour, 85, host of *Gilmour's Albums,* CBC Radio's longest-running, highest-rated one-man show, died of heart failure in Toronto on Nov. 7. Gilmour began his career as a newspaper reporter in his home town of Medicine Hat, Alta. In 1956, he began *Gilmour's Albums*, his slightly eccentric selection of music from a wide variety of genres and assorted tidbits like old train whistles. Originally booked on a 13-week contract, *Gilmour's Albums* ran for 40 years and eight months–a weekend fixture on CBC Radio and a listening ritual for thousands of households–until he retired last June. The half a million Canadians who tuned into his show each week will still be able to listen to rebroadcasts from the CBC archives until August.

GILMOUR'S ALBUMS, *a weekly disc-jockey program on CBC Radio hosted by film and record columnist Clyde Gilmour, was known for its eclectic mixture of music, from jazz to grand opera, and its longevity, from 1956 to 1997.*

A Funny Thing Happened...

Increasingly, American Comedy Turns Out to be CanWit

AMERICANS seem to get a laugh out of Canada. To wit, the one they like to tell about how Canada got its name: Spanish explorer sails up the St. Lawrence, shouts for a report from the crow's nest, and the lookout calls back, "Aca nada!" (Nothing here!). But the main way they get a laugh out of the northern neighbor is from Canadian comedians who cross over. There is a straight line (so to speak) that runs all the way from Mack Sennett in the 1910s to Jim Carrey in the 1990s. They, and dozens of others–more often than not unidentified as Canadians in the Great Big South–are knock-'em-dead expatriates of the Great White North.

As it happens, Great White North itself is a coinage of comedians Rick Moranis and Dave Thomas, whose Bob and Doug McKenzie act as beer-loving hosers from north of the border made it big on U.S. TV and in Hollywood (*Strange Brew*, 1983).

But back to Mack Sennett (1880-1960). Born Mikall Sinnott in Danville, Quebec, he showed an early comic bent in burlesque, next as a performer-writer-director with D.W. Griffith's Biograph Studios and then, from 1912 to 1935, as a producer of hundreds of short, silent slapstick flicks from his Keystone Company, featuring The Bathing Beauties, The Keystone Kops, Charlie Chaplin

MIKE MYERS, LIKE OTHER Torontonians before him, graduated from gigs with Second City to a place in the Saturday Night Live *lineup from 1989 to 1994, and then into movies:* Wayne's World *in 1992,* Austin Powers: International Man of Mystery *in 1997, and, in 1999, an Austin Powers sequel,* The Spy Who Shagged Me.

THE MCKENZIE BROTHERS, Bob (aka Rick Moranis), and Doug (aka Dave Thomas) during the eh-days of the Canadian comedy show SCTV *(1976-1983), and then plugging Molson's beer on American TV, reinforced the American idea of the hick-typical Canadian.*

and Fatty Arbuckle, W.C. Fields and Harold Lloyd. He won fame for picking on the foibles of the advancing mechanized society.

Sennett was a precursor of Canadian comics galore up to and including Carrey, who spoofs the absurdities of fin-de-siècle urban rituals. A laff riot.

1914 Marie Dressler, the Inimitable

Margaret Bell – OCTOBER 1914 **N**owadays, audiences are divided into two classes—the quantitative audience and the audience of quality. There are certain stars who make an especial appeal to the quantitative audience. Excessive avoirdupois, accentuated so that it appears even more excessive, will extract a laugh from the most stone-faced of audiences.

One of the greatest laugh producers of recent years concerned a certain awkward person with a super-abundance of flesh and the propensity to fall asleep. During these sleeps, she sometimes dreamed. One took her on shipboard. Tillie, the dreamer,

MACK SENNETT, BORN MIKALL SINNOTT at Danville, Quebec, to parents who moved south when he was 17, was aiming for a career in opera when he drifted into acting work and thence to churning out silent slapstick from the Keystone film company he co-founded in 1912.

MARIE DRESSLER LEFT HER COBOURG, Ontario, home at 14 to perform with travelling theatre troupes, changed her name from Leila von Koerber and gained fame as a comedienne in American vaudeville and films, winning a best actress Oscar for her performance in Min and Bill *(1930).*

was not a good sailor. After a gruelling siege of more or less indelicate stage tactics, which made her audience rock back and forth in unrestrained mirth, she made a very awkward exit over the side of the ship, into a fictitious sea. The coffers of the aforementioned Tillie are full.

It is of Marie Dressler that we speak. Just fifteen years after she was born, Marie Dressler became an actress. Lake Ontario [Dressler was from Cobourg, Ontario] seems to be noted for the girls who have left to enlist in the army of musical comedy and avoirdupois.

Her first play was *Under Two Flags*. She travelled around. By the end of the century she was gradually turning her efforts toward farcical comedy. Marie Dressler's turn came in 1905 with her joining Joe Weber's company in the Weber Music Hall [on Broadway]. So great was the hit she made that the next season she toured the country with Weber. She was the cleverest comedienne of her type.

It was time to try her luck in other lands. London, through the medium of the Palace Theatre, saw her in 1907. London shook her sides with laughter. And Marie Dressler loved London. So much so that she stayed there for three seasons.

America next saw her in that typical Dressler sort of comedy, *Tillie's Nightmare*. Since then, she has made no outstanding success in any role, being content to rest, for a while, on the laurels won already, and incidentally the profits from this elaborately staged comedy.

1958 Don Harron's Losing Struggle to Sidestep Stardom

Alice Griffin and Barbara Moon – APRIL 12, 1958 His name is Donald Harron and, at 33, he is an internationally successful stage, radio and TV actor, playwright, comedian and gag writer [later celebrated as co-writer, with Norman Campbell, of the *Anne of Green Gables* musical performed annually in Charlottetown and for his Charlie Farquharson hick act].

DON HARRON was better known across Canada by the names Charlie Farquharson and Valerie Rosedale, and as a host of CBC Radio's Morningside *and CTV's* Don Harron Show.

Ripened by four years of undergraduate Harron skits at the University of Toronto, Harron patter now sells like hotcakes. The New Play Society's annual Spring Thaw review depends heavily on his comic sketches. His best-known auto-creation is Harry Shorthorn, a malinformed Ontario rustic who tours the Canadian National Exhibition midway and says things like, "I take everything I see in this Middleway with a dose of salts. Take that there two-headed boy from Borneo. Oh, I know he's got two heads right enough, but I got my doubts he's really from Borneo."

A few years ago, the CNE offered Harron a contract to present Shorthorn in a nightly one-man act—at the time, an unprecedented offer to a hometown boy. He turned it down. He said he didn't want to get typed as a comedian.

1991 Making Fun in Four-Part Harmony

Cecily Ross – DECEMBER 30, 1991 The four members of CBC Radio's popular comedy troupe, the Royal Canadian Air Farce, are gathered in a Toronto office to put the finishing touches to a routine that will wind up their 1991 season. The glass door from a hallway bursts open and a young man in a sheepskin coat enters. "I don't want to bother you," he announces. "But I was just passing by and I wanted to tell you that I'm an enormous fan of yours." Roger Abbott, Don Ferguson, Luba Goy and John Morgan are a little embarrassed by the unexpected adulation. But such incidents are becoming more common for a group that has spent 18 years taping shows before live audiences across Canada. During that time, the four performers say, they have developed a sense of what Canadians are thinking and feeling. Said Abbott, 45, a Montreal

THE ROYAL CANADIAN AIR FARCE, a satirical quartet on CBC Radio from the early 1970s and then on CBC-TV from 1993, comprised John Morgan, Luba Goy, Roger Abbott and Don Ferguson, who is shown here in a skit with Reform Party leader Preston Manning in 1995, pronouncing the word "reform."

broadcaster who was a founder of the Air Farce in 1973: "You walk out on that stage and you can tell the mood of the community."

In the past year, typically, the troupe performed in 32 Canadian communities. And as problems in the country deepen, it seems that laughter is good medicine. All four members stress that what they do is comedy, not satire. Said Ferguson, 45, a former audiovisual producer from Montreal who specializes in impersonating Brian Mulroney, Joe Clark and Pierre Trudeau: "With satire, half the audience agrees and the other half is turned off." Added Goy, 46, who was raised in Ottawa and often plays Mila Mulroney and Queen Elizabeth II: "My job is to get up there on stage and make people laugh."

About half of the group's material is written by Morgan, 61, a Welsh-born former journalist. An easy camaraderie characterizes rehearsals and performances. "It's amazing how much you can accomplish if no one cares who gets the credit," says Abbott, whose on-air characters include Jean Chrétien.

The Air Farce has given Canadians more than just laughs. The group donates most of the proceeds from its taping shows to charities in the communities where they are held. Fans have toasted the Air Farce with screech in St. John's, Nfld., and presented them with cowboy hats in Calgary. On a wall of the group's Toronto offices hangs a citation from the Edmonton branch of the Canadian Mental Health Association honoring the Air Farce for its "contribution to the mental 'wellness' of all Canadians."

1993 Kids on the Ball

Joe Chidley – JULY 26, 1993 **K**ids in the Hall is the thinking cynic's comedy team, satirizing politics, sex, family–you name it–with cerebral wit. Right? "I think of the troupe as one big fat dumb guy," replies member Kevin McDonald. "He doesn't think about issues–he thinks about the comedy."

Forget the name: the Kids, all between 30 and 35, are comedy veterans. In 1984, Ottawa's Mark McKinney, Calgary's Bruce McCulloch and Torontonians McDonald

FROM ITS EARLY DAYS, Canadian TV began providing comedy shows that featured playlets or sketches. This format carried on from 1989 to 1997 with Kids in the Hall: *Kevin McDonald, Bruce McCulloch, Scott Thompson, Dave Foley and Mark McKinney.*

and Dave Foley teamed up to take on the Toronto club circuit. Scott Thompson, of North Bay, Ont., joined in 1985. By 1989, Lorne Michaels was in the Kids' corner as executive producer of their half-hour show for the CBC and the U.S. cable station HBO until last season, when it moved to CBS.

Filmed in Toronto, the show is pervaded by an urban absurdity that produces odd, yet oddly relevant, characters. The mix works: every Friday night, Kids in the Hall draws more than 500,000 viewers in Canada and a U.S. audience of six million. "Americans respond the same way Canadians do," says McDonald. "Nothing's getting lost in the translation."

By 1995, the Kids plan to release their first feature film. Its plot? "It'll be about five guys being funny," McDonald says. No kidding.

1993 Wise Guys

Brian D. Johnson – JULY 26, 1993 **C**anadian humor? To some, it's an oxymoron, like British cuisine or Yankee modesty. After all, our idea of a joke is spending a year debating a constitutional accord as if it were a matter of life and death, then changing the subject. Canada is a nation without a punch line. But perhaps that's just the point: sobriety is the mother of comic invention. Canada serves as straight man to the States. And for a country that gets to watch the riotous adventures of America through the wide screen of the 49th parallel, a sense of humor becomes indispensable.

In Canada, comedy is serious business. It is our biggest cultural export. We produce comedy stars almost as prolifically as we produce hockey players: Dan Akroyd, Mike Myers, Michael J. Fox, Leslie Nielsen, Martin Short, John Candy, Rick Moranis, Jim Carrey, Alan Thicke, Catherine O'Hara, Howie Mandel, André-Philippe Gagnon, the Kids in the Hall. . . . Canadians seem to have a hammerlock on the

American funnybone. And the shadowy figure behind this comic conspiracy, the man who knows where all the bad jokes are buried, is Canadian producer Lorne Michaels, godfather of NBC's *Saturday Night Live*.

Since Michaels launched *SNL* in 1975, it has incubated some of the biggest comedy stars of the past two decades. His career now spans two generations of stars, from Akroyd to Myers. Last summer, Michaels and Myers parlayed an *SNL* sketch about a couple of heavy-metal yahoos into the hit movie *Wayne's World*. The picture went through the roof, ranking fifth in North America with a gross of more than $150 million–of which 23 per cent was earned in Canada.

Canada, of course, is the ultimate suburb of the United States–which might explain why Canadians find America funny. They grow up watching the dominant culture while laughing behind its back. "For me," says Michaels, "people start to be funny early in their lives, when they notice the

JOHNNY WAYNE AND FRANK SHUSTER, here on The Ed Sullivan Show *in New York (Sullivan in the middle), got their professional start as comedians on CBC Radio in 1941, then as Second World War army entertainers, and eventually moved to television in 1954, doing parody sketches with a cast of character actors.*

difference between the official version and what their eyes and ears tell them. The official version tends to be south of the border. It's like living next to Imperial Rome."

With the longevity of *SNL*, he has a track record unmatched by almost any producer in TV comedy. *SNL* started out as a ground-breaking adventure, the first show that really delivered the 1960s sensibility of sex, drugs and rock 'n' roll to network television. Michaels is the first to admit that it fails as often as it succeeds. But that has always been the case–it is live, and the capacity to fail is the secret of its success. "It doesn't go on because it's ready," says Michaels. "It goes on because it's 11:30."

Michaels, who changed his name from Lorne Lipowitz in the 1960s, grew up infatuated with show business. His grandparents owned a small movie theatre in Toronto, the College Playhouse, where his mother ran the box office. His father, a furrier, died when Lorne was 14. His high-school sweetheart was Rosie Shuster. And her father, comedian Frank Shuster, became a surrogate dad, a mentor and, eventually, a father-in-law. (Twice divorced, Michaels is now married to Alice Barry, his former assistant at *SNL*.)

Frank Shuster originally tried to dissuade Michaels from entering show business. "I discourage the world from going into show business," Shuster, 76, told *Maclean's*. "But anybody who wants it badly enough is going to do it anyway." In fact, Shuster was "a tremendous influence," says Michaels.

After attracting some notice in 1964 by producing U.C. Follies, a successful revue at the University of Toronto, Michaels graduated with a BA in English and never looked back. Like Wayne and Shuster, he performed on CBC Radio, doing satirical sketches with partner Hart Pomerantz in 1967. Taking his talent south, Michaels wrote for Woody Allen and Joan Rivers, and spent a year writing for TV's *Laugh-In*, churning out jokes as part of a large pool of writers.

LORNE MICHAELS *drew on his experience as a comedy writer-performer and on such funny fellow Canadians as Dan Akroyd as well as Gilda Radner when he began producing* Saturday Night Live *for NBC-TV in 1975. He went on to other shows, including* Kids in the Hall.

Returning to Toronto in 1969, he and Pomerantz co-hosted a TV variety show, *The Hart and Lorne Terrific Hour*. Then, back to the United States in 1973, he co-produced a series of Emmy-winning TV specials for Lily Tomlin. Their success led NBC to consider his radical proposal for *Saturday Night Live. SNL* helped usher in the age of irony–television about television. During the show's second season, in 1976, a Killer Bees sketch ended with the camera dropping to the floor and Michaels stepping onstage to fire the director. Now, in the post-Letterman era, self-referential TV is everywhere. "Like everything else," says Michaels, "brilliant people do it, then less brilliant people, then everyone does it and you get tired of it."

Michaels does not spend a lot of time thinking about Canada. But he visits Toronto about twice a year. "The Toronto I grew up in doesn't exist any more," says Michaels. "I remember going to the CNE [Canadian National Exhibition] when it was an overgrown country fair. It was during the polio scare of the 1950s. You could go and catch polio. I went and I loved it–strip shows and freak shows and all the stuff that Toronto became embarrassed about. And the Food Building, which was a purely Canadian thing–to have a food building!"

Now, Michaels has brought his own sideshow to America, his world of Coneheads and metal-heads and cross-dressing comedians. But he presides over it with the cool discrimination that is the very soul of Canadian humor.

Perhaps the key to "CanWit" is an affection for the absurd, the sense of detachment that reflects our ironic distance from America–and from each other. Mort Sahl had it. So did Marshall McLuhan and Pierre Trudeau. They messed with the medium and the message. Whenever interviewers ask Mike Myers what's so funny about Canadians, he likes to quote a line from Martin Short: "Americans

JOHN CANDY, a player of gentle-loser roles, acquired his grounding with the Second City comedy troupes in Chicago and home town Toronto, which paid off in a string of mainly comic Hollywood roles from 1984 to his death at age 44 while filming in Mexico in 1994. Here, he and fellow SCTVers Martin Short and Rick Moranis appear to be holding imaginary drinks.

watch television, while Canadians watch American television." It is a fine distinction, like the gap between a laugh track and a laugh. You don't have to be Canadian. But it helps.

1995 Headline High Jinks

John DeMont – FEBRUARY 20, 1995 Somewhere deep in the warehouse-style room in downtown Halifax, Cathy Jones is screaming into a telephone receiver. The noise provides an edgy backbeat for the rest of the mid-morning chaos: the two TV screens tuned to the O. J. Simpson murder trial; Rick Mercer and Greg Thomey lost in an improvised commercial for "stool-flavored vodka" made out of the icebergs that flow into St. John's harbor; Mary Walsh explaining that "the Shaq"–nickname for American basketball star Shaquille O'Neal–is actually hockey warhorse Eddie Shack. "It's Monday morning," shrugs Gerald Lunz, creative producer of the satirical television show *This Hour Has 22 Minutes*. Which means the room is already crackling

THE FOUR NEWFOUNDLANDERS who created the comic satire show This Hour Has
22 Minutes *on CBC-TV in the 1990s—Cathy Jones, Greg Thomey, Mary Walsh and Rick
Mercer—drew an average weekly audience of more than a million viewers across Canada.*

with the manic energy that comes from the knowledge that the team has just five days
to put together another 22-minute show.

By any measure, they consistently deliver. The idea—combining sketch comedy
with a mock TV newscast that sends up the week's events—is hardly new. But the cast of
This Hour brings a zany new spin to the genre. "It's the best format in television,"
declares Mercer, 25. "It allows us to be topical and unapologetically Canadian." The
four cast members bring extensive experience to the show. Mercer had toured the country with his hysterical one-man stage productions. The rubber-faced Thomey, 32, has
written and acted in his own satiric plays. Jones, 39, and Walsh, 42, are two of the country's best-known comic actors, whose experience includes 20 years as members of the
outrageous CODCO comedy troupe, which had its own CBC show from 1986 to 1992.

What they share—along with a grounding in the salty, irreverent humor of
Newfoundland, where they have all spent most of their lives—is the ability to create a
startling array of characters. "Writing for these people is like having a cast of thousands," says writer Alan Resnick.

*JIM CARREY, a Hollywood king of the funny in the 1990s, rounded off a century of Canadian
invasions into the American comedy limelight. Carrey's elastic face and pratfalls made him a
direct descendant of the slapstick delivered by Mack Sennett in the early years of the century.*

'This is the Big Time'

Canada Boasts More Than Its Fair Share of Star Entertainers

MAKE a list of Canadian performing artists who have ascended to what Rompin' Ronnie Hawkins loved to shout during a major gig–"Big Time, this is Big Time!"–and in jig time the roster is scores of names long. Thinking alphabetically gives an idea of the late-century range–from rocker Bryan Adams and dancer Frank Augustyn, band leader Tommy Banks and orchestral conductor Mario Bernardi, through musical performers Cynthia Dale and Céline Dion, actor-directors Jean Gascon and Richard Monette, stage stars Eric Peterson and Christopher Plummer, and on to singers Jon Vickers and Gilles Vigneault, actor Al Waxman and rocker Neil Young.

Pick a category, Hollywood's Academy Awards, say, and find among other Canadian winners three best-actor champions in a row–Mary Pickford (*Coquette*), 1929; Norma Shearer (*The Divorcee*), 1930, and Marie Dressler (*Min and Bill*), 1931.

Hawkins's big time meant at least the United States (whence the rock-'n'-roller migrated to Canada in the 1950s), but brevity would require winnowing the list down to those who stay mainly with the homeland and evade the temptations of assimilation abroad. That shrinks the all-star team, but retains a galaxy of grand entertainers.

Perhaps the grandest was Glenn Gould. A musical giant who crouched at his

GLENN GOULD, here in his youth, possessed a prodigious talent. He began his studies at the Royal Conservatory of Music in Toronto at age 12, became a piano soloist with the Toronto Symphony at 14 and had graduated to concert tours by the time he was 19.

piano. A performer who abandoned the concert hall (except for playing in an empty Toronto auditorium) in favor of the recording studio. A Canadian who behaved weirdly (overcoat, muffler, cap and gloves regardless of the season). A pianist who gave the world two different renderings of Bach's Goldberg Variations, each of them compelling. A genius who left too soon, at age 50, killed by a stroke in 1982.

1923 Canada's Queen of Song

Charles H. Gibbons – DECEMBER 1, 1923 **Y**ears ago there was born in the little village of Chambly, near Montreal, la petite Emma Lajeunesse, a little French-Canadian girl whose name was to take its place with Jenny Lind and that multitude of great singers whose art has remained an enduring memory in so many hearts.

Madame Albani ruled as royally as any potentate in her world of art. She sang in palaces and in humble orphanages. She sang in the mines at Kimberly, from balloons that all might hear, and in the closed seraglios of the great Indian Empire.

Through her, Canada and the American continent first gained recognition and representation in the high courts of genius. At eighteen she had "arrived" as a regnant prima donna, an achievement for buoyant youth that has not been duplicated. Her reign was the longest of any of the acknowledged queens of opera and oratorio– even as that of good Queen Victoria, her near and dear friend, at whose funeral she was the only soloist, was unique for a modern monarch. Yet further distinction is hers as the inspired creator of more operatic and oratorio roles than any other soprano of past or present.

Many took to their hearts this petite Emma. They still do homage to her as Madame Albani, latterly grown exceedingly frail, a white-haired septuagenarian living now in her memories. Vast wealth slipped like water through her slim fingers, her generosity and her impracticality being boundless. For her today the drudgery of teaching.

When the small singer was fourteen, her family removed to Albany, N.Y., where she was engaged soon after at the Church of St. Joseph as organist and teacher of the choir, in which also she sang as first soprano. Soon she was on her way to Naples, where her art education was completed. Her professional name was adopted, not in compliment to the New York state capital, as commonly supposed, but on a teacher's suggestion, Albani being the patronymic of an honored but extinct noble house of Italy.

DAME EMMA ALBANI, born Marie-Louise-Cécile-Emma Lajeunesse at Chambly, Quebec, made her stage name world famous as a brilliant operatic soprano in the late 19th century, but remained a star of the concert tour in Canada and abroad during the first years of the 20th century.

Her return to her dear Mo'real [in 1883] was in the nature of a triumph. The Mayor declared a civic holiday. In state she was escorted to the Hotel de Ville and seated on the mayoral throne, after that, a great public reception. Other visits to Canada were made in 1889 (when she and her husband were guests of Sir John A. and Lady Macdonald), in 1903 and in 1906, Mlle. Eva Gauthier, relative and protégé of Sir Wilfrid Laurier, on that last occasion being the contralto of her touring company.

1937 Lombardo Style

Arthur Mann – JULY 15, 1937 It was a trio of violin, flute and drum–brothers Guy, Carmen and Liebert Lombardo. Then piano pupil Freddie Kreitzer joined by invitation. Guy Lombardo was 14, Carmen and Freddie 13, Liebert, 11. They practised so much–such intricate popular melodies as "Belgian Rose" and other hits of 20 years ago–that Papa Lombardo had to step in when prolonged musical fervor threatened their studies at St. Peter's Parochial School.

DANCEBAND LEADER AND violinist Guy (Gaetano Alberto) Lombardo, here with brothers Victor, Carmen and Liebert in 1943, made his Royal Canadians orchestra popular enough to sell some 300 million records over a 50-year span from the 1920s to his death at 75 in 1977.

The quartet gained a reputation after one appearance at a Mothers' Club luncheon. They were swamped with invitations. Guy combed the neighborhood for boy musicians, quickly augmented his band with players of the saxophone, banjo, guitar, trombone and tuba. When another drummer joined up, Liebert Lombardo abandoned the drums to become one of the best trumpet players in the world.

This is the human tale of a simple beginning. A group of healthy energetic kids from London, Ontario, became one of the highest-paid dance bands in North America. Money, fame, hard work and some ten thousand songs played over the radio haven't changed their smooth natures, nor their smoother music.

In 1920-1921, you will remember, Paul Whiteman's dignified interpretation of jazz music swept the continent. Straightaway there appeared hot orchestras. Guy Lombardo, only 18, decided that dancing was for people in love–for couples gliding over the floor, pressed close, whispering, sighing–and so he planned his music always to fit this mood. Their reward came in 1924 at the Port Stanley Casino, a Lake Erie resort south of London. The Lombardos and their soft music drew not only the patrons but a modest vaudeville contract. Guy billed his band as "The Royal Canadians."

• *Guy Lombardo and His Royal Canadians–"the sweetest music this side of heaven"–endured for more than 60 years. Even after Guy Lombardo's death at 75 in 1977, the band continued, under the leadership of Lombardos and others, into the 1990s.*

1950 The Not So Happy Gang

June Callwood – FEBRUARY 1, 1950   There is nothing in Canadian radio to compare with The Happy Gang. Broadcast across the country for a lunchtime half hour five days a week, its tireless good humor has won the program a record for longevity in daytime variety shows. It is currently in the gala throes of its 13th season. The Happy Gang has but one outstanding peculiarity. When it's not on the air it isn't happy.

The Happy Gang (10 men and a woman), with one or two exceptions, feels nothing warmer than respect for the boss, leader Bert Pearl, and it is possible one-half the Gang would cheer happily if the other half was fired. The final incongruity is that the unhappiest man is Bert Pearl, billed on the show as "that slap-happy chappie." One CBC producer says: "I know. It's killing him to slosh around with that always-smiling routine."

The Happy Gang, despite the rumblings, is heard by more than 2-1/2 million Canadians, beating the soap operas by hundreds of thousands. It is the most successful daytime show in Canada.

• *In all, the music-and-jokes show ran for 22 years, 1937-1959, with such star instrumentalists as Bob Farnon and later Bobby Gimby on trumpet; clarinetist and soprano saxophonist Cliff McKay, keyboard player Jimmy Namaro, bassist Joe Niosi and organists Kay Stokes.*

OSCAR PETERSON made a joyful noise unto the world as a boy jazz pianist on Montreal radio, went national via the CBC at the close of the Second World War and gained a wider audience after a performance at Carnegie Hall in 1949. In the 1990s, he was still delivering his syncopated, swinging jazz at the occasional concert.

1965 If Oscar Peterson Isn't the Greatest Living Jazz Pianist, Somebody's Fooling His Banker

Jack Batten – APRIL 17, 1965   The piano that Oscar Peterson, the Canadian jazz musician, played during his concert at Massey Hall in Toronto late last January was his own–a sleek, black, seventy-five-hundred-dollar Steinway grand that, on the platform stage, suggested nothing so much as a finely tooled racing car. The piano resides for most of the year in an upholstered warehouse stall and is rolled out only infrequently for public appearances.

The concert was by way of being a special occasion for Peterson and he was anxious that everybody, including himself and the grand, perform at a level close to their peak. The concert was, for one thing, his first appearance in a series that will take him this season back and forth across North America half a dozen times and once around Europe, and bring him fees of close to one hundred thousand dollars. It was also his first concert appearance in two years before an audience in Toronto, where he has lived since 1954 when he moved from Montreal, his birthplace. Peterson is one of the few Canadian artists who have reached international success on a grand scale and have retained Canada as their home base, and proudly.

His opening selection–played, as Peterson's music customarily is, to the rhythm accompaniment of bassist Ray Brown and drummer Ed Thigpen–set the pace for the evening: the three musicians propelled their jazz with a sweeping momentum that never waned.

Oscar Peterson's career has been uniquely blessed. For him at any rate, applauding audiences have always been there, and the affluence–though his childhood was marked by fairly difficult poverty–came quickly. In the same style, he emerged out of the audience onto the stage at Carnegie Hall on the night of Sept. 18, 1949, to win rave reviews in *Down Beat* magazine and an international audience that has never deserted him. Leonard Feather, probably the most widely read jazz critic in North America, sums up Peterson's career simply: "Oscar Peterson is the greatest living jazz pianist."

1987 In the Vanguard for the Arts

Mark Nichols – DECEMBER 28, 1987 **S**he is recognized as Canada's first lady of classical music, but singer Maureen Forrester is not a lady who puts on airs. Her zestful sense of fun was in evidence last July when she began an address to a breakfast meeting of the Canadian Bar Association in Ottawa by declaring, "You see before you a woman who has had her teeth capped, her chin lifted, no appendix, no gallbladder–so I'm a perfect catch." Then she turned to the serious part of her talk, on the importance of fostering the arts in Canada. "We have a lot of natural talent in Canada," she says. "It's a shame when that talent has to go somewhere else to make a living."

It is a message she never tires of delivering and one she presses with vigor. As chairman of the Canada Council since 1983, Forrester, 57, has outspokenly opposed the government's attempts to reduce the autonomy of the council, which provides financial support to individual artists and cultural organizations. At

MONTREAL-BORN MAUREEN FORRESTER, pictured here in 1981, developed her rich contralto voice into a fine concert instrument at an early age, turning professional at age 21 in 1951 and giving guest performances with symphony orchestras and opera companies around the globe.

the same time, she has travelled across North America and to Europe and Asia to demonstrate the vibrant quality of her lush contralto voice. Sums up Walter Homburger, the recently retired general manager of the Toronto symphony, "She has made a most valuable contribution to the cultural life of this country."

1989 A Milestone in Music for a Laureate of Song

D'Arcy Jenish – DECEMBER 25, 1989 **A**s she wraps up a two-hour show at Pittsburgh's Benedum Center, Anne Murray dances over to a corner of the stage and picks up a batch of long-stem yellow roses. She struts across the stage tossing flowers into the crowd. By the time she has disappeared behind the curtain, the fans in the first few rows are on their feet cheering wildly and soon the rest of the crowd of 2,500 has joined in a thunderous standing ovation. Then, Murray reappears, and calls out in her husky voice, "Are we having fun or what?" After 20 years as a professional entertainer, record sales of 20 million and four Grammy awards, Anne Murray works a crowd with poise, polish and confidence.

In a business where today's instant sensation can be tomorrow's forgotten star, Murray, 44, has proved to be remarkably durable. She has released her 30th album. Last summer, her home town of Springhill, N.S., opened the Anne Murray Centre, a $1.6-million tourist attraction devoted to the life and career of the singer. Her unpretentious references to her roots demonstrate her attachment to her native country—and reinforce Canada's attachment to her.

1992 Songs for All the People

Bob Levin – DECEMBER 28, 1992 **S**he had the dream, the drive, the gift. Music pulsed in her blood. She is the youngest of 14 children of Adhémar and Thérèse Dion of Charlemagne, Que., 20 km east of Montreal, and at five she belted out Ginette Reno songs from a tabletop in her parents' piano bar. At 12, in her basement, she recorded a song written by her mother, and the demonstration tape won her an audience with Reno's mentor, Montreal impresario René Angélil. Soon, under Angélil's guidance, Céline Dion became a major Quebec star, a wholesome, girl-next-door success with a soaring voice as big as her ambitions. At 18, chafing at her little-girl image, she took a year off to make herself over, emerging as a permed, spike-heeled pop princess ready to invade the English market. That invasion now is in high gear. Says Dion: "Every time someone asks me, 'Céline, has your dream come true?' something else happens. I still feel like this is just the beginning."

ANNE MURRAY (above left), the contralto from Springhill, Nova Scotia, won worldwide popularity with her country-style pop singing in the 1970s and became a national sweetheart for many Canadians with her wholesome look and manner and such superhits as "Snowbird" in 1970.

NEIL YOUNG (left), gained an international name as a founder in 1966 of the Buffalo Springfield band in Los Angeles. After going solo, he teamed up for concerts and records with David Crosby, Stephen Stills and Graham Nash. He chalked up a long string of enduring songs to his credit, from "Heart of Gold" to "Rockin' in the Free World."

CÉLINE DION (above right), the youngest of 14 in a musical Quebec family, released her first hit single at age 13 in 1981, was French Canada's most popular chanteuse by the late 1980s and, after studying Berlitz English, recorded an English album in 1990, developing into a belt-'em-out superstar in America and overseas.

331

1993 Master of Surprise

Barry Came – DECEMBER 27, 1993   The moment is pure theatre, offering a glimpse of Robert Lepage's quirky imagination. There is a December bite in the Montreal morning and the celebrated actor-writer-director, invited for breakfast at the city's

THE HOTTEST YOUNG CANADIAN actor-directors in the closing years of the century were prizewinners at the 1998 Toronto International Film Festival: Toronto's Don McKellar, cited for the best Canadian first feature, Last Night, *and multitalented Quebecer Robert Lepage, for best Canadian feature film,* No.

elegant Ritz-Carlton hotel, is warmly bundled in a bright blue coat. But beneath the winter gear, his outfit is anything but conventional. He wears formal evening dress–black tie, black tails and a starched white shirt as crisp as the frosty air. "I thought it was expected," he says, while a mischievous twinkle lights his eyes. "This is, after all, the Ritz."

Lepage's infinite capacity to surprise is his hallmark. It is an unerring gift and it has catapulted the 36-year-old son of a Quebec City taxi driver to the heights of international renown. Widely recognized as the most innovative theatre director in Canada after a two-year stint as director of French theatre at Ottawa's National Arts Centre, he has over the past 18 months established himself as a performing arts force on three continents–acclaim in London for setting Shakespeare's *A Midsummer Night's Dream* in a mud bath, rapturous reviews in New York for his one-man show *Needles and Opium*, and a hectic stay in Tokyo reprising *Needles and Opium* as well as directing five Shakespeare plays, three in French and two in Japanese.

Earlier this year, the Quebec Conservatory of Dramatic Arts graduate set out on an entirely new path by directing a double bill for the Canadian Opera Company–Bartok's *Bluebeard's Castle* and Schoenberg's *Erwartung*. The avant-garde production won top prize at the Edinburgh International Festival. Yet another departure came when he joined Peter Gabriel, designing and directing the rock star's latest concert tour.

Beneath Lepage's eclecticism, there is an underlying unity that revolves around his entire notion of the purpose of theatre. "Just as photography liberated traditional art forms, so have film and television liberated traditional theatre," he explains. "It should no longer be realistic or naturalistic. It has reached the stage where it should be free to be cubist or impressionist or surrealist, or all of that. It should be an experimental forum to change our perspective, to see how we can view things in a different way, to make us wonder."

1995 Talent and Timing

Rick Phillips – NOVEMBER 13, 1995 **M**any singers, and especially tenors, work for years to reach the international limelight. Then, if they finally make it, the demands on them increase a hundredfold. Suddenly, they are asked to learn many roles, travel the globe and make recordings. The stress on the singer and the voice can be devastating. That, however, does not apply to Canadian tenor Ben Heppner, 39, a fast-rising star on the opera scene. Heppner's management of his career, his refusal to accept new roles before he is ready, show an artist of intelligence–and longevity. He waited until this fall to release his first two solo albums. *Ben Heppner Sings Richard Strauss*, recorded with the Toronto Symphony Orchestra under Andrew Davis, shows off the artist's brilliant tone and his ease with the taxing music. *Great Tenor Arias*, with the Munich Radio Orchestra conducted by Roberto Abbado, reveals the warmth and shadings of his voice.

Despite his long road to stardom, Heppner, who lives in the Toronto suburb of Scarborough, has resisted its pressures. He seems determined to take his time with his career and to enjoy it. Born in rural Murrayville, B.C., near Vancouver, he was the youngest of nine children in a Mennonite farming family. He studied music at the universities of British Columbia and Toronto. While a member for several seasons of the Toronto-based Canadian Opera Company's ensemble–an apprenticeship group–he scraped out a living as a music teacher, church choir director and restoring houses. Meanwhile, he and his wife, Karen, were raising three young children. But then, in 1988, he won an award at the Metropolitan Opera Auditions in New York City, and that was the springboard to an international career. He is now in demand at prestigious opera houses around the world.

Canada has been blessed with a long list of world-acclaimed tenors–Edward Johnson, Leopold Simoneau, Richard Verreau, Ermanno Mauro and Paul Frey–but Heppner is most often compared to heroic tenor Jon Vickers, the Saskatchewan-born singer who rose to world prominence in the late 1950s and is now a legendary name in the annals of opera. And if Ben Heppner continues to pace himself, Canada will have another name to add to the list.

1996 'Hello Icon, Hello Darling'

Diane Turbide – DECEMBER 23, 1996 **W**illiam Hutt, the venerable actor, is describing his 30-year-long association with Martha Henry, actor and director. "I've played Martha's brother, uncle, lover, husband and father, and, if she'd been available for *The Importance of Being Earnest*, I'd have played her mother," he says, rolling out the punch line with a comic's perfect timing. In the past three years, the two have enjoyed

DUE IN GREAT PART to grants and services from the Canada Council for the Arts, set up in 1951, repertory theatres opened in major centres and summer drama festivals enriched the activity. The Stratford Festival, which began in 1953, boasted such acting talents as William Hutt and Martha Henry, pictured here.

their most creative collaboration, in the Ontario Stratford Festival's productions of *The Stillborn Lover*, which Timothy Findley wrote for them, and in Eugene O'Neill's *Long Day's Journey into Night*.

"Hello icon, hello darling," Hutt greets Henry, as they settle in for lunch at a popular restaurant in Stratford where they both live. Hutt teases Henry by repeating the accolades they received for *Long Day's Journey* for two Stratford summers. They re-created those roles in David Wellington's 1996 film version. "First, we were called the Lunts, then we were theatre royalty, now we're icons," says the 76-year-old actor.

Henry is wary of putting the intangible into words, but plunges in anyway. Once an actor has studied the text of a play, she says, "All the elements have to be there—a good text, the right cast, the right audience—for that electrical communication to happen. It rarely does, but with *Journey* it happened just about every night." Henry, 58, won a Governor General's Performing Arts Award for lifetime achievement, an award Hutt received in 1992.

1997 A Woman Who Loves to Dance

Barry Came – DECEMBER 22, 1997 **A**s usual, Karen Kain is at rehearsals, hard at work preparing the National Ballet of Canada for another season. But as she paces the polished hardwood in the ballet's main gymnasium on Toronto's waterfront, the shoes on her celebrated feet are not pointe slippers but suede boots. She wears not tights nor leotards but an elegant wool sheath, belted in brown leather. And there are no sudden, breathtaking flights of physical daring, the kind that earned her reputation as the National Ballet's—and Canada's—undeclared prima ballerina assoluta. For Kain is moving on this year, having retired from the ballet last October at the age of 46. "Now, I'm doing a little coaching," she says during a break in the activity. "Just because I've hung up my slippers with the ballet doesn't mean I'm going home to lie down and die. There's still lots I want to do."

In her 27 illustrious years with the National, Kain set the standard by which all other Canadian ballerinas are likely to be judged. She has been an international star. But it all came to a formal close in Winnipeg on Oct. 4, 1997, when Kain danced her last role as a principal with the ballet, ending a seven-city, cross-country farewell tour. "I felt very sad for a couple of weeks," she says. "But then I did some coaching in Europe, danced in New York, and suddenly my enthusiasm returned."

KAREN KAIN—here dancing in Winnipeg with Rex Harrington in 1997—succeeded Lois Smith, Canada's first prima ballerina, as the National Ballet of Canada's principal female dancer. Frank Augustyn, who frequently partnered Kain, took over from David Adams, the National's first principal male dancer, who partnered Lois Smith both on the stage and in wedlock.

A CHRONOLOGY OF THE CENTURY

LANDMARKS, LOW POINTS, AND MATTERS OF MUCH ADO

1901: The first cross-Canada royal tour begins on September 16, when the Duke and Duchess of Cornwall and York (the future King George V and Queen Mary) arrive in Quebec City from England.

Prince Arthur of Connaught, grandson of Queen Victoria, is one of the group on April 19, 1906, who were "running the slides," a sport born of the business of getting timber to the mill by river power and the ancestor of the thrill sport of whitewater rafting at the other end of the century.

1904: The North-West Mounted Police, formed in 1873, receive from King Edward VII on June 24 the right to use the prefix Royal "in recognition of 30 years of loyal service." The force retained the honorific when it merged in 1920 with the Dominion Police to create the Royal Canadian Mounted Police.

1905: The provinces of Alberta and Saskatchewan are established from the North-West Territories lands on September 1.

1908: Quebec City, which was founded in the summer of 1608 by Samuel de Champlain, celebrates its 300th anniversary from July 20 to July 3, with the Prince of Wales (the future King George V) in attendance for most events.

1909: Aviation pioneer J.A.D. McCurdy, 22, makes the first powered flight in Canada in the Silver Dart, a plane chiefly designed by him, at Baddeck, Nova Scotia, his

1912: Calgary's first Stampede Rodeo opens on September 2 as a six-day event featuring "the bucking horse ride, steer wrestling, calf roping and trick and fancy riding."

1914: Canadian authorities refuse to admit more than 350 passengers, mainly Sikhs, who arrive off Vancouver from Hong Kong in May aboard the Japanese freighter *Komagata Maru*, forcing the freighter and its passengers finally to depart for Calcutta on July 23. Thousands of Vancouverites throng the docks, cheering.

- Britain declares war on Germany on August 4, automatically drawing Canada and other British Empire countries into the conflict. The first Canadian troops leave for England on October 3.

1916: On January 28, Manitoba women win the right to vote and to stand for political office—the first in Canada to gain those entitlements.

- A fire that breaks out in the parliamentary reading room in Ottawa in the evening of February 3, kills seven people and destroys Parliament's Centre Block. The replacement structure, including the Peace Tower, is completed in 1922.

1917: The Canadian Press (CP) is founded by the daily newspapers as a news-sharing co-operative that grows into a bilingual circulator of staff-written as well as member-provided regional, national and international news, photos and voice reports for radio and television.

- On June 7, in Alberta, Louise McKinney becomes the first woman elected to a legislature in Canada (and in the British Empire).
- The Military Service Act of August 29, which provides for the conscription of young men for war service, provokes protests among Western farmers, organized labor and French Canadians. Subsequent efforts by military police to enforce the draft triggers rioting. The monthly enlistment rate actually declines and the entire affair inflicts lasting damage on national unity.

- In two of the Great War's most testing and terrible battles, Canadian troops capture Vimy Ridge in France (April 9 to April 12, 1917) and Passchendaele, Belgium (October 26 to November 20, 1917).

1918: German and Allied leaders sign an armistice at 11 a.m. on the 11th day of the 11th month of 1918. It stops the fighting on front lines that snake across northern France and southern Belgium (Canadian troops have just

A Silver Star Mother in Saint John in 1918

advanced into Mons, Belgium). The terms commit Germany to give up ships, planes, tanks and guns and to pay Allied occupation costs.

1919: A permanent Canadian federal law allowing women to vote (earlier enfranchisements were temporary wartime measures) takes effect on January 1.

- A general strike in Winnipeg, called by the city's Trades and Labor Council on May 15 after the

Prince of Wales to Participate in the Quebec Tercentenary Celebration

MAY 1908

In mid-summer, 1608, the intrepid French explorer and navigator, Samuel de Champlain, founded at Quebec the first permanent settlement in Canada. The three hundredth anniversary of this historic episode, which will be observed in July next, will be signally honored by the presence of H.R.H. the Prince of Wales, Prince George, as he is popularly known.

The programme of the Quebec Tercentenary is in brief as follows: The Prince will arrive on the morning of July 22nd, and will be received by the Governor-General and presented with an address of welcome from the Dominion Parliament. On July 23rd, the scene of the landing of Champlain will be reconstituted; 24th, dedication of battlefield of Plains of Abraham, followed by military and naval review; 25th, review of the assembled fleets; 26th, special thanksgiving services; 27th, naval display ashore, followed by bombardment of Quebec; 28th, children's day; 29th, Prince leaves the port on return trip home.

The Silver Dart, a replica of which is pictured here, undertook Canada's first foray into powered flight in 1909.

birthplace, on February 23, completing a project of the Aerial Experiment Association under Alexander Graham Bell, inventor of the telephone. (Americans Orville and Wilbur Wright made the first-ever such flight on December 17, 1903, near Kitty Hawk, North Carolina.)

• The Department of External Affairs is formed in Ottawa on June 1, with Charles Murphy as minister, Joseph Pope as chief (undersecretary) along with two clerks, two typists, a messenger and an annual budget of $13,350.

• The University of Toronto beats Parkdale Canoe Club of Toronto in the first Grey Cup Game on December 4 at Rosedale Park in their home city. Governor General Earl Grey is late ordering his trophy for "the amateur rugby football championship of Canada," so the cup is not presented until March, 1910.

1910: The Naval Service Act of May 4 officially establishes the Royal Canadian Navy.

---

breakdown of contract talks in the building trades, leads to the jailing of strike leaders and, on June 21, to "Bloody Saturday," when armed and mounted police charge demonstrators, resulting in many injuries and one death. The strike is called off on June 25 but leaves a bitter national legacy. In *Maclean's*, publisher John Bayne Maclean

Planning Soviet Rule in Canada

AUG. 1919

On June 21, 1919, when mounted police charged Winnipeg people on strike, the act ensured the establishment of a European-style them-us class system in Canada.

Lieut. Col. J. B. Maclean – *August, 1919* The defeat of the Revolutionists in Winnipeg [June 21, 1919] by the arrest of the leaders has not by any means ended the dangers to Canada. The Germans are spending money more freely; and from a purely business standpoint it will pay them to pour out many millions more in their efforts to promote strikes, create discord among returned soldiers and otherwise cripple Canadian and other allied trades while they—far better organized than we are—will undersell us in our own markets.

Clear, undisputed evidence is in the possession of the authorities that their agents and dupes are preparing Eastern Canada for the revolutions; that the money comes from German sources; and finally that the whole movement is directed from one source in the United States and by one German, in New York. This man is Sauteri Nuorteva, alias Nyberg, a German ex-convict, head of the German propaganda bureau in New York—the body which directed the bombing, fires and explosions in the munition plants and ships in the U.S.

reflects the business community's paranoia following the 1917 Russian Communist revolution in ascribing the strike to a German conspiracy to foment Bolshevism and destabilize Canada.

• The Treaty of Versailles, concluded in the suburban Paris palace on June 28 by German and Allied leaders—including Canadian Prime Minister Robert Borden—is even more demanding of Germany than the armistice. It requires the vanquished country to cede land to neighbors and to pay the victors reparations amounting to more than the world's known gold resources. Marshal Ferdinand Foch of France, Allied supreme commander, is quoted stating presciently: "This is not peace, it is an armistice for 20 years."

1920: The Group of Seven painters open their first exhibition at the Art Gallery of Toronto on May 7. Reviews are favorable, but the show is not popular, and only three of more than 100 works are sold. Only later were the Group's landscapes to grip the Canadian imagination.

1921: The schooner *Bluenose* is launched on March 26 at Lunenburg, Nova Scotia. Skippered by Angus Walters, the sleek sailboat wins International Fisherman's Trophy races five times from 1921 to 1938 and is featured on the back of the dime coin. In 1942, the schooner goes to work as a West Indies freighter, wrecking off Haiti in 1946. It is reproduced as *Bluenose II*, a charter vessel, on July 24, 1963.

• In the federal election of December 6, Agnes Campbell Macphail (Grey South East, Ontario) becomes the first woman MP, a member initially of the Progressive Party and later of the Co-operative Commonwealth Federation (CCF); J.S. Woodsworth (Winnipeg North Centre), an acquitted leader of the 1919 Winnipeg General Strike, a charter member of the Independent Labor Party and later the CCF's founding leader, is the first avowed socialist elected to Parliament.

1923: Frederick Banting and his research supervisor at the University of Toronto, J.J.R. Macleod, receive the Nobel Prize in physiology/medicine "for the discovery of insulin," first used in 1921 against diabetes mellitus, previously a fatal disorder. Banting, who at first threatened to decline the honor because it excluded research associate Charles Best, gave Best half his prize money. Macleod shared his with assisting biochemist J.B. Collip.

• Radio announcer Foster Hewitt (1902-1985) makes his first hockey broadcast on March 23 (a Senior League game between Toronto Parkdale and Kitchener, Ontario). He thus launches a radio-television career that runs for 55 years and makes his nasal play-by-play coverage familiar coast to coast, especially on Saturday nights—*Hockey Night in Canada*—via CBC.

1925: The United Church of Canada is formed on June 10 from the union of the Methodists, almost all Congregational churches and roughly two-thirds of the Presbyterian churches.

• On June 11 at Waterford Lake, Nova Scotia, coal miner William Davis is killed by company police during a bloody fight, the culmination of four years of strikes and strife between Cape Breton miners and steelworkers and their communities on one side and, on the other, the provincial police and the British Empire Steel Corporation of Montreal, which had reduced wages and cut off credit at the local company stores. The date of Davis's death was marked each year thereafter as Miners' Memorial Day.

1926: The leaders of Britain, Canada and the other partly independent former British colonies agree in London on November 19 that the members of "the British Commonwealth of Nations" are autonomous and equal in status. That is affirmed in law on December 11, 1931, with Britain's Statute of Westminister. *Maclean's* reports that, henceforth, "the Dominions can, if their people so desire, move to a status of complete independence."

1927: The Judicial Committee of the Privy Council in Britain, the

FEB. 1927

Fruits of the Imperial Conference

J. A. Stevenson — *February 1, 1927*
Another Imperial Conference has come and gone. Attention is properly concentrated upon the portentous document known as the Report of a Committee on Inter-Imperial Relations, which was appointed by the main conference to examine the constitutional arrangements of the Empire. Its chairman was Earl Balfour, and included in its personnel were all the Dominion premiers. The report which they presented was formally adopted by the conference on November 19, 1926.

An extraordinary diversity of opinion prevails. On the one hand it is acclaimed as the "Magna Charta of the Empire" and on the other, so high an authority as the *London Times* declares that "it is essentially a register of conditions as they exist already rather than a programme for the future; and the majority of the Conservative press of Canada regard it in the same light."

Early in its pages, we find a definition of the status of the group of self-governing communities composed of Great Britain and the Dominions as follows:

"They are autonomous communities within the British Empire, equal in status, in no way subordinate one to another in any aspect of their domestic or external affairs, though united by a common allegiance to the Crown, and freely associated as members of the British Commonwealth of Nations."

The problem of appeals to the Judicial committee of the Privy Council was also considered, but was sidestepped by a negative declaration to the effect that, if any Dominion wishes to abolish the right of appeal it is at liberty to do so.

In the sphere of foreign relations, the step toward the assumption of independent powers in the negotiation of treaties which was taken by Canada in 1923 in connection with the Halibut Treaty with the United States, was confirmed and developed further.

The constitutional and political results of the conference do set up a sort of political framework within which the Dominions can, if their people so desire, move to a status of complete independence without unnecessary friction.

Nellie McClung gained celebrity as a 20th-century frontierswoman in the rights-of-women struggle.

JUNE 1927   *Voted Greatest Living Canadian*

In the opinion of a majority of *Maclean's* readers who answered the question, "Who is the greatest living Canadian?" Dr. F.G. Banting, discoverer of insulin, is that man. Dr. Charles E. Saunders, to whom Canada owes the gift of Marquis wheat, is the nominee of the second largest group; Sir Robert Borden [former prime minister] comes third, and Sir George Foster [former finance minister], fourth.

It is significant that Drs. Banting and Saunders—two scientists, the one in medicine, the other in agriculture—should head the list. Neither of these men has attained prominence in politics; neither of them has made the accumulation of riches his goal; neither of them commands the power that comes to the successful politician or financier, but both of them have wrested new knowledge from Nature which makes life more livable in Canada, or in the world, for that matter. If the letters received are representative—and there is every reason to believe they are—it is obvious the Canadian ideal is that of service as opposed to personal aggrandisement: a striking valuation to come from a people confronted at every turn by the starkly material.

One other point: Letter after letter commends Banting and Saunders for refusing to leave Canada in order to assure themselves of large financial returns. Canadians, it would seem, admire most those who elect to stay in their own country and devote their genius to its services.

---

highest court of appeal for Canada on constitutional issues until 1949, in a Labrador boundaries ruling on March 1, effectively awards all of Labrador to the Dominion of Newfoundland, rejecting Quebec's claims to the land.

• Events marking the Diamond Jubilee of Canadian Confederation on July 1 include the first coast-to-coast radio network broadcast—Parliament Hill celebrations, also beamed overseas. The inaugural recital of a new carillon in Parliament's Peace Tower features *O Canada*, *The Maple Leaf Forever* and *God Save the King*.

• A Dominion-Provincial conference of first ministers in Ottawa, November 3 to November 10, launches a quest for agreement on constitutional reform that continues intermittently for 55 years when—still lacking unanimity—a revised version of the British North America Act of 1867 is Canadianized without Quebec's assent.

1929: The Judicial Committee of the British Privy Council decides on October 18 that Canadian women are indeed "persons," overturning a 1928 ruling by the Supreme Court of Canada that the term referred only to males in constitutional law governing Senate appointments. Four months later, on February 20, 1930, Canada's first woman senator—Cairine Reay Wilson—takes her place in Parliament.

• A stock market crash in New York and Canadian exchanges on October 29 heralds the beginning of the Great Depression, which spreads hardship in North America and overseas throughout the 1930s.

Canada Has Completed Era of Tremendous Development

JULY 1927

A.W. Blue – *July 1, 1927* There is no more comprehensive, impressive or colorful picture of Canada's rise to financial independence and wealth, to the status of nationhood, than that indicated in a statistical survey of her achievements in the major departments of her national activities. Canada today occupies a unique position.

Although she has bridged but sixty years of nationhood, she stands third among the nations of the world from the standpoint of per capita wealth, exceeded only by that of the United States and Great Britain. Her volume of foreign trade per capita exceeds that of any other country, and it is interesting to note that her present total, with a population of slightly more than nine millions, approximates the total trade of the United States when her population stood at seventy-five millions.

In all lines of primary and secondary activity, Canada has made tremendous strides in the past few years, and, while agriculture is still the basic industry, Canada is making a name for herself through her vast mineral and forest wealth, as well as through her extended industrial development.

Canadian sprinter Myrtle Cook anchored the winning sprint relay team at the 1928 Olympics—the first where women competed—and became a hero at home.

1930

1930: The first British Empire Games (later the Commonwealth Games) open on August 16 in Hamilton, Ontario.

- Harold Oswin (1903-1991), an employee of Neilsen Ltd. in Toronto, invents the Crispy Crunch bar—a mixture of peanut butter, toffee and chocolate—which many Canadians regard as the world's greatest chocolate bar. Oswin, for his invention, wins a $5 bonus.

1932: On August 1, a Calgary meeting of socialists, farmers and pro-labor people forms the Co-operative Commonwealth Federation, with labor MP J.S. Woodsworth as leader. At its first party convention the next year in the Saskatchewan capital, the CCF's Regina Manifesto sets such goals as the socialization of health services, the financial system, utilities and natural resources.

It vows to work for equal economic opportunity regardless of gender, nationality or faith. At its 1961 convention in Ottawa, the party formalizes its alliance with organized labor and changes its name to the New Democratic Party.

1935: The Bank of Canada begins operations in Ottawa on March 11 with a government mandate to regulate credit, to protect the exchange value of the Canadian dollar and "generally to promote the economic and financial welfare of the Dominion."

- On August 22, the three-year-old Alberta Social Credit Party under William (Bible Bill) Aberhart, advocating the distribution of money to increase purchasing power in a depressed economy, wins the provincial election. Aberhart remains premier until

1943 and his party retains power in Alberta until 1971. Social Credit governs British Columbia from 1952 to 1991 (except for an NDP interregnum, 1972-1975). The party is represented in Parliament by western Canadian MPs from 1935 to 1968. A Quebec offshoot, the Ralliement des Créditistes, holds parliamentary seats between 1962

and 1980. Preston Manning, the son of Aberhart successor Ernest Manning, Alberta's premier from 1943 to 1968, draws on his right-wing populist roots to help form the western-based Reform Party of Canada in 1987.

1936: King Edward VIII, after almost 10 months as monarch of

King George VI and Queen Elizabeth in Halifax at the commencement of their 1939 visit, designed to drum up enthusiasm for the British Empire as war clouds loomed over Europe.

1940

1942: By order of the federal cabinet on February 26 (almost 12 weeks after Japan bombed the U.S. fleet berthed in Pearl Harbor, Hawaii, on December 7, 1941), more than 20,000 British Columbians of Japanese descent, three out of four of them Canadian nationals, are incarcerated or exiled inland from the Pacific coast, their homes, boats and other assets seized in the name of national security. A postwar deportation program is repealed by Ottawa in 1947, but the dispersal project goes on until March 31, 1951. In 1988, Ottawa provides a sum of $12 million "as symbolic redress for those injuries" to the National Association of Japanese Canadians, which distributes the money to promote the community's "athletic, artistic and academic development."

1945: VE Day, celebrating Victory in Europe, May 8, followed by VJ Day (Victory in Japan) on August 14, each prompt nationwide jubilation—coast-to-coast party time with dancing in the streets. In Halifax, VE Day turns into ugly rioting and looting after authorities shut liquor outlets.

- On July 20, Ottawa mails its first "baby bonus" cheques to the mothers of Canada under the 1944 Family Allowances Act. The first universal welfare program pays every mother set monthly amounts per child under 16, slightly more for older teen-agers. Those cheques may have helped stimulate the baby boom, the highly fertile years from 1945 to 1967.
- In Ottawa on September 5, Igor Gouzenko, a code clerk at the embassy of the Soviet Union, defects with 109 documents containing evidence that Soviet-run spy rings have

| JAN. 1947 | Greetings, Fellow Citizens |

Arthur Irwin — *January 1, 1947* Canada welcomes many new adult citizens every year; up to now they had good reason to be puzzled by their status in this free country. Even native Canadians weren't official Canadians. The New Citizenship Act, to be proclaimed January 1, changes all this. Whatever our origin we are now all Canadians—which is as it should be.

The new Act will also bring some dignity and solemnity to the procedure of naturalization. Up to now, it has taken far less ceremony to become a Canadian than to become a Rotarian, or an Elk. New citizens were sworn in by the batch, like traffic offenders. In future it's hoped to have classes to teach the new citizen the principles of Canadian democracy. The Oath of Allegiance will be administered with due ceremony and even a little pomp.

penetrated the Canadian government and the atomic research facilities at Chalk River, Ontario, which had contributed to the development of the A-bombs dropped on the Japanese cities of Hiroshima and

Nagasaki a month earlier. After two days of rebuffs by official Ottawa, and an attempt by Soviet agents to seize him, Gouzenko persuades Canadian authorities to place him, his pregnant wife and their young

England—and Canada—chooses on December 10, 1936, to give up the throne rather than Wallis Simpson, the twice-divorced American woman he loves and later marries, but whom the British establishment will not accept as a future queen consort. His last kingly act is to grant royal assent to a law dethroning him on December 11, thereby making his younger brother King George VI. The abdication creates an international sensation, particularly in Canada, where Edward was widely popular. As Prince of Wales, he had served at Canadian Army headquarters in Europe at the close of the First World War and had visited Canada four times, purchasing a cattle ranch in Alberta on his first grand tour in 1919. *Maclean's* runs verbatim texts of Edward's message to the British Parliament, his radio address "to the peoples of the Empire" and the abdication law, including the assertion that "Canada has requested and consented to the enactment of this act."

1937: Trans-Canada Air Lines, a Crown company (later Air Canada, privatized in 1988 and 1989), begins regular flights on September 1, initially between Vancouver and Seattle.

1938: Disgruntled Relief Camp workers and others occupy the main Vancouver Post Office in a protest that turns ugly when the police forcibly extract the men on "Bloody Sunday" (June 19), and 35 people are wounded.

• On August 18, Franklin D. Roosevelt becomes the first U.S. President to visit Canada. After presiding with Prime Minister Mackenzie King at

On May 21, 1939, during the first visit to Canada of a reigning monarch, the King and Queen attended the unveiling in Ottawa of the national memorial to the tens of thousands of Canadians killed while fighting alongside the British in the First World War.

the opening of the international Thousand Islands Bridge across the St. Lawrence River, he addresses an audience at Queen's University in nearby Kingston, Ontario.

1939: The first visit to Canada by a reigning monarch begins with the arrival of King George VI and Queen Elizabeth by ship at Quebec City on May 17. They criss-cross Canada by a specially fitted royal train, encounter cheering crowds, make a five-day side trip to the United States and, on June 15 in Halifax, embark for a one-day visit to St. John's on the voyage home.

• Canada declares war on Germany on Sunday, September 10 (seven days after Britain's declaration). During the six-year Second World War, Canadians engage in combat against Germany and Italy in Europe and on the North Atlantic, and against Japan in Asia, with armed forces that number more than one million men and women. About the same number are employed in the war industry at its production peak in 1943.

During a bitter strike by steel workers in Hamilton in 1946, union members used boats to block company vessels carrying strikebreakers and supplies to the Stelco plant. Here, workers aboard the *Whisper* patrol Hamilton Bay.

son under protection. His information eventually leads directly to the conviction of 11 people on espionage charges, including Canadian MP Fred Rose; Sam Carr, an officer of Canada's Communist Party, and British atomic scientist Allan Nunn May. Gouzenko, he and his family with assumed names and at a secret Canadian address, lives until 1982. Many people regard his action in September, 1945, as the launching deed of the Cold War. The often menacing global power struggle between Soviet communism and American-led capitalism outlasts Gouzenko, its closure taking place in two stages—the breakup of the Soviet bloc of East European states in 1989 and of the Soviet Union itself two years later.

1947: A law creating Canadian citizenship takes effect on January 1. Previously, the legal status of a person born in Canada or naturalized was "British subject," with the sub-identification "Canadian national."

• The Imperial Oil Company launches a productive new petroleum era in Western Canada with a major dis- covery—Leduc No. 1, a well 50 kilo- metres south of Edmonton that is inaugurated ceremonially on February 13. The company, having drilled 133 dry holes up to 1946, had decided to try one more line of wildcat wells across Alberta. A crew led by toolpush Vern (Dry Hole) Hunter starts drilling on November 20, 1946, and strikes Leduc oil 12 weeks later at a depth of 1,544 metres.

1949: Newfoundland, which spurned Confederation at Canada's founding, becomes the 10th province at midnight on March 31, after two referendums produce a narrow decision for joining the Dominion. Liberal Joseph R. (Joey) Smallwood, who led the Yes forces, is the new province's first premier.

• The Supreme Court of Canada, established in 1875, becomes Canada's court of last resort with the abolition of appeals in civil cases to the Judicial Committee of the Privy Council in Britain (appeals to London in criminal cases had been abolished in 1933).

Joseph R. (Joey) Smallwood employed in full measure his puckish manner and his gift of the gab to persuade Newfoundlanders in 1949 to join Canada as its 10th province—which, it turned out, he would run as premier for the next 23 years.

1950

1950: British Columbia, Alberta, Saskatchewan, Manitoba, Ontario, and Prince Edward Island sign an agreement with Ottawa on April 25, 1950, for the construction of the Trans-Canada Highway. Work begins that summer and is completed in 1970.

1952: Following 17 successive British office holders, Vincent Massey, 65, becomes the country's first Canadian governor general on February 28. A former president of his family's farm implements company, Canada's first envoy in Washington in the 1920s and its high commissioner in London during the Second World War, Massey had only the previous year completed his greatest contribution to Canada: As head of the Royal Commission on National Development in the Arts, Letters and Sciences, his recommendations in 1951 spawned the Canada Council and other instruments of Canada's cultural enrichment.

1957: Ellen Fairclough becomes the first woman to serve in Canada's

T.C. (Tommy) Douglas, as premier of Saskatchewan, introduced Canada to publicly run and funded universal medical care. The program was instituted in the province on July 1, 1962, and Ottawa inaugurated national medicare five years later.

federal cabinet on June 21, when she is sworn into office as secretary of state in John Diefenbaker's newly elected Progressive Conservative government.

• Opposition MP Lester B. Pearson, former external affairs minister and soon to be leader of the Liberal Party (and prime minister from 1963 to 1968) is awarded the Nobel Peace Prize on October 14. As external affairs minister the previous fall, he had been instrumental in separating the combatants in the Suez Crisis—Britain, France and Israel versus Egypt—with the organization of a United Nations Emergency Force on borderlands in the Sinai Desert and the Gaza Strip.

1958: On March 31, Prime Minister John Diefenbaker, seeking to expand on his government's fragile minority status in Parliament since its election in June 1957 leads his Progressive Conservatives to the largest Commons majority on record in a general election—a total 208 members in the 265-seat House. In a *Maclean's* interview published two days before the election, Diefenbaker says he went into public life to fight discrimination based on race or ethnic antecedents. "I am the first prime minister of this country of neither altogether English nor French origin," he notes, "and I determined to bring about a Canadian citizenship that knew no hyphenated consideration."

1959: The Diefenbaker government, in a cost-saving decision announced on February 20, kills the Avro Arrow, a supersonic jet fighter built by A.V. Roe of Canada in the Toronto suburb of

1960

1961: On March 15, at a Commonwealth leaders' meeting in London, Canada's John Diefenbaker plays a pivotal role in promoting a statement committing Commonwealth members to cultivate "equality of opportunity for all, irrespective of race, color or creed" and provokes South Africa to quit the organization. (South Africa rejoins the Commonwealth in June 1994 after abolishing apartheid and enfranchising the country's non-white majority.)

1962: The Saskatchewan Medical Care Insurance Act, forerunner of the national medicare program six years later, comes into effect on July 1. Almost all the province's doctors strike in protest. A settlement is reached a month later.

• Canada's first communications satellite, *Alouette I*, is launched into earth orbit on September 29 by

JUNE 1967

EXPO '67

It's simply indescribable. From one end of its 1,000 acres to the other, Expo '67 is a conflagration of wondrous images, that words and pictures can only hint at. It's a cliché by now—but it really is the best show ever. Everywhere you turn, dazzling colors and fantastic shapes startle the eye.

Expo is the biggest exhibition ever presented anywhere, but what really sets it apart from ordinary fairs is the fascinating pull of its attractions. You don't just go to see Expo. You get caught right up in everything. At some point you realize that without you, multiplied a million times over, there wouldn't be an Expo '67. One young matron spent three days being happily "taken in" by such spectacles as the U.S. geodesic dome and La Ronde's people-eating Gyrotron, then reported to her friends, "You shouldn't go to Expo unless you're willing to become involved!"

From April through October 1967, a prime focus of celebration in the centennial year of Confederation was Expo '67, an amalgam of activity and sparkle on an expanded St. Lawrence island off Montreal, Ile Ste-Hélène, and a people-built one, Ile Notre-Dame.

Headline Makers

We polled the editors of all Canada's dailies and invited them to pick Canadian men and women whose works or words or personalities excite the most attention. John Diefenbaker placed first, followed in a hairline finish by Lester B. Pearson. The score was 23 to 22. The top ten was top heavy with other political figures: C.D. Howe got 15 votes, Maurice Duplessis of Quebec 12, Dr. Sidney Smith, the new minister of external affairs, 11, and ex-prime minister St. Laurent 9.

The most interesting woman? Firebrand Charlotte Whitton [see inset photo] (16) by a country mile over Secretary of State Ellen Fairclough (8) and cook-commentator Kate Aitken (2). [Ottawa's Mayor] Charlotte polled only one less than Governor-General Vincent Massey, and easily outstripped such other prominent women as singers Gisele MacKenzie and Lois Marshall, golfer Marlene Stewart Streit and swimmer Marilyn Bell Di Lascio, each of whom was mentioned twice.

Except for the Montreal rocket, Maurice Richard, athletes as a group rate low in interest with the editors, especially in comparison with writers and artists. Richard (8) stood even with B.C. premier W.A.C. Bennett and writer Bruce Hutchison and two behind playwright Robertson Davies. Outside Richard, no athlete was mentioned more than twice, but actor Gratien Gélinas, pianist Glenn Gould and novelist Hugh MacLennan each polled five votes.

In the professions physician-scientists have a special appeal for the editors, led by famous neuro-surgeon Wilder Penfield (13), Dr. Hans Selye (5) and Dr. Charles Best, co-discoverer of insulin (3).

Perhaps indicative of the perishable quality of public interest is the fact that the four surviving Dionne quints, who would surely have rated near the top in interest 20 years ago, now merely split a vote with Papa Oliva, on the same level as poet Ned Pratt and Eskimo carver Oshaweetuk.

Charlotte Whitton of Ottawa made her mark on the life of Canada by winning election as the country's first woman mayor in 1951 and then by flaunting her feminism in showdowns with antagonistic males.

Downsview and first test-flown on March 25, 1958. As a result, A.V. Roe lays off 14,000 employees, many of whom moved to the United States, where Canada thereafter buys its military planes.

- On June 26, Queen Elizabeth II and President Dwight D. (Ike) Eisenhower officially open the St. Lawrence Seaway, a joint project of the Canadian and U.S. governments, permitting navigation between the Atlantic Ocean and the Great Lakes, in a ceremony at St. Lambert Lock, Montreal. Almost 40 years later, after several years of declining traffic and three years of financial losses, Ottawa transfers management of the Canadian sections of the seaway on October 1, 1998, to a private, non-profit corporation under a 10-year lease.

In the year of flower power, the new Prime Minister of Canada plucked a tulip in Ottawa in the middle of May.

the U.S. National Aeronautics and Space Administration (NASA).

- Two hangings in Toronto's Don Jail during the first minutes of December 11—Arthur Lucas, a Detroit mobster who slew an FBI informant and his common-law wife hiding out in Toronto, and Ronald Turpin, who killed a Toronto policeman—prove to be the last judicial executions in Canada.

1964: On March 31, after four years of haggling, Canada, the United States, British Columbia and Washington state interests proceed with provisions of the controversial Columbia River Treaty, whereby the Canadians build three dams on their stretch of the border-crossing river and British Columbia pre-sells the Americans its share of the hydro power produced in Washington. In March 1999, under renegotiated terms, British Columbia regains control of its Columbia power to use or sell as it chooses.

1965: After years of indecision and bickering, and a protracted debate in Parliament over replacing the Red Ensign (a Union Jack in one corner), Canada's new, red and white Maple Leaf flag flies for the first time officially on February 15 at a ceremony on Parliament Hill.

1967: Canada celebrates the Centennial of Confederation all year in many ways, from the construction of Centennial arenas to July 1 barbecues. The main event is Expo '67, the Montreal world's fair named Man and His World, a 62-nation extravaganza that draws 50,306,648 visitors, 53 per cent of them Canadians, in its six-month stretch from April 27 to October 29.

- President Charles de Gaulle of France, one of many leaders welcomed to Canada during Centennial year, offends many Canadians when he cries "Vive le Québec Libre" from the balcony of Montreal City Hall at the end of a speech closing the Quebec part of his tour on July 24. Prime Minister Lester Pearson makes it the end of the tour altogether, sending de Gaulle home by describing his words as "unacceptable to the Canadian people and its government."

1968: The Medical Care Insurance program, a federal-provincial shared-cost service enacted by Parliament and negotiated in with the provinces, takes effect on July 1. Saskatchewan and British Columbia join, with the other provinces set to follow.

1970

1970: The kidnapping of British envoy James Cross in Montreal on October 5, followed by the seizure of Quebec labor minister Pierre Laporte on October 10, avowedly by the violently separatist Front de Libération du Québec, ignites "the October Crisis." Ottawa calls out the army and invokes the War Measures Act on October 16, suspending civil liberties and authorizing the police to round up and arrest without charge more than 450 Quebecers. The following day, Laporte's strangled body is found in the trunk of a car. Laporte's killers eventually serve prison time. Cross is freed, his kidnappers permitted through negotiation to accept exile to Cuba for a time.

1975: Legislation making the beaver a symbol of Canadian sovereignty becomes law on March 24.

Conservative MP Sean O'Sullivan pushes the measure through Parliament to protect Canada's longstanding regard for the beaver as a national icon—hitherto unofficially—from proposals in neighboring New York State to adopt the animal as its emblem.

- The metrification of Canada, a process launched with a policy-setting federal White Paper on Metric Conversion on January 16, 1970, begins in practice on April 1 with the use of Celsius temperatures in weather reports. Changes from imperial standards of measurement to the metric system follow over the next 10 years.

1976: Federal legislation abolishing capital punishment (except for some military offences) becomes law on July 16, two days after its approval by 130 votes to 124 in

René Lévesque, who led his Parti Québécois to electoral victory on November 15, 1976, retained office as premier of La Belle Province for nine years.

AUG. 1976 *Doing It Up Royally*

Michael Enright — *August 9, 1976* They had been standing there in the sun for a couple of hours, the Imperial Order Daughters of the Empire, Moncton chapter. They had trooped over to Chatham in northern New Brunswick because the Queen was to sign the town guest book and walk in the park. Now they waited, loyalist and royalist, a formidable wall of rock-bottomed allegiance. The Queen eased down the line in the hot sun, looking a bit tired. When she reached the IODE emplacement, she smiled tightly: "And how *are* the Daughters today?"

There it was. A relaxing sense of recognition on both sides. The Daughters smiled as one. The connective linkages were still in place. For Canadians, this 13-day royal visit was a low-key renewal of affection. Queenship has a compelling sense of occasion for Canadians. They may have seen it all before but they turned out to line up again.

What they saw was a 50-year old woman who stands five-four but with a tiara looks a head taller. She has fixing blue eyes, a high forehead and a wide mouth. In her twenty-fifth year as Queen, she is sixty-third in a line of sovereigns going back 1,000 years. She knows about queenship in all its details, that to be regal is to be distant and formal. Yet she is said to be direct in conversation, quick to laugh and well-informed politically. She drinks sparingly, usually gin and tonic, and she never smokes.

Officially she came to Canada to open the Olympic Games in Montreal. But the

Queen also came to cheer her daughter, Anne, who was the first member of a British royal family to compete in the Olympics. The visit became very much a family holiday when the three princes—Edward, Andrew and Charles—joined their parents at Bromont, Quebec, to watch the equestrian events. It was the first time the entire family had been together outside Britain.

The people running the tour worried openly about Quebec. They knew the Quebec political leadership was not happy with the Queen's prominent role at the Olympics because it underscored a dramatic federal presence. And there was the vision of the Queen being in Quebec at all. She had not been to Montreal since 1967 and then had toured only the Expo islands. She had not been seen widely or publicly since her 1964 visit, which turned ugly when Quebec City police rioted against a group of students shouting separatist slogans.

In Montreal, security was the tightest since the War Measures crisis of 1970. They need not have worried. Her visit was of no interest to serious indépendantistes. She was viewed in the main as an item of curiosity, an adjunct to the Olympics or a minor sport like archery. During one reception at Place des Arts, a group of five separatists stood across the road with a sign reading QUEBEC FRANÇAIS. A young Mountie watching them was asked if the RCMP could handle the demonstration. "I think so," said the cop, "especially since two of them are ours."

AUG. 1976

Heroes of the XXI Olympiad

Michael Posner – *August 9, 1976* For 16 days last month, the attention of millions was riveted on the city of Montreal and the Games of the XXI Olympiad. Nothing rivaled it. For several hours every day North Americans sat enthralled before their television sets. The world's leading newspapers ran Olympics stories on page one. No fewer than seven magazines displayed the pubescent form of gymnast Nadia Comaneci—the first woman to score a perfect mark in the Olympics—on their covers. In Montreal, scalpers exchanged $30 seats for $200 in hard cash. Spectators lined up for hours to secure standing room tickets. Telly Savalas, Mick Jagger and Queen Elizabeth came to call. In the streets of a city in which even the women who hawk Jehovah's Witnesses literature are chic, there were people singing until 3 a.m.

It was an occasion. Conceived in fantasy and reared amid controversy, the Montreal games—to the surprise of everyone—were executed with near-flawless precision. Predictably, there were complaints about security, but the indefatigable presence of Canadian army officers clearly had its intended effect. The closest approximation to an incident was the crashing of the closing ceremonies by a lone streaker. In the end, even Roger Tailibert's Stade Olympique, an edifice of classic proportions, was ready (if not finished). And though the debt for this fortnight's festival was estimated at $1.5 billion and still climbing, Montrealers seemed to accept it with Gallic indifference. Spent or mis-spent, the money had already changed hands; one might as well enjoy it.

Queen Elizabeth II, on one of her many visits to Canada in the last half of the century, inspects a Canadian guard of honor on July 16, 1976, before moving on to formally open the Montreal Olympics.

the House of Commons. (In 1966, Parliament had restricted the death penalty to cases of treason or the killing of peace officers.) In later years, the abolitionist argument is reinforced when justice authorities overturn a number of murder convictions—in several cases as a result of so-called DNA fingerprinting, whereby forensic science learned during the 1990s to precisely compare an individual's cellular DNA to human tissue found at a crime scene. Notable among the judicial reversals: Donald Marshall in Nova Scotia on May 10, 1983, after 11 years in prison; David Milgaard, who spent almost 23 years in prison, in Saskatchewan on July 18, 1997; Guy-Paul Morin, convicted in 1992, in Ontario on January 23, 1995; Gregory Parsons, found guilty in 1994, in Newfoundland on February 2, 1998; Peter Frumusa, imprisoned for more than eight years, in Ontario on June 25, 1998.

- Montreal, with a spectacular new if unfinished stadium and other freshly built facilities, is host to the summer Olympics. The 16-day competition is formally opened on July 17 by the Queen, whose entire immediate family is in Canada for the occasion, with Princess Anne competing in an equestrian event.

1980: Terrance Stanley (Terry) Fox, an athlete and student from New Westminster, British Columbia, whose right leg had been amputated after he contracted bone cancer, attracts international attention while attempting a cross-country "Marathon of Hope" run to raise money for cancer research. After setting out on April 12 at St. John's, Newfoundland, he is forced to stop on September 1 in Thunder Bay, Ontario, after he is found to have cancer in his lungs. Donations to his cause during his run totalled about $25 million and Ottawa made him a Companion of the Order of Canada. Following his death on June 28, 1981, a month short of his 23rd birthday, he received many posthumous honors, including annual running events to fund the quest to find a cure for the disease that took his life.

- *O Canada*, composed by Calixa Lavalée in 1880, with French lyrics by Judge Adolphe-Basile Routhier and the English by Stanley Weir, is finally made the national anthem of Canada by law on June 27, 1980.

1982: After decades of fruitless effort to reform and patriate the Canadian constitution—the British North America Act, an 1867 statute of the British Parliament—Queen Elizabeth and Prime Minister Pierre Trudeau preside at the Parliament Hill ceremony Canadianizing the document on April 17.

- Parliament changes the name of the July 1 national holiday to Canada Day from Dominion Day on October 26, completing a process whereby "Dominion," the designation devised by the Fathers of Confederation, gradually fell into official disuse (the Dominion

Bureau of Statistics became Statistics Canada on May 1, 1971). The Canada Day legislation slips through a near-empty Commons in July without forewarning, debate or vote and, in the fall, survives Senate opposition by a single vote. Retentionists vainly remind abolitionists that "Dominion" was taken from the Bible's Psalm 72 to define the land's expanse (Atlantic to Pacific, St. Lawrence to the North Pole): "He shall have dominion also from sea to sea, and from the river to the ends of the earth." Abolitionists counter that French lacks a good translation of the word. But after all the sound and fury, the amended and patriated 1982 Constitution retains the historic title: the provinces, the country's fundamental statute still declares, "shall form and be One Dominion."

1984: From September 9 to 20, Pope John Paul II tours Canada, the first papal visit.

1986: Expo '86, the Vancouver World's Fair featuring transportation and communication themes, draws almost 21 million visitors—far beyond expectations—from May 2 to October 13.

1987: The Royal Canadian Mint in June begins circulating the loonie, the 11-sided, bronzed nickel dollar with the Queen's head on the front and a portrayal of the common loon on the tails side. Many people, notably in western Canada, turn against the coin. But it becomes a fixture in purses and pockets as the dollar bill, while remaining legal tender, pretty well disappears from circulation by the end of 1989.

For years after Terry Fox's cross-Canada Marathon of Hope ended in 1980 with his death from cancer, annual runs raised money for research into the disease.

1988: Calgary stages highly successful Winter Olympic Games from February 13 to 27, presiding over what visitors and residents alike praise as a two-week people party.

MAY 1982

Rebirth of a Nation

Robert Lewis – *April 26, 1982* The Queen called it "a defiant challenge to history." Prime Minister Pierre Trudeau described it as "an act of defiance against the history of mankind." For all that, Saturday, April 17, was a quintessentially Canadian day. There was poetry and pageantry, pride and patriotism, political potshots and petty patronage. True to tradition, there were no shots fired in anger—only the 21-gun salute to a sovereign who reigned over the whole parade, even as the heavens opened at the magic hour. But despite downpour and disclaimers, after 115 fractious years, Her Majesty Queen Elizabeth II could fairly proclaim that the Constitution "is truly Canadian at last."

It also was assailed and besmirched—inevitable, if hardly fitting. The government of Quebec denounced a process in which, said Vice-Premier Jacques-Yvan Morin, "we are being royally screwed." Trudeau responded in French from the platform on Parliament Hill: "By definition, the silent majority does not make a lot of noise; it is content to make history." But Trudeau could have no answer for the gods. As he sat down with the Queen to sign the proclamation at 11:35 a.m. (EST) Saturday, the first drops of an eventual downpour spattered the hand-lettered parchment crafted from Manitoba flax. Errant droplets smudged the Queen's red-lettered introductory protocol greeting and the black Mont Blanc ink signature of André Ouellet, the trouble-prone registrar general who affixed the Great Seal of Canada. Instead of a quick trip to the printer and distribution across the nation, the proclamation was dried out during the weekend under the watchful eye of calligrapher John Whitehead. "After 50 years of discussion," Trudeau said proudly, "we have finally decided to retrieve what is properly ours." The dominant item of the new Constitution Act 1982 is Trudeau's treasured Canadian Charter of Rights and Freedoms. Starting this week, the charter will launch the nation on an American-style pursuit of rights in the courts.

Among whereases and notwithstandings in the rest of the 60-section act, there are seeds for flowers—and for weeds. An amending formula that eluded politicians nine times since 1927 now permits constitutional changes with the approval of Parliament and seven provinces, representing 50 per cent of the population. But up to three legislatures can opt out, producing a scenario for the checkerboard Canada that Trudeau once lamented.

As Trudeau stressed, "the process of constitutional reform has not come to an end." The new act, for example, guarantees that yet another federal-provincial conference must be held within 12 months to deal with native rights. Indian, Inuit and Metis leaders felt betrayed by the clause that entrenches "existing aboriginal and treaty rights" on the grounds that it sounded suspiciously like a further erosion of their claims to land and valuable resources. As a result, native people were strikingly absent from the patriation ritual. They staged protests around the country.

Walking elegantly through the fray was Elizabeth II, a 55-year-old veteran of 30 years on the throne, making her 10th visit to Canada. Adoring crowds pressed forward with bouquets during her 20-minute walkabout on Parliament Hill. There were shouts of "Way to go, Bess," and, "Yea, Queenie." Even battle-scarred reporters, not a few republicans among them, lapsed into exuberance during a pre-patriation party for the press. The Queen allowed that she was "sad" that Quebec was out of the deal. She professed puzzlement about Canada's chronic inability to come to terms with constitutional change.

Trudeau can reflect on the realization of a lifelong dream. "He stuck with it when many others would have quit," said former NDP leader Tommy Douglas in a rare Opposition tribute. "Today the Canadian people owe him a real debt of gratitude for what he's done." Trudeau, of course, had plenty of help—from Jean Chrétien and Jean Wadds to women and the handicapped. Whether proclamation is "a fresh beginning," as Trudeau asserted, remains to be seen.

At Woodroffe Public School in Ottawa last week, there seemed little doubt. Principal Dick Zadow handed out government-supplied flags and decals, and 400 kids sang *O Canada* in both official languages before plunging gleefully into an oversized cake with a frosted maple leaf. Wow, rejoiced one Grade 6 student, we are free. At Ecole Pierre Laporte in Trudeau's own Mount Royal riding that day, it was a different tale. "There's nothing happening," said Vice-Principal Gerald Janelle. "It's not St. Jean Baptiste Day."

So goes the gulf between French and English in places, the kind of regrettable dichotomy between founding peoples that first drew Trudeau to Ottawa in 1965. He saw a new constitution as the vehicle that would transport English and French to a new state of harmony and mutual respect. With the Constitution now in force, the true test of the vision will not come in the courts but in the hearts and minds of men and women who are boys and girls today. The two solitudes, alas, were entrenched too long ago to be bridged by words on parchment.

OCT. 1984 *Rivers of Change*

Morley Callaghan — *October 1, 1984* A remarkable thing about the Pope's visit is that it provided a revelation to Canadians about themselves. It has told us how much we have changed in the 40 years since the Second World War and that we are probably still changing—from a place where the power and ideas of the White Anglo-Saxon Protestant were dominant. We have had the great immigrations from Europe, Asia and the Caribbean. We have just had about 16 years of Trudeau, hardly a WASP in thought or deed. But the Pope's visit showed us what we may only have suspected: we are a racial and cultural mosaic in fact as well as ideal, but a mosaic in motion.

For one thing, such a visit by a pope would have been unthinkable in the Canada of 40 years ago. He simply would not have been welcome. For another, the pageantry of the Pope revealed our moving mosaic dramatically, by the nature of the picture of the great crowds, by the breaking down of barriers between people. And I believe the change is continuing. People will flow together. We are becoming something else.

As the Pope moved across the country, he kept repeating what a wonderful thing it is to have all these cultures here, that all these cultures should be preserved. Well, all right. But from watching what is happening across the country, I do not believe people can be held within the confines of those mosaic patterns, with everybody remaining in the ghetto of the mosaic. People move. Young people meet. Love laughs at cultural locksmiths.

Three years after John Paul II paid the first papal visit to Canada in 1984, he returned to drop in exclusively on the Northwest Territories village of Fort Simpson (population around 1,200), which the Pope had been forced by bad weather to stand up the first time around.

1990

1995: In a Quebec referendum on October 30, a followup to the 1980 province-wide poll that fell short of supporting the province's separation from Canada, the voters reject independence by a sliver—50.6 per cent of them opposing secession.

1996: The toonie, the two-dollar coin instantly nicknamed to rhyme with the loonie of 1987, goes into circulation on February 19 to gradually supplant the two-dollar bill. Complaints and ridicule—including early claims that the bronze centre of the coin breaks out of its sur-

rounding nickel—are shorter-lived and more subdued than the grumbling that greeted the loonie.

1997: A mining discovery portrayed as the gold find of the century, a venture by Calgary-based Bre-X Minerals Ltd. on the Indonesian island of Borneo, turns out in March to be the mining hoax of all time. Investigators later report the project involved falsification of ore samples "without precedent in the history of mining anywhere in the world." On March 27, after Bre-X's new American partner reports "insignificant amounts of gold" in its test drillings, investors sell off Bre-X stock at a pace that soon vaporizes its multi-billion-dollar market value. Many scalded shareholders launch lawsuits against Bre-X and its chief executive, David Walsh.

Figure skater Elvis Stojko won the world championship three times—in 1994, 1995 and 1997. He built on a Canadian title-winning record that stretched from Donald Jackson (1962) and Donald McPherson (1963) through Brian Orser (1987) and Kurt Browning (1989, 1990, 1991, 1993).

• On May 31, the Confederation Bridge connecting Prince Edward Island and New Brunswick is opened with celebrations and lingering doubts

Prince Charles and Diana, with their boys William and Harry, bid farewell to Toronto from the deck of the Royal Yacht *Britannia* on October 27, 1991. A little over a year later, on December 9, 1992, the royal marriage broke up in an official separation.

Celebration

December 22, 1986 The most striking celebrations often are as gaudy and exuberant as American poet Walt Whitman's sprawling poem *Song of Myself*. The most memorable may be those in which people joyfully behave, as Whitman wrote, to "celebrate myself and sing myself."

It happened that way at Vancouver's Expo 86, where the world fair's transportation theme was overtaken by people enjoying themselves and other people, swelling British Columbian pride.

It began in May when Prince Charles and Diana, Princess of Wales, officially opened Expo 86. By the time it closed in October, Expo had counted almost 21 million visitors.

Making the Magic Last

Bob Levin – *March 7, 1988* Suddenly, the party was almost over. The days were dwindling away, and the other Olympics—the ones in the Calgary streets in which Games-goers vied to have the most enjoyable time imaginable—were in their final, frenzied phase. On the Stephen Avenue mall, under a sparkling blue sky, strollers gobbled fat hotdogs, watched jugglers and listened to reggae and rock. They traded pins feverishly. As a choir at Olympic Plaza sang *Over the Rainbow*, 28-year-old Brian Arnelien of Clifford, Ont., summed up the prevailing mood. "Nobody wants the Games to end."

It was a moment that defied mere logic. It went beyond sport to something very much like magic. During the last week of the Games, as calm, northerly air broke down the tumultuous Pacific flow that had forced 22 postponements, Canadians embraced a host of new heroes.

The world had come to Calgary on a cold February afternoon and, 16 eventful days later, it was preparing to go. Ahead lay Calgary's collective hangover—and perhaps an Olympian let-down. But in the waning days last week, Calgarians seemed intent on making the magic last, on savoring the moment. "If I stayed here 100 years," said Mick Butson, doorman at the VIP-packed Palliser Hotel, "I'd never see anything like this again. Never."

---

among some Islanders about the wisdom of building the fixed link to mainland Canada. The bridge, almost 13 kilometres long, is the world's longest span over waters that are ice-covered part of the time. It replaces a three-hour ferry ride with a car trip that takes about 10 minutes when traffic is moving at normal travelling speeds.

- The death of Diana, Princess of Wales, from injuries sustained in a Paris car crash early on August 31, touches off an emotional response among many people in Britain and elsewhere, including Canada. For reasons not entirely clear, an outpouring of negative sentiments develop toward the British royal family, including Queen Elizabeth as well as Prince Charles, Diana's ex-husband. Many commentators question—as they had with increasing frequency through the 1990s—

whether the monarchy would long survive. For Canada, the questioning raises the possibility—albeit with little public discussion—that Canadians, without a head of state, would be required to alter their form of government.

1998: The Supreme Court of Canada, responding on August 20 to constitutional questions submitted by the federal government in 1996, advises in a 78-page unanimous opinion that Quebec does not have the right to declare its independence of Canada unilaterally, but "a clear majority vote in Quebec on a clear question in favor of secession would confer democratic legitimacy on the secession initiative which all the participants in Confederation would have to recognize." There would then have to be "principled negotiation" on the terms of sepa-

Inuit leader Paul Okalik hugged his son after being sworn into office as a member of the legislative assembly of the new Territory of Nunavut, created on April 1, 1999, with Okalik Senior as its first premier.

ration between Quebec and the rest of Canada. Regarding a Quebec referendum, "It will be for the political actors to determine what constitutes 'a clear majority on a clear question.'" Politicians on both sides of the Quebec question publicly

express satisfaction with selected features of the court's opinion.

- On September 24 in Ottawa, South African President Nelson Mandela becomes the first foreign leader to be honored as a Companion of the Order of Canada. He addresses the House of Commons in what, at age 80, he calls "something of a farewell" and expresses gratitude to "a people that has made our aspirations their own" in promoting human rights in his country. The following day in Toronto's SkyDome stadium, he addresses 45,000 schoolchildren—and many more across the country via television—to promote the Canadian chapter of the Nelson Mandela Children's Fund, declaring that "children are the most important asset of any country."

What a visitor from Mars would discover

A visitor from Mars, you see, arrives in Canada and can't figure out this debate on whether Quebec is going to separate or not. On examination, the puzzled visitor would find:

1. For 29 of the last 30 years, the prime minister of Canada has come from Quebec.
2. The current prime minister of Canada, in his second term, is from Quebec.
3. The chief justice of the Supreme Court of Canada is a francophone from Quebec.
4. Three of the nine justices on the Supreme Court of Canada–or 33 $\frac{1}{3}$ per cent–are, by law, from Quebec, whose population of Canada is now down to 25 per cent.
5. The head of the Canadian Forces is a francophone from Quebec.
6. The Governor General of Canada in Rideau Hall is a francophone.
7. The Clerk of the Privy Council is a francophone from Quebec.
8. The Canadian ambassador to the United States in Washington is a francophone from Quebec.
9. The head prosecutor of the International War Crimes Tribunal in The Hague is a Quebec-born francophone.
10. The finance minister of Canada is from Quebec.

The perplexed visitor from space would then go to the history books. The visitor would discover that the problem goes back to the early morning of Sept. 13, 1759.

Louis-Joseph de Montcalm-Grozon, Marquis de Montcalm de Saint-Véran, was a soldier at 12 and was severely wounded and made prisoner at the Battle of Piacenza. In the Seven Years' War, he assumed command of the French troops in North America in 1756, and captured the British post of Oswego and also Fort William Henry, where some of the prisoners (men, women and children) were massacred by the Indian allies. In 1758, with a small force, he successfully defended Ticonderoga and then moved to Quebec City with 5,500 troops and prepared to defend it against a British attack.

James Wolfe, born in a vicarage in Kent, served against the Scottish Jacobites at Falkirk and Culloden. As a major-general, and commanding 9,000 men, he sailed from England in February of 1759 and in June landed below the cliffs of Quebec. His attack on Montcalm's strong position was completely foiled. Until at dawn on Sept. 13, when he scaled the cliffs at an insufficiently guarded point with 4,500 men and found himself on the Plains of Abraham.

The French were routed, Quebec capitulated and, as the history books say, "its fall decided the fate of Canada." Wolfe died in the hour of his victory. Montcalm, mortally wounded, expired the next morning.

In most all historic struggles–the Battle of Waterloo, Trafalgar, the U.S. Civil War–there is a clear winner and a clear loser. What happened on the Plains of Abraham that September was that the French thought it was a TIE!

The distinguished American historian Henry Steele Commager once wrote that "never in the history of colonial wars has the victor treated the vanquished so generously."

The English, as we know, gave the French special protection for their Roman Catholic religion, their language, their civil law. Montreal, today, must be the only place in Christendom with a Protestant school board and a Catholic school board.

The result is that, in 1998, for the first time in recent memory, with Preston Manning, we have a leader of Her Majesty's Loyal Opposition in the House of Commons–Joe Clark taught himself French quite well–who cannot express himself intelligibly in French.

Every separatist in Montreal can swear that they personally know someone who, after the war, went into Eaton's on Ste-Catherine and was told to "speak white." They were probably correct.

We are down to a situation where we are told that the only way for the country not to be destroyed is for the curly-headed leader of the federal Conservative Party of Canada, Jean Charest, to give up his principles and give in to the overwhelming pressure and become the provincial leader of the Liberals in Quebec.

It recalls the old stand-up line: "I'm a politician and I have principles. If you don't like them–well, I have other principles."

Daniel Johnson Jr. should be given a Victoria Cross for, knowing he simply doesn't have the personality or verve to compete with St. Lucien Bouchard, valiantly falling on his sword, thus preventing the Parti Québécois from calling a quickie spring election.

The Great Unwashed, out there before the voting booth, may not have IQs up there with Einstein, but they have great common sense and fairness. They know that any government that tries to take advantage of the confusion and weakness of the Opposition seeking a new leader would be punished mercilessly at an election. St. Lucien, knowing as much, has admitted as much.

He perhaps knows that a Manitoba Tory government, trying that gig, was astonishingly unhorsed by a young Ed Schreyer of the NDP who had been a leader for barely 18 days and hadn't had time to unpack his Ottawa bags.

The visitor from Mars would find this a very funny country. The visitor from Mars would be right.

Photo Credits

Prelims:
Page 1: *Maclean's*/Peter Bregg; Page 8: Western Canada Pictorial Index; Page 10: Canadian Press/Tom Hanson; Page 12: Canadian Press/Ron Poling; Page 14: Western Canada Pictorial Index; Page 15: New Brunswick Archives; Page 16: National Archives of Canada/C-24559; Page 17: National Archives of Canada/PA-30802; Page 18: Bayne Stanley.

Progress and Perils:
Page 21: Archives of Ontario; Page 22: National Archives of Canada/C-063257; Page 23-4: Western Canada Pictorial Index; Page 25: Canadian Press; Page 26: (left) City of Toronto Archives; (right) Detail of National Archives of Canada/C-020548; Page 27: Detail of National Archives of Canada/PA-059591; Page 28: William James Topley/National Archives of Canada/PA-11616; Page 30: *Toronto Sun* Archives; Page 31: John Sylvester.

Tweedletory, Tweedlegrit:
Page 33: National Archives of Canada/PA-123990; Page 34: L.P. Picard/National Archives of Canada/C-3930; Page 35: Nelson Quarrington/W. Howard Measures Collection/National Archives of Canada/PA-148532; Page 36: Canadian Press; Page 37: (top) Canadian Press; (middle right) Bill Fox; (middle left) Canadian Press/Dave Buston; (bottom) Detail of National Archives of Canada/C-014140; Page 38: Duncan Cameron/National Archives of Canada/PA-117107; Page 39: Canadian Press/Ryan Remiorz; Page 40: (left) Canadian Press; (right) National Archives of Canada/PA-17222.

The Longest Revolution:
Page 43: *Toronto Sun* Archives; Page 44: *Toronto Sun* Archives; Page 45: City of Toronto Archives; Page 46: National Archives of Canada; Page 47: (top) Western Canada Pictorial Index; (bottom) *Toronto Sun* Archives; Page 48: (top) National Film Board/National Archives of Canada/PA-117582; (middle left) Canadian Press Air Photo/*Toronto Sun* Archives; (middle right) Canadian Press; (bottom) *Toronto Sun* Archives; Page 49: Canadian Press; Page 50: City of Edmonton Archives; Page 51: City of Toronto Archives; Page 52: (left) Canadian Press; (right) *Toronto Sun* Archives; Page 53: Canadian Press/Tom Hanson.

The Peaceable Kingdom at War:
Page 55: Ivor Castle/National Archives of Canada/PA-001093; Page 56: National Archives of Canada/C-006097; Page 57: (top) National Archives of Canada/C-067449; (bottom) National Archives of Canada/PA-107909; Page 58: National Archives of Canada/PA-133760; Page 59: (left) National Archives of Canada/PA-1679; (right) City of Toronto Archives; Page 60: (top) National Archives of Canada/C-14104; (bottom) National Archives of Canada/PA-001326; Page 61: National Archives of Canada/PA-001654; Page 62: Department of National Defence; Page 63: Department of National Defence; Page 64: (top) Department of National Defence; (bottom) National Archives of Canada/PA-114799; Page 65: (top) National Archives of Canada/PA-141663; (bottom) Department of National Defence; Page 66: (top) York University Archives; (bottom) Canadian Press; Page 67: City of Toronto Archives.

Generation Lucky:
Page 69: Grant Collingwood Collection; Page 70: (left) *Edmonton Sun* Archives; (right) Grant Collingwood Collection; Page 71: *Montreal Gazette* Archives; Page 72: National Archives of Canada/PA-111390; Page 73: Grant Collingwood Collection; Page 74: Grant Collingwood Collection; Page 75: Western Canada Pictorial Index.

'The Old Game was Tougher':
Page 77: Canadian Press/Jeff McIntosh; Page 78: Hockey Hall of Fame; Page 79: (top) National Archives of Canada/PA-151013; (bottom) City of Toronto Archives; Page 80: Canadian Press/Paul Chiasson; Page 81: City of Toronto Archives; Page 82: (left) Canadian Press; (right) Canadian Press/Paul Chiasson; Page 83: *Toronto Sun* Archives/Greig Reekie; Page 84: Canadian Press/Ryan Remiorz; Page 85: Canadian Press; Page 86: National Archives of Canada/PA-151001; Page 87: National Archives of Canada/PA-150983; Page 89: *Montreal Gazette* Archives; Page 91: Canadian Press/Frank Lennon; Page 92: *Toronto Sun* Archives/Ken Kerr; Pages 94-5: (clockwise from top) Canadian Press/ Paul Chiasson; Doug MacLellan/ Hockey Hall of Fame; Hockey Hall of Fame; Imperial Oil: Turossky/Hockey Hall of Fame; Canadian Press; (clockwise from left) Hockey Hall of Fame; Hockey Hall of Fame; Hockey Hall of Fame; Canadian Press; Frank Prazak/Hockey Hall of Fame.

A Question of Survival:
Page 97: National Archives of Canada/PA-89114; Page 98: (top) National Archives of Canada/C-005945; (bottom) National Archives of Canada/C-059556; Page 99: M.O. Hammond/Metropolitan Toronto Reference Library; Page 100: (top) Canadian Press; (bottom) *Maclean's*/Phill Snel; Page 101: (left) Canadian Press; (right) National Archives of Canada/PA-172792; Page 102: (left) Canadian Press; (right) Vancouver Sun Archives; Page 103: University of Toronto Archives.

The Mosaic and the Glue:
Page 105: National Archives of Canada/C-15020; Page 106: (top) National Archives of Canada/C-038613; (bottom) National Archives of Canada/C-023555; Page 107: Department of National Defence; Page 108: British Columbia Archives; Page 109: Canadian Press; Page 110: William James Topley/ National Archives of Canada/PA-010237; Page 111: Western Canada Pictorial Index: Pages 112-13: City of Toronto Archives; Page 114: Western Canada Pictorial Index; Page 115: National Archives of Canada/C-19134; Page 117: E. D'Angelo/National Archives of Canada/PA-91100; Page 121: New Brunswick Archives; Page 122: National Archives of Canada/PA-093521 (used with permission of the Communist Party of Canada); Page 123: Canadian Press/Nick Procaylo.

The Forces of Disunity:
Page 125: National Archives of Canada/C-005110; Page 126: *Montreal Gazette* Archives; Page 127: Canadian Press/ Tom Hanson; Page 128: *Montreal Gazette* Archives; Page 129: City of Toronto Archives; Page 130: Rodolophe Carrière/ National Archives of Canada/PA-074624; Page 131: (top & bottom) *Montreal Gazette* Archives; Page 132: MacLean/National Archives of Canada/C-079010; Page 133: (top) Canadian Press; (bottom) *Montreal Gazette* Archives; Page 134: *Montreal Gazette* Archives; Page 135: Canadian Press; Page 137: Canadian Press; Page 138: Canadian Press/Ron Poling; Page 139: Canadian Press.

Passing Fads and Fleeting Fancies:
Page 141: York University Archives/Don Grant; Page 142: City of Toronto Archives; Page 143: York University Archives/Frank Grant; Page 144: Western Canada Pictorial Index; Page 146: Canadian Press/Len Wagg; Page 147: (top) Canadian Press/Kip Frasz; (bottom) Canadian Press; Page 149: *Toronto Sun* Archives.

From 'Curiosity' to 'Love Affair':
Page 151: Metropolitan Toronto Reference Library; Page 152: Metropolitan Toronto Reference Library; Page 153: National Archives of Canada/C-000623; Page 154: *Montreal Gazette* Archives; Page 155: (top) Archives of Ontario; (bottom) New Brunswick Archives; Page 156: *Montreal Gazette* Archives; Page 158: York University Archives; Page 159: York University Archives; Page 160: General Motors.

When Things Go Fatally Wrong:
Page 163: *Maclean's*/Christopher Morris; Page 164: Canadian Press; Page 165: (top to bottom) National Archives of Canada/PA-030289; National Archives of Canada/C-066464; Canadian Press/Kerry Doubleday; Page 166: City of Toronto Archives; Page 167: Canadian Press; Pages 168-9: City of Toronto Archives; Page 170: Western Canada Pictorial Index; Page 171: National Archives of Canada/PA-4315; Page 172: York University Archives.

The Years of Desperation:
Page 175: City of Toronto Archives; Page 176: (top) National Archives of Canada/C-020594; (bottom) National Archives of Canada/PA-35133; Page 177: National Archives of Canada/PA-029399; Page 178: National Archives of Canada/C-55451; Page 180: Ontario Archives; Page 181: Western Canada Pictorial Index; Page 182: Western Canada Pictorial Index; Page 183: (left) Provincial Archives of Alberta; (right) National Archives of Canada/C-027900; (bottom) Western Canada Pictorial Index.

The Seething Sixties:
Page 185: *Montreal Gazette* Archives; Page 186: *Toronto Sun* Archives; Page 187: National Archives of Canada; Page 188: York University Archives; Page 189: *Montreal Gazette* Archives; Page 190: Showtime Music Archives (Toronto); Page 192: Canadian Press; Page 193: (left) Canadian Press; (right) National Archives of Canada/PA-139986; Page 194: National Archives of Canada/PA-152498; Page 195: Canadian Press.

Big-Neighbor Factors:
Page 197: National Archives of Canada/United Press International/PA-117603; Page 198: National Archives of Canada/C-003569; Page 199: (top) Canadian Press; (bottom) National Archives of Canada/PA-097869 (reprinted with permission of the Communist Party of Canada); Page 200: Canadian Press/Jose Goitia; Page 201: *Montreal Gazette* Archives; Page 203: *Toronto Sun* Archives; Page 205: Canadian Press/Scott Applewhite; Page 206: Canadian Press/John Lehmann; Page 207: Canadian Press/Patrick Pettit.

An Attachment to the Arctic:
Page 209: Canadian Press/James Stevenson; Page 210: Northwest Territories Archives; Page 211: Vancouver Sun Archives; Page 213: Northwest Territories Archives/Ted Grant; Page 214: *Maclean's*; Page 215: Canadian Press/Kevin Frayer; Page 217: Fred Bruemmer; Page 218: *Toronto Sun* Archives; Page 221: Northwest Territories Archives/Mary Kunzler-Larmann; Page 223: Vancouver Maritime Museum; Page 224: Fred Bruemmer; Page 226: Northwest Territories Archives.

From Torments to Triumphs:
Page 229: Canadian Press/Shaney Komulainen; Page 230: Royal British Columbia Museum; Page 231: (left) *Maclean's*/Brian Willer; (right) Canadian Press; Page 232: National Archives of Canada/PA-48475; Page 233: (left) National Archives of Canada/PA-122481; (right) *Toronto Sun* Archives; Page 234: National Archives of Canada; Page 236: Canadian Press/Tom Hanson; Page 237: Canadian Press; Page 238: Canadian Press/Andrew Vaughan; Page 242: Western Canada Pictorial Index; Page 243: Canadian Press/Fred Chartrand; Page 244: Canadian Press/Nick Procaylo.

Color Canada Dusty Green:
Page 247: *Toronto Sun* Archives; Page 249: City of Toronto Archives; Page 250: City of Toronto Archives; Page 252: (left & right) *Toronto Sun* Archives; Page 253: Canadian Press/Michael Creaghan; Pages 254-5: (left) Canadian Press; (right) *Toronto Sun* Archives; Page 256: Canadian Press; Page 257: Canadian Press/Chuck Stoody; Page 259: Canadian Press/Nick Procaylo.

Drains and Gains in Brain Power:
Page 261: Canadian Press; Page 262: (left) Canadian Press; (right) Canadian Press/Tobbe Gustavsson; Page 263: Canadian Press/Peter Bregg; Page 265: (top) National Archives of Canada/C-9071; (bottom) National Archives of Canada/PA-9192; Page 266: Canadian Press/Tim Clark; Page 267: Canadian Press/Tobbe Gustavsson.

The Real Stuff *à la* Canuck:
Page 269: Canadian Press; Page 270: Canadian Press; Page 271: Canadian Press; Page 272: Canadian Press/Fred Chartrand; Page 273: Canadian Press/Tom Hanson; Page 274: (top) Canadian Press; (left) Canadian Press; (right) Canadian Press/Peter Bregg; Page 275: Canadian Press.

Canada's Expositors:
Page 277: *Maclean's*/Brian Willer; Page 278: (left) *Maclean's*; (right) *Toronto Sun* Archives; Page 279: (left) National Archives of Canada/PA-137071; (right) National Archives of Canada/C-018347; Page 280: (left) *Maclean's*/Peter Bregg; (right) National Archives of Canada/C-011299; Page 281: National Archives of Canada/PA-145189; Page 282: (clockwise) *Toronto Sun* Archives; *Toronto Sun* Archives; Canadian Press; Canadian Press/Chris Lund; Canadian Press; *Montreal Gazette* Archives; Page 283: (left) Canadian Press; (right) Random House of Canada; Page 284: Art Gallery of Ontario, Toronto/Carlo Catenazzi.

A Presence on the Silver Screen:
Page 287: National Film Board of Canada/National Archives of Canada/PA-111745; Page 288: (top) Canadian Press; (bottom) National Archives of Canada/C-80901; Page 289: Canadian Press/John Lehmann; Page 290: City of Toronto Archives; Page 291: (top) National Archives of Canada/C-052029; (middle) Grant Collingwood Collection; (bottom) Canadian Press/Kevin Argue; Page 293: National Archives of Canada/PA-158833; Page 294: Canadian Press; Page 297: CBC Picture Service; Page 298: Canadian Press.

Television:
Page 301: National Archives of Canada/C-080917; Page 302: (top) Gazette/National Archives of Canada/PA-077934; (bottom) Canadian Press; Page 305: CBC Still Photo Collection; Page 306: (left) George Hunter/National Archives of Canada/PA-108419; (right) *Toronto Sun* Archives; Page 307: Canadian Press; Page 308: (top) Canadian Press; (bottom) Canadian Press/Peter Bregg; Page 309: Canadian Press.

A Funny Thing Happened…:
Page 311: *Maclean's*/Phill Snel; Page 312: Canadian Press; Page 313: (left) Canadian Press; (right) *Maclean's*/Hurrell; Page 314: Robert Baillargeon, McLaughlin Planetarium; Page 315: Canadian Press/Rodney Daw; Page 316: Canadian Press; Page 317: *Toronto Sun* Archives; Page 318: Canadian Press; Page 319: *Toronto Sun* Archives; Page 320: Canadian Press; Page 321: Canadian Press/Moe Doiron.

'This is the Big Time':
Page 323: Canadian Press/Wheeler Newspaper Syndicate; Page 324: National Archives of Canada/C-029722; Page 326: Canadian Press; Page 328: *Maclean's*/Brian Willer; Page 329: Canadian Press; Page 331: (top left) *Maclean's*/Brian Willer; (right) *Maclean's*/Peter Bregg; (bottom) *Toronto Sun* Archives/Mark O'Neill; Page 332: Canadian Press/Rene Johnston; Page 334: Canadian Press/Peter Bregg; Page 335: Canadian Press.

Chronology:
Page 336: (top) National Archives of Canada/C-000037; (bottom) City of Toronto Archives; Page 337: (top) Department of National Defence; (bottom) Western Canada Pictorial Index; Page 338: *Toronto Sun* Archives; Page 339: National Archives of Canada/PA-150994; Page 340: National Archives of Canada/C-036285; Page 341: (top) National Archives of Canada/C-006545; (middle) Partridge/National Archives of Canada/PA-120526; (bottom) Canadian Press; Page 342: (top) *Toronto Sun* Archives; (bottom) Malak/National Archives of Canada/C-030085; Page 343: (top) Canadian Press; (bottom) Canadian Press/Chuck Mitchell; Page 344: Canadian Press; Page 345: Canadian Press; Page 346: *Toronto Sun* Archives; Page 348: (top) Canadian Press; (bottom left) Canadian Press; (bottom right) *Maclean's*/Peter Bregg; Page 349: Canadian Press.